CONRAD: EASTERN AND WESTERN PERSPECTIVES
general editor: Wiesław Krajka

VOLUME I

CONRAD'S LITERARY CAREER

edited by

Keith Carabine, Owen Knowles, Wiesław Krajka

EAST EUROPEAN MONOGRAPHS, BOULDER
MARIA CURIE-SKŁODOWSKA UNIVERSITY, LUBLIN
DISTRIBUTED BY COLUMBIA UNIVERSITY PRESS, NEW YORK

1992

EAST EUROPEAN MONOGRAPHS, NO. CCCLIII

Printed in the United States of America

TABLE OF CONTENTS

ABBREVIATIONS

I. Conrad's Works

AF	*Almayer's Folly*
AG	*The Arrow of Gold*
LE	*Last Essays*
LJ	*Lord Jim*
MS	*The Mirror of the Sea*
N	*Nostromo*
NLL	*Notes on Life and Letters*
NN	*The Nigger of the "Narcissus"*
OI	*An Outcast of the Islands*
PR	*A Personal Record*
Res	*The Rescue*
SA	*The Secret Agent*
SS	*A Set of Six*
TLS	*'Twixt Land and Sea*
TS	*Typhoon and Other Stories*
TU	*Tales of Unrest*
UWE	*Under Western Eyes*
V	*Victory*
WT	*Within the Tides*
YS	*Youth: A Narrative, and Two Other Stories*

All references to Conrad's works in the following essays are to the Dent Collected Edition (1946-55) or the World's Classics Edition, whose pagination is identical.

II. Conrad's Letters

CL	*The Collected Letters of Joseph Conrad*
	ed. F. R. Karl and L. Davies (Cambridge: C.U.P., 1983-), 4 vols.
LL	*Joseph Conrad: Life and Letters*
	ed. G. Jean-Aubry (London: Heinemann, 1927), 4 vols.

Juliet McLauchlan
Oxford University, Department for Continuing Education,
Oxford, England

Opening Address for Conrad's Polish Footprints.
I International Joseph Conrad Conference
at UMCS Lublin, Poland,
Baranów Sandomierski 8-10 September 1991

I want to say something to you all but, chiefly I think, to our Polish hosts and hostesses and all our Polish friends in this splendid group. This is almost essential because my paper is not a "keynote" piece. When I was writing it I did not know that I was to be the first of your guests to speak. That is a great privilege, and I am delighted to be able to say briefly why I am, personally, so happy to be in Poland again – apart from the fact that Poland and its people readily endear themselves. I hope I may be speaking for many of your guests when I offer preliminary thanks to the conference organizers for bringing us all together in these wonderful Polish surroundings.

I have come here, of course, for Conrad. In my view he is the greatest writer of fiction in English. In that sense he is an English *writer,* but not an *English* writer. For Conrad was, supremely, a Pole and remained, I believe, supremely, a Pole. I have always found it very moving that Conrad ultimately came to feel that his sons must know more about their Polish background, even though he had so deliberately brought them up to be as English as possible. There seems to be absolutely no doubt that Conrad made this sacrifice to avoid domestic conflict *and* any inner conflict for the boys themselves. Certainly, Borys Conrad assured me on numerous occasions that this was the case.

In *Poland Revisited* Conrad records his hope (as they were about to start for Poland) that in "these young beings...unless Heredity is an empty word, there should have been a fibre which would answer to the sight, to the atmosphere, to the memories of that corner of the earth where my own boyhood had received its

1

earliest independent impressions." (*NLL,* 146) Towards the end
of the first chapter of *A Personal Record* he wrote:

> That which in [his sons'] grown-up years may appear to the world about
> them as the most enigmatic side of their natures and perhaps must
> remain for ever obscure even to themselves, will be their unconscious
> response to the still voice of that inexorable past from which his work of
> fiction and their personalities are remotely derived. (25)

We therefore considered it "meet that something more [his
memoirs] should be left [for them]" than his own "hard-won
creation."

All this, I am convinced, came from the depths of Conrad's
own Polish nature. I quote again from *A Personal Record* where
Conrad begs his readers to allow for:

> the part of the inexplicable...in appraising the conduct of men in
> a world where no explanation is final...No charge of faithlessness ought
> to be lightly uttered...The inner voice may remain true enough in its
> secret counsel. The fidelity to a special tradition may last through the
> events of an unrelated existence, following faithfully, too, the traced
> way of an inexplicable impulse. (35-6)

I would maintain that this sort of fidelity to the special Polish
tradition remained always in the counsel of Conrad's heart and
was expressed throughout his own "hard-won creation," which,
though distinctively Polish, is felt to be universal.

So Conrad is yours; Conrad is ours; but we especially need
Poland and need you to help us to recognize and value the Polish
particular in the Conradian universal. We all hope to learn much
from you, and with you, in the course of this conference.

Claude Maisonnat,
University Lumière Lyons 2,
Lyons, France

Discursive Deception and the Quest for Meaning in *Almayer's Folly*

With tongue in cheek presumably, Conrad once wrote in *A Personal Record*: "What is interesting to a writer is the possession of an inward certitude that literary criticism will never die, for man...is, before everything else, a critical animal" (96). He will no doubt be proved right once more as I propose to take a critical view of the controversial allegation that he made in connection with *Almayer's Folly,* and according to which he became a writer by pure accident. He justified this first statement by adding: "The conception of a planned book was entirely outside my mental range when I sat down to write" (68). I wish to challenge such an affirmation by showing that his very first novel is a rather cleverly constructed work whose literary merits are frequently under-estimated.

However Conrad himself, apparently in partial contradiction to his initial statement, has shown elsewhere that he had a specific interest in the construction of story and plot and in the planned production of effects. In an essay entitled *A Glance at Two Books* written in 1904 in which he reviewed John Galsworthy's *The Island Pharisees* and W. H. Hudson's *Green Mansions,* he insisted that the problem with the British novelist as opposed to the European and particularly the French one was that he

> seldom regards his work...as an achievement of active life by which he
> will produce certain definite effects upon the emotions of his rea-
> ders...He does not go about building up his book with a precise
> intention and a steady mind. (*LE,* 132)

Conrad seems to show here an acute awareness of the techniques of the craft of fiction worthy of a master and incompatible with the idea that *Almayer's Folly* was a sort of natural product free of the literary standards required of his other books. At any rate Conrad never dismissed his first novel as being below standard in any way, which should be a good enough reason for us to examine its real status in the Conradian corpus. The first explanation that comes to mind is therefore that *Almayer's Folly* provided him with the very field of experimentation he needed to explore his writing skills even if his knowledge of great masters (the French in particular) had already made him acutely aware of the necessity of mastering such skills years before he took pen in hand.

Indeed, in the past a few perceptive critics have extolled the merits of the novel and even waxed lyrical when trying to convince their readers, without substantiating their claims with adequate evidence. H. L. Mencken, for example, unreservedly praised the novel and exclaimed in a rather grandiloquent manner: "I challenge the nobility and gentry of Christendom to point to another Opus 1 as magnificently planned and turned out as *Almayer's Folly*" (Mencken, 158). More recently, critics like Ian Watt or Cedric Watts took a more temperate and academic view in their own revaluation of the narrative.

In a much less flamboyant manner, the aim of this paper will be limited to providing textual evidence that *Almayer's Folly* was from the start, from its opening words indeed, a remarkably professional piece of work in so far as it reveals an extremely subtle and detailed attention paid to the way its very discourse produces and at the same time blurs and withholds meaning, deceives expectations and disrupts character, narrator and reader unity.

Furthermore I shall argue that the quest for, and the questioning of meaning represented in the novel and which concern all narrative levels, reach far deeper than mere reader manipulation, although that is undeniably at work too, and already contain, at least in a primitive form, the seeds of deconstruction. In a quite perceptible way, five years before *Lord Jim* and sixteen years before *Under Western Eyes,* Conrad's first novel, by emphasizing the unreliability of its own discourse and the inherent duplicity characteristic of verbal communication, initiates a reflection on the status of fictional works, and, thereby situates its author among the pillars of early modernism.

The constantly thwarted quest for meaning which is the hallmark of *Almayer's Folly*, will be examined on three different levels successively. Firstly it will be shown to be at work on the diegetic level, in the story proper, in which all the characters are seen to be engaged in endless verbal cheating and lying in order to deceive others and further their own ends. Secondly on the narrative level where an overall strategy of reader and character manipulation turns the reading of the novel into a highly uncertain activity; and, finally, on the level of *enunciation* where it will appear that the very status of the narrative agency, the subject of the *enunciation* is questioned so that the reliability of the whole text eventually is sapped as if it has been submitted to a process of deconstruction.

The Pursuit of Meaning: From Quest to Question

Since all the characters in *Almayer's Folly*, including such minor ones as Jim-Eng the Chinaman, seem to spend more time talking to one another or spying on their neighbours, that is to say trying to find a meaning for their behaviour than actually doing things, it is no wonder that the ever-baffled quest for meaning and consequently for truth should be so overwhelmingly foregrounded in the novel. Its general effect, however, is to cast severe doubts on the reliability of the discourses held and the messages received. For example, the reader frequently comes upon such ominous statements as the following: "With inborn suspicion they would not believe the simple account of himself the young trader was always ready to give." So much emphasis is put on the unreliability of the characters' actions and speeches, that what applies here to Dain's too obvious explanations for his apparent activities and which seems suspicious to the people in the settlement, could also apply to the text itself.

To start with, on a primitive level, the quest for meaning and truth usually takes the form of deciphering and decoding the outside world in order to bring out its potential meaning. Indeed a good deal of spying and eavesdropping goes on, which testifies that in fact meaning and truth are not readily available but can only be reached through an act of will and personal effort. A good illustration of this is Babalatchi's discovery of the love affair between Dain and Nina by dint of observing the nightly nautical movements on the river Pantai. This secretly acquired knowledge will subsequently enable him to understand the exact nature of Dain's connections with the settlement, providing him with a definite superiority over Almayer who is deceived by the trader almost to the end.

Similarly in chapter one, as Almayer is waiting in the dark for Dain's long-expected return, he tries to identify unknown paddlers on the river and must strain his senses of hearing and sight before he is able to realize that it's not Abdulla's men, as he wrongly surmised, but Dain himself. To make this clear to the reader, the text insists massively on the process of gradual discovery of the truth through Almayer's perceptions, stressing thereby the fact that his main activity is to decipher the signals he receives from the outside world. First he *detects* a splash of paddles, then he can hear the paddles *distinctly,* then he hears the *sharp sound* of paddles falling into the canoe.

As Almayer is far from being the only character to devote himself to this deciphering activity, the whole novel appears to be an omnipresent quest for meaning. Simultaneously all the characters in the novel give themselves up, albeit in a different mode, to that never-ending quest, through the mediation of language this time, as they try to find out the truth contained in the messages they receive from others. But the most remarkable feature of the narrative is that all the speakers seem to be suspicious of the sincerity and truthfulness of the speeches they hear. This general suspicion transforms the world of the novel into a sort of hazy, and mysterious world, in which nothing is clear or certain and final meaning constantly delayed.

The signifiers of deception and duplicity keep cropping up in the narrative, as if reaching at the truth of things is an obsession with all the cast of characters, and as if the only aim in life of their interlocutor is to cheat them. Hence the numerous accusations of lying that are constantly bandied forth by everyone, irrespective of class, sex or nationality. Here is a short sample: Almayer to Nina (about her decision to go away and live with Dain):"I do not believe you. You lie" (163); "Oh! Nina! I do not believe" (164). Dain to Almayer: "Who would doubt a white Tuan's words? I shall not go to the Arabs their lies are very great" (53). Dain to Nina: "I swear: this a white man's lie" (178). Mrs. Almayer to Nina: "They [the whites] speak lies and they think lies because they despise us" (151). Babalatchi to Lakamba: "Who is there here for me to deceive, O Rajah?...All I have told you I believe to be true...This is no time to harbour suspicions" (127). Lakamba to Dain: "Can I believe what you tell me? It is like a tale for men that listen only half-awake" (127).

This clearly shows that all the characters are involved in a constant tampering with meaning and truth, that they alternately find themselves in the position of encoding or decoding trumped-up messages, that hinder the construction of meaning and prove most inconvenient for the reader. It should be noted too, that these characters are never more untrustworthy than when they claim to speak the truth. The slave Taminah provides a good illustration of this trick: "'I have seen him not long ago' she said at last. 'The talk is true; he's dead'" (111). She does not hesitate to confirm Dain's death to Reshid when she knows full well that he is safe and hiding in a clearing waiting for Nina. She follows her own course of action in order to attract Dain's attention upon her person but in the unfolding of the narrative such a piece of information is highly disturbing for the reader who has been left in doubt about Dain's fate for a long time.

In the same way when Dain returns from his failed expedition downriver and meets Almayer eagerly waiting for him, his answer to Almayer's question about the ship appears remarkably ambiguous: "The brig is where no Orang Blanda can lay his hands on her" (13). On the one hand it may mean that the ship is safe and well out of the authorities' reach after a successful illegal mission, and this is the reading Almayer selects because it fits his purpose. On the other, it may also mean that the ship has been destroyed so that no authority will ever be able to find her and consequently that the mission has failed. This is of course the interpretation the reader is encouraged to make as the narrator gives him a clue with his own comments on Dain's words: "said Dain with a gloomy tone in his voice which Almayer in his elation failed to notice" (14).

It is important to note however that things are not so simple and clear-cut because in both cases the literal meaning is partially true so that there's no actual lie. It is true that Taminah has seen Dain shortly before meeting Reshid, but he wasn't dead. Similarly it is true that the ship is out of reach of the Dutch authorities, but not in the sense Almayer construes, since Dain had to sink it to escape.

With these last two examples of the way the characters deceive one another we are also led to take into account the fact that not only are the characters deceived and manipulated in the story but the reader is too, so that the suspicions the characters entertain about discourse in the novel are seen to be an echo, a duplication of the suspicion the reader is bound to feel when confronted with the narrative, with the text of the novel which must henceforth be considered as unreliable. I will now study the extent to which the narrative agency in *Almayer's Folly* manipulates the reader's response to the text and renders it utterly unreliable.

Textual Unreliability: The Strategy of Discursive Deception

The text of *Almayer's Folly* can rightfully be compared to a box with a false bottom: what the reader gets out of the surface narrative is never the whole story, there are always extra elements which make sense afterwards or rather which acquire a new layer of meaning retrospectively, once he or she is possessed of the relevant connections. In his *A Personal Record,* Conrad recalls being worried about the readability of the novel for that very reason, even before it was completed. Indeed there were only nine chapters in existence when Conrad asked his first reader to give him his opinion on his work and expressed his concern: "it occured to me that there was a good deal of retrospective writing in the story as far as it went" (17). Then he adds that revealing clause: "as if already the story-teller were being born into the body of a seaman" (17). This marked interest in the construction of his first novel should be enough to show that he was far more conscious of the importance of technique in the writing of fiction than he claimed to be. In other words there was no abrupt break between his two lives: the preoccupations of the craft-conscious novelist were already of prime importance to the professional sailor so that the two careers seem to have overlapped for quite a while, at least during the long years it took him to write *Almayer's Folly*.

It is worth pointing out here the wonderfully relevant polysemic dimension of the expression "retrospective writing." Understood on the diegetic level, it refers classically to the conventional idea of resorting to the flashback technique. On the narrative level it applies to the trick of deferring meaning which is the object of our present study. On the fictional level it could also be a reference to the standard Conradian conviction that: "a novelist lives in his work. He stands there, the only reality in an invented world, among imaginary things, happenings and people. Writing about them, he is only writing about himself" (*PR*, xiii), so that the very phrase "retrospective writing" appears to be a perfect definition of Conrad's style of writing in all its complexity.

The technique of deferring meaning in the novel (perhaps a superficial manifestation of Derrida's *differance,* before the letter) implies a good deal of reader-involvement. In fact the narrative surface of the text could be seen as an interface between the meaning-producing potentialities of the text and the meaning-producing activity of the reader. As a result, the latter does not merely collect information, adding up items of unproblematic status from the narrative but is called upon to produce his own meaning through an active process of decoding, exactly as we have seen the characters in the novel do on the diegetic level. In short, the text presents itself as an all-out reader's trap which posits the necessity of retrospective, that is to say repeated, reading, and we will now examine the various modalities of the text's ultimate unreliability.

In its attempt to lead its readers astray, the narrative agency of *Almayer's Folly* resorts to two major devices which are well--known but none the less extremely complex in their interaction – firstly the strategy of concealment, then the jig-saw puzzle strategy.

The strategy of concealment aims at hiding the true meaning of a statement by first suggesting a readily available apparent meaning which turns out to be the wrong one. Thus, the first interpretation to which the reader is led functions like a sort of screen preventing further enquiries as it seems quite plausible at least for a while, but it is essential that the mistaken deduction should be exposed later on or otherwise the device would be self-defeating. The device most frequently used to conceal meaning in *Almayer's Folly* is quite naturally irony, particularly under the guise of dramatic irony. Irony being roughly speaking the art of saying the contrary of what is intended, the distinctive feature of dramatic irony lies in the important fact that the speaker is, as it were, taken in by his own discourse; irony is therefore unintended on his part and he does not know what he really says. The speaker loses control and mastery of his own language, which betrays his inadequacies. The speaker is therefore the victim of his own discourse. The main character submitted to the process of dramatic irony is Almayer, but it must be stressed that the reader who is frequently left in the dark like him, at least long enough for the narrative agency to send him on a wrong trail, is to a large extent deceived too, although, contrary to Almayer, he is undeceived by the end of the narrative.

When Almayer addresses his daughter in chapter one: "You cannot imagine what is before you" (18), he simply means to say that as she has never been to Europe she can have no idea of the wonderful life they are going to lead once they are in Amsterdam. The first ironic element is of course that Almayer himself has never been to Europe either. However, the reader with a retrospective eye will find out that Almayer (and incidentally he himself too) was utterly wrong, since at the time these words were spoken Nina knew quite well what was in store for her because she had already planned to elope with Dain. She was waiting for Dain too, but with a different purpose. Furthermore the power and the glory Almayer promised her in Amsterdam will in fact be hers, but, to Almayer's great dismay, in Bali as the wife of a mighty Malay rajah, not as the daughter of a respected and successful white trader. Such is the dramatic irony in *Almayer's Folly* that what Almayer says *is* true in a way but with a twist which ironically misfires upon him. In a subtle way the narrative agency plays here on the gap between *énoncé* and *enunciation*. What Almayer says as a subject of the *énoncé* seems therefore quite unproblematic, but what the subject of the *enunciation* means the reader to understand is the opposite, even if he doesn't always provide him with the adequate signals there and then. Thus the gap between *énoncé* and *enunciation* becomes a gap between temporary and final meanings.

The narrative is constantly manipulated in the sense that it does send signals that are deciphered on one level, but which turn out to have quite another meaning on a different level, and consequently the reader is confronted with a text whose reliability must be questioned. For instance in chapter one when Dain, on his return from the failed expedition says to Almayer: "Nothing could have stopped me from coming back here...Not even death" (13), the reader who is not yet acquainted with the Dain/Nina relationship, wonders why Dain seems so keen on helping Almayer in his economic venture when the latter has hitherto been described as isolated from the trading community in Sambir.

These ironic statements can be seen as signals sent to the reader but which can only be deciphered correctly on a second reading. Thus in chapter three as Almayer seems at a loss to understand Nina's reaction after the visit of Abdulla who wanted to buy her for his nephew Reshid, he exclaims: "Damn those women! Well! If the girl did not look as if she wanted to be kidnapped!" (47). There is, of course, an element of truth in his exclamation but he is unable to perceive it because it functions on a different level. What Nina wants from her father is the recognition of her identity, of her status of autonomous subject;

but she will only find it with Dain, who has to take her away from her father first. Kidnapped she will be indeed (from Almayer's point of view of course), but in fact she will elope with Dain, her father's friend or rather temporary ally, not with Reshid his enemy as he feared. Hence the ironic dimension of the narrator's remark in chapter three: "Almayer had now a friend" (49). This friend, by an ironic reversal, will become in due time his worst enemy. In this way, apparently plain and unproblematic segments of the text can acquire a new meaning, in fact see a complete reversal of their original meaning.

I shall now turn to another modality of the strategy of discursive deception: lying. Just as all the characters in the story are adepts at the art of lying, so the narrative agency also resorts to that trick to conceal the real meaning of statements and events in a bid to manipulate the reaction of the reader. Suspicion is, however, also a characteristic of verbal exchanges in the novel, and Dain sends a warning signal to the reader when, addressing Lakamba, he insists on the truthfulness of his words: "All that I have said is true, and there is nothing more" (52). As it turns out there is something more – it is related to Nina and will determine the end of the story. In the same way the narrative agency comments on Dain's visit by instilling doubts into the reader's mind by saying: "With inborn suspicion they would not believe the simple account of himself the young trader was always ready to give." However after that indirect warning, it proceeds to lure the reader into accepting the surface truth of the events by adding quite treacherously: "Yet it had all the appearance of truth" (57).

Chapter seven offers a good illustration of the way in which the narrative agency manipulates the reader by suggesting interpretations which are really lies. As Dain gets ready to cross the river, the narrator paves the way for the identification of the dead body as Dain's by having Lakamba remark: "He may get drowned" (87). Then the reader witnesses Mrs. Almayer's despair and hears Babalatchi's forceful arguments that finally convince Almayer that the body is Dain's. This is followed by the description of Almayer's own breakdown as his last hopes of fortune are smashed and by Nina's strange reaction: "'and so Dain is dead' she said coldly, when her father ceased speaking" (101). Her words read as her desperate efforts to overcome her grief after Dain's sudden death and not to reveal her relationship with him now that her father's plans are doomed. In fact a retrospective reading shows that she tries not to give in to the last remnants of the affection she feels for her father in an attempt to avoid betraying the plan Dain, she, her mother and Babalatchi have concocted in order to deceive the whole settlement, the Dutch officers, Almayer and eventually the reader too. The narrative voice is definitely unreliable in the novel because of its tendency to lie to the reader. But, as we shall see, fictional lies can also be construed as the means whereby truth can be glimpsed.

However, the effects of discursive deception are even more complex in *Almayer's Folly* and we shall now examine the second series of devices used to ruin textual reliability, the jig-saw puzzle strategy. It consists in breaking up an element of information into several smaller units which are distributed in an apparently random way throughout the text, but which in fact function as a coherent series which must be put together in order to become meaningful, rather in the same way as the reader looks for clues when dealing with a detective story. Two main modalities of the process can be identified: first the disruption of the traditional time-scheme and the imposition of a non-chronological order on the narrative that force the reader to re-construct, to re-tell the story as it were. Secondly the recourse to intra-textual riddles, namely some sort of narrative grey areas which cannot receive any explanation on the spot but which eventually make sense retrospectively when connected one to the other. In both cases ultimate meaning is deferred until the reader is in possession of all the elements of the story. He must then be active in re-constructing the whole story to come up with a slightly different interpretation.

The temporal structure of the story is the first mystery offered to the reader. For the new reader, the text presents itself as a juxtaposition of segments set up in an order whose logic is not apparent. Indeed the very first words of the novel put the text under the aegis of fragmentation and puzzlement. The words: "Kaspar! Makan!" (3) are in Malay and the reader has to wait for the end of chapter one to find out what they meant exactly. It was merely Mrs. Almayer calling her husband for supper, but the important element here again is not in the literal meaning of the expression, but in the fact that the message to the reader is delayed. It's a fitting opening for a novel whose basic working principle seems to be discursive deception.

Similarly, the reader has to wait till the end of chapter six to understand the succession of events and realize that the novel actually begins on the day of Dain's return and that the story occupies a very short span of time. The day after Dain's return is densely packed with events. It starts with the discovery of the dead body and ends with the visit of the Dutch officers and Taminah's betrayal of Dain and Nina. The next day sees the final depature of the couple. The last six pages only are devoted to the time elapsing until Almayer's death. Having thus reconstructed the chronological sequence of events and taken into account the few flashbacks concerning Almayer's, Nina's and Mrs. Almayer's past, the reader discovers with some surprise that the bulk of story takes place in only two days and nights. It is clear now that the main function of temporal dislocation is to disturb the reader's awareness of time and thus that it participates in a very effective way in the strategy of discursive deception.

The narrator also resorts to intra-textual riddles to make sure that the reader remains active. The narrative of *Almayer's Folly* is punctuated with a series of mysterious noises and visions which may appear so unimportant that the reader might not bother to elucidate them. And yet these narrative grey areas, even if they help reinforce the atmosphere of mystery, also function as a sort of subordinate story within the story, running parallel to the main scheme but not unrelated to it. For example, in chapter nine involving Almayer and Dain, minor events take place in the background which participate in the main scheme but which are only intermittently brought to the awareness of the reader. They involve minor characters and follow strictly the logic of events, strengthening its coherence in fact. In chapter nine, an argument arises between the Dutch officers as one claims to have heard voices that the other failed to perceive: "'Did you hear that?' he asked? 'No!' said the other. 'Hear what?' 'I thought I heard a cry. Ever so faint. Seemed a woman's voice. In that other house. Ah! again! Hear it?' 'No,' said the lieutenant after listening a while 'you young fellows always hear women's voices'" (146). In fact the first officer hadn't dreamt. We subsequently learn in chapter ten that those were the voices of Nina and Mrs. Almayer on their last meeting, the latter trying to prevent Nina from seeing her father one last time as he lies dead drunk and asleep.

The next example is even more striking, as each element in the series could be construed as a sort of reality effect, needing no further justification for its presence. One explanation is that they could illustrate the troubled and restless mind of the various characters at a time of acute crisis when in fact it is a clue as to the progression in space of a character: "On the other side of the creek there was a rustle in the long grass" (150); "This time she fancied she had heard a faint noise, like the echo of her own sigh" (154); "she appeared to be listening to some noise behind the shed…'There are strange noises,' she whispered" (155); "a vague shape flitted out from amongst the stalks of the banana plantation" (156); "and from the stars under his feet rose a whisper full of entreaties and tears" (158).

In fact what puzzles successively Nina, Mrs. Almayer, Babalatchi and Almayer turns out to be the slave girl Taminah who, despairing of being noticed by Dain, has decided to betray Dain and Nina's plans of escape. There's no doubt, here again, that the meaning of each episode depends on its being related to the progression of the girl through the jungle and ultimately on the reader's ability to go through the story backward before connecting these elements and deducing their real purpose, so that the grey areas now become absolutely clear and coherent with the whole narrative. If we recall Ian Watt's concept of "delayed decoding," then it is clear that *Almayer's Folly* exemplifies it in a remarkably extensive way.

If the reader is constantly manipulated as we have shown and if he is bound to question the text in such a radical way, it is perhaps because the novel as narrative is also a questioning of the status of narrative. We are now going to examine to what extent *Almayer's Folly* is a reflection on the nature of fiction in the same way as, say, *Lord Jim* or *Under Western Eyes*.

From Lies to Truth: An Ethical View of Fiction

Post-Saussurean linguistics have taught us that words, languages, discourses, and ultimately fictions as products of those three elements are represented as unreliable in *Almayer's Folly* on account of the unavoidable structural gap existing between sign and referent and between *énoncé* and *enunciation*. This gap renders all forms of verbal expression liable to manipulation and thus potentially undermines the truthfulness of any utterance; hence the suspicion that fiction, in so far as it is a product of language, can be equated with telling lies. This seems to have been an obsessive preoccupation with Conrad as early as 1900 when he wrote *Lord Jim,* and remained a foremost object of speculation in such major works as *Heart of Darkness* (1902) or *Under Western Eyes* (1911). In this final section I would like to suggest that not only did Conrad show an amazingly modern awareness of the problematic of fiction, but that in his very practice of creative writing (at its best) he came to grips with the paradox of providing truth out of lies by adhering rigidly to an ethical code of writing which acknowledges the inescapable and unpredictable connection betwen the writing subject's unconscious desires and his creative urges mediated through the symbolic code of language.

Firstly, we should bear in mind the extent to which the status of fiction is challenged in the novel. To complete the analysis of textual unreliability, I would like to show that the very position of the narrative agency in *Almayer's Folly* is not as secure as it at first seems. In fact on close scrutiny, the text appears to be the juxtaposition of a series of episodes whose linguistic status differs. The characters in different scenes should logically speak different languages in accordance with their national origins (Dutch, Malay, Arab, Chinese and English). The narrative agency is thus supposed to play the role of translator, with the English language as a unifying element. However, if some verbal exchanges are linguistically identified in the narrative, others are not, thereby introducing a certain degree of narrative inconsistency which undermines the reliability of the text and questions the linguistic identity of the narrator himself. The disruptive effect of these features on the process of *enunciation* in the novel is confirmed by the fact that the very medium of fiction in *Almayer's Folly,* the English language, is presented as a double--edged weapon. Dain, speaking to Almayer exclaims: "Tomorrow we talk Tuan, now I know you...I speak English a little, so we can talk and nobody will understand" (53).

In so far as identification of the narrative agency is made more difficult and thus encourages confusion between author and narrator, we are justified in assuming that a process of deconstruction is at work in the constructed narrative of the novel. How conscious this process may be, is a moot point; but what is beyond dispute is the fact that textual unreliability, because it is to be found at all levels of the writing process (language, discourse, *enunciation,* and eventually fiction), cannot be said to be the outcome of chance factors. We are a far cry from the supposed technical innocence Conrad claimed was his lot. As a self-conscious work of fiction, *Almayer's Folly* heralds the major interrogations of Conrad's later fiction from *Heart of Darkness* to *Under Western Eyes.*

To be sure, the fact that *Almayer's Folly* was Conrad's first novel has prompted a number of critics to take a contrary view and ascribe its inconsistencies to its author's lack of skill. Thus John McClure writes: "*Almayer's Folly* is very much a first novel...[whose]...narrator seems to interpret omniscience as a license for self-contradiction." (101). In response I would argue that what McClure calls self-contradictions are none other than the manifestations, in the novel, of the paradox of fiction in general, one that can be formulated in this way: What sort of truth can be reached through fictional lies? The narrative inconsistencies of the novel would then appear to be Conrad's fumbling way of tackling the problems of writing and not to be the consequence of want of skill.

It is perhaps worth noticing in this respect that what the novel consciously achieves on the ideological level, namely the debunking of the romantic stereotypes of the white man's view of non-white cultures, it also achieves in a less sophisticated way on the epistemological level by interrogating its fictional status; and it does so by foregrounding its self-questioning and paradoxical relation to truth, which, in the end, amounts to deconstructing its own status as artifice.

Furthermore if all fiction equates ambiguously with lies as Conrad was later to maintain, then *Almayer's Folly* is doubly problematic since it is a novel representing characters who keep lying to one another. In that sense it bears a close resemblance to such masterpieces as *Heart of Darkness* and *Under Western Eyes,* both novels in which the question of truth and lies is central. What might be added, however, is that in *Almayer's Folly,* it would seem that lying to others is not so dangerous as lying to oneself if we bear in mind the fate of Almayer whose tragic flaw is that he keeps lying to himself about his real situation and status. For Conrad, this fact may well imply that a work of fiction which would not take into account its own fictional status, which would be blind to its internal contradictions would no longer deserve to be called literature and would rank among those pieces of writing of inferior value, just like Bulwer-Lytton's novels which he derided in *The Nigger of the "Narcissus"* by denouncing the insincerity of their sentences. *Almayer's Folly's* claim to modernity, however, does not rely on this tentative attempt at deconstruction only, but also on the idea that truth and fidelity to the writer's sensations and emotions imply that confrontation with unconscious forces should not be eschewed.

The final point I would like to make is that Conrad like all great modern writers was keenly, and frequently painfully, aware that the truly creative process of writing fiction involves dealing in some way with one's unconscious conflicts as we can infer from his often quoted "Preface" to *The Nigger of the*

"Narcissus" in which he describes the unconscious as "that lonely region of stress and strife" where the artist, "if he be deserving and fortunate...finds the terms of his appeal."

Conrad's ethical conception of writing is therefore twofold. On the one hand it consists in not cheating the reader by foregrounding the unreliability of fictional representation, on the other hand it requires absolute truth to the writer's own desire. How can this be achieved then?

Conrad maintained that: "To have the gift of words...[was] no such great matter" (*NLL,* 9). He obviously meant that writing fiction of a literary status (what he respectfully called Letters) could not be limited to the mere jotting down of words on a page. These words had to be produced out of some state of urgency, which alone could guarantee their truthfulness. What it means in Lacanian terms, is that this guarantee of truthfulness could only be won through a process of intersubjective dialectics between the Imaginary and the Symbolic. Moreover since the writing subject is by essence a subject of the unconscious he must register the desire of the Other that speaks through him.

Similarly, it must be strongly emphasized that creative writing could no more be the pouring forth of supposedly unconscious fantasies than it could be verbal juggling. What must necessarily be at work to preclude any drift towards those two extremes is the process of symbolic castration. Thus the process of creative writing can be defined as the locus of the relationship established between a subject and his discourse in so far as his unconscious desires and conflicts are taken into account, that is to say expressed in an oblique way in the signifying chain, and are not allowed to overrule him. In the process of creative writing it is the writer himself who is ultimately created.

Conrad seemed well aware of this danger when he wrote in *A Personal Record*:

> But the danger lies in the writer becoming the victim of his own exaggeration, losing the exact notion of sincerity, and in the end coming to despise truth itself as something too cold, too blunt for his purpose – as, in fact, not good enough for his insistent emotion. (xviii)

It would appear then that, for Conrad, the writing process was a constant battle against the lure of imaginary identifications that alienate the subject and a battle to enforce his submission to the Law of Language (Symbolic castration) whose aim is to acknowledge the subject's structural division by endlessly displacing him in the signifying chain and thus from his alienating imaginary identifications.

Such an attitude to writing is doubly ethical because it not only protects the writer from alienating imaginary identifications that devalue his work, but also prevents the reader from falling into the same traps thereby granting him the status of a subject with his autonomy and freedom. The paradox is then that narrative manipulation, and avowed textual unreliability, far from being instruments of reader alienation, are ultimately the means of precluding it in a most effective way.

Eventually we can say that *Almayer's Folly* is very much a transitional novel as it is to a large extent a classic realist text with a real story, identifiable characters and a movement of narrative towards final disclosure. Nevertheless we have seen that it is simultaneously a text embodying the rudimentary elements of its own deconstruction, (equivocation, reader snares and contradictions) and as such it no longer belongs to the classic realist category. On the contrary, it clearly belongs to the precursors of the post-modernist creed and must be considered beyond doubt as the forerunner of Conrad's later interrogations on fiction. This ambivalent status is perhaps the reason why the novel did not receive all the critical attention it deserved, and the implicit aim of this paper whose opening statements challenged Conrad's far too modest pronouncement on his achievement has been ultimately to show that it is far more successful than he assumed.

WORKS CITED

McClure J. A. *Kipling and Conrad: The Colonial Fiction.* Cambridge and London: Harvard University Press, 1981.

Mencken H. L. *A Selection.* New York: Random House, 1919.

Watts C. *Joseph Conrad: A Literary Life.* New York: St. Martin's Press, 1989.

Watt I. *Conrad in the Nineteenth Century.* London: Chatto and Windus, 1980.

Adriaan M. de Lange,
Potchefstroom University for Christian Higher Education,
Potchefstroom, South Africa

Conrad and Impressionism: Problems and (Possible) Solutions

One of the most compelling features of Conrad's early work is its evocation of a distinctive, yet elusive atmosphere. From the earliest novels, through to *Suspense,* the fiction invariably deals with a bewilderment caused by discontinuities in the experience of space and time. The feeling and mood of a scene are vital constituents in the cumulative process of disorientation, and each scene is therefore carefully structured to produce the elusive atmosphere which is essential to the whole. Richard Curle, the first Conrad critic, commented in 1914 that "the secret of Conrad's atmosphere eludes me as a critic, though emotionally it is as clear as the day" (66). Edward Garnett also shared this sentiment, stating that "the whole shifting atmosphere of the sea, the horizon, the heavens" was "felt by the senses as mysteriously near us, yet mysteriously aloof" (107). The point is made finally by the Symbolist poet, Arthur Symons who captured the elusive yet compelling nature of Conrad's fiction in the following words:

> Only great painters have created atmosphere to the extent that Conrad has: and Conrad's is if anything more mysterious, menacing and more troubling to the senses than theirs; he creates thrilling effects by mere force of suggestion, elusive as some vague mist, full of illusion, of rare magic, which can become poisonous or sorcerous. (24)

Symons's description touches upon three matters not much attended to in discussions of Conrad's impressionism: the atmosphere itself realized in the fiction, the specific connection between the fiction and visual impressionism, and the ontological dimension underlying the fiction. This paper wishes to outline briefly the debate around the notion of impressionism, contextualize Conradian impressionist criticism against this

21

background, suggest a possible method with which to approach Conrad's atmospheric descriptions and illustrate its practicability by a reading of the first chapter of *The Nigger of the "Narcissus"*.

The definition and analysis of literary movements[1] and periods – arbitrary as such divisions may be – fill many volumes and have provided a sound theoretical and historical basis for the development and functioning of critical discourse about the specific trend or period in question. Yet the same cannot be said of Impressionism, a nebulous concept which can be likened – as indeed Davies (67) has done – to a sponge, changing its form and shape according to the kind of pressure applied to it. Three examples will prove this point: For example, Nagel (ix) states that while he was researching his book *Stephen Crane and Literary Impressionism,* he was astonished to discover that even such an authoritative source as the *Literary History of the United States* (Fourth Edition) does not even mention the term, thereby implying that "despite the enormous impact of Impressionism on painting and music, the movement had no influence on American literature whatsoever." It is only as recently as 1978 that Bender could venture to make the statement that "the concept of Literary Impressionism is gaining acceptance as an explanation of the movement from Victorian to Modernist conventions" (231). And finally, in the preliminary research for this study, only one source dealing explicitly with literary impressionism could be located.

This critical neglect of Impressionism is all the more peculiar when one considers the important but hitherto neglected role it played for a substantial period at the turn of the century during the transition from Naturalism to Modernism. The notions of reality and the writer's representation of reality fulfilled central roles in all of these movements. Naturalism had as its basis a positivist approach to reality, which could only be known through scientific exploration, by negating metaphysical concerns in favour of sensory experience, and by describing the concrete moment of reality in precise detail. Translated into novelistic practice, this involved the analytic and objective observation of characters in their environment with emphasis on the linearity of time, and the precise description of setting. The naturalistic plot was structured on the principle of causality, and consisted of the stringing together of scenes which were described in great detail. Reality is therefore knowable and traceable. Modernism, on the other hand, questioned especially the mimetic representation of reality and the logical-sequential structure of time and causality. The development of the modernist novel has manifested four great preoccupations which emphasize its quarrel with naturalism on the one hand and its link with impressionism on the other, namely the complexities of its own form, the representation of inward states of consciousness, the assumption of a nihilistic disorder behind the ordered surface of life, and the freeing of the narrative from the determinations of an onerous plot (Bradbury and McFarlane, 393).

Impressionism found itself midway between these two movements in its attempts to grapple with the problems of reality and its representation in a fragmented, relativistic, accidental, subjective and forever-accelerating world.[2] Being neither a "movement" – in the strict sense – nor a critical invention, it existed on a set of shared assumptions, aiming to "catch and reproduce the shifting, fleeting intangible impressions by which the outside world impinges on our senses" (Brown 80). In attempting to do this, the Impressionists were forced to abandon causality, formal logic, and the desire to fit their "impressions" into existing generic forms. When framed by a problematic whose main terms are *reality, perception* and *representation,* a consideration of the many prominent British and American writers randomly described as "impressionist" (Poe, Swinburne, Whitman, Wilde, and Conrad all fall into this category and in turn influenced writers such as Virginia Woolf, Ford, Lawrence, Crane and Faulkner) suggests the need for readjusting our critical thinking in order to accept Impressionism as a central rather than a peripheral concept.

A logical question to ask is: why then this apparently strange phenomenon of neglect? A number of possible answers seem to present themselves. One major reason certainly has to be the lack of agreement as to what exactly is signified by the concept, and by *literary* impressionism in particular.[3] This vagueness consequently gave rise to two extreme and diverse practices, both detrimental to the study of Impressionism. One avenue was to reject even the validity of the term for literary studies, as Cuddon's testy remark – "The terms *impression* and *impressionist* have crept into literary criticism, but they are vague terms which we might well dispense with" (326) – indicates. The other extreme was to focus on the inclusiveness of the concept by conflating its manifestation in many disciplines, thereby never really focusing on the most important *literary* aspects of the concept. And it is because of this "all-inclusiveness" that Moser (123) states rather cynically: "The history of literary impressionism remains to be written...[and][it]...probably never [will]." While the study of Impressionism will clearly remain a problematic project because of the immense scope of such an interdisciplinary brief, it is my contention that one way to contribute toward the writing of Moser's history is first to provide clearer definitons of the concept within the context of the work of individual authors – such as Conrad – and, second, to read these definitions and descriptions against a broader ontological background.[4]

The same lack of agreement and diversity of approach bedevils Conrad criticism.[5] The many conflicting statements about the form and nature of his impressionism prove that it is still a bone of contention among Conrad scholars, despite the attention afforded to it, and that a rigorous examination of the arguments regarding Conrad's impressionism is called for.

It is a basic premise of this paper that Conrad's link with Impressionism provides an important perspective on his work as a whole, as well as on his position straddling the nineteenth and twentieth centuries.[6] A study of Conrad's impressionism not only provides important clues to the changes in artistic sensibility of the transitional period, but will also delineate Conrad's idiosyncratic position with regard to contemporaries such as James, Wells and Crane.

The differences of opinion with regard to Conrad seem to arise from disagreement in two areas, namely that of definition and method. Most of the studies mentioned above have concentrated on Conrad's epistemology, thereby using an interpretative paradigm or reading strategy which ignores the more basic level apparent in his work, that of his ontology. Pavel (100) has suggested that writers create fictional worlds which seem to possess stable dimensions. Benson's approach (1989) offers suggestions for a new approach and method which not only add some clarity to the impressionism debate, but which will show that Conrad's fictional worlds are not so stable as they seem at a first reading. Benson (1989, 30) argues that despite the unusual and elusive nature of Conrad's atmosphere, "it is surprising that no systematic attempt has been made to determine just what this atmosphere is and how it might bear on interpretation." His thesis and method offer a new and valid starting-point for a re-examination of Conrad's works based on a study of their informing ontological realities, realities which not only provide significant patterns of the *fin-de-siècle* bewilderment in Conrad's work as indicated by Armstrong (1987), but which also underscore Lothe's (1989) thesis that the intriguing interplay of form and content remains the most significant constituent aspect of his narrative method.

The impressionistic elements in two of Conrad's most famous works, *Heart of Darkness* and *Lord Jim* have been considered by a number of others (Krajka 1984; Watt 1980) and will not be dealt with here. An intratextual approach will indicate that not only these two texts, but a significant number of Conrad's work portray significant impressionistic elements. I wish to pursue the dialogue between Conrad's literary and non-literary texts, and show that there is a constant awareness of, and sensitivity to the impressionistic rendering of atmosphere which started as early as 1894.

If we take as a point of departure this aspect of atmosphere that is so frequently evoked by Impressionist painting, we have to focus on two crucial aspects, the visual and through it, the ontological. Impressionist atmosphere, says Benson (1989, 30), can be explained in terms of its commitment to the natural eye, that renders what the eye actually sees, a world of light and colour relationships. Atmosphere represents the mingling of colour reflections under various conditions of light, shade and distance. Edges are softened, ambience becomes luminous or hazy, and pictorial space is rendered by means of light and colour rather than geometric perspective.

A study of the letters written between 1896-1899 reveals Conrad's major concern with the notion of metaphysical darkness and the construction of a fictional world. The preoccupation with space and atmosphere was compelling enough to have structured his experience of the imaginative process. In a letter to Marguerite Poradowska of 29 March 1894, Conrad described his creative process in terms which show a spatial and atmospheric framework, as well as the sense of objects materializing out of a formless mist:

> Inspiration comes to me while gazing at the paper. Then there are vistas that extend out of sight; my mind goes wandering through great spaces filled with vague forms. Everything is still chaos, but, slowly, ghosts are transformed into living flesh, [and] floating vapours turn solid. (*CL*, 1, 151)

A similar concern with atmosphere figures in Conrad's response to Garnett's impressionistic sketches of London. There is a clear indication that the reading experience at once conceals and reveals, moves and lives:

> You do not jump on me. You grow – so to speak – around me. Your sentences luxuriate in your own atmosphere, they spring up on every side – till at last the picture is seen through the crafty tracery of words, like a building through leaves, both distinct-and hidden.
> Light and gloom...wave before our eyes in the stir of sentences – and one feels the greatness, the mistiness of things amongst which lives...a crowd mysterious.... (*CL*, 1, 331-2)

The letters written at the time of the publication of *The Nigger of the "Narcissus"* provide an interesting perspective on his concern with concepts which are impressionistic in nature and emphasize the notions of sensory impressions and the interplay between description and thematics. In a letter to E. L. Sanderson (17 October 1897), Conrad states that "I am impressionist from instinct" and that he can consequently only respond to Sanderson's poem emotionally; he suggests that Sanderson change the word *hoarse* in the line "The ocean's hoarse reverberating roar" to something that would convey the "persistent tumultuous *voice* of the sea" (*CL,* 1, 398-9; my italics). The insistence on sensory impression is also evident in a letter addressed to Edward Garnett (5 Dec. 1897), where Conrad comments on Crane's impressionism in his much quoted line – "He is the only impressionist and only an impressionist" – but goes on to imply that while Crane has vision, outline, color and movement, he is not popular because his work lacks something else such as the interplay between form and content. (*CL,* 1, 416-7)

Finally, his letter to an anomymous reviewer of *The Nigger* dated 9 Dec. 1897 provides an important insight into matters formal and thematic:

> I wanted to give a true impression, to present an [sic] undefaced image. And You, who know amongst what illusions and self-deceptions men struggle, work, fail – You will only smile with indulgence if I confess to You that I also wanted to connect the small world of the ship with that larger world carrying perplexities, fears, affections, rebellions, in a loneliness greater than that of the ship at sea. (*CL,* 1, 420-1)

This extract provides an unusual biographical perspective on Conrad's concern with creating a fictional space[7] in his work which would be representative of his larger thematic concerns. It also provides an important contrast between the work of impressionist painters and that of Conrad. While the painters often show "man in harmony with nature, and nature resplendent with a shimmering, congenial sunlight," Conrad's impressionistic passages induce "a sense of absurdity, rather than harmony, and a sense of nature's antipathy rather than congeniality to man" (Watts, 141).

Conrad's narrative techniques and descriptive ability show a marked sophistication during the crucial five years between the

publication of *Almayer's Folly* (1895) and *Lord Jim* in 1900.
It was especially during this period that distinctive impressionist
techniques were forged which later became the common properties of narratives such as *Heart of Darkness, Lord Jim,
Nostromo* and *The Secret Agent.* The use of episodic scenes,
a strong reliance on sensory images – especially those of colour
– and the shifts in narrative stance to emphasize the relativity of
perspective and perceptual distortions brought about by alter-
nating authorial or omniscient narrative with descriptive passages are all to be found in varying degrees in the works of this
period.

A second point which needs to be raised before turning to the
first chapter of *The Nigger* is that narrative and descriptive
techniques are inextricably interwoven with Conrad's moral
concerns, and, in fact, actually function as foregrounding
devices for thematic issues. This point is emphasized by Watt
(96) when he states Conrad uses concrete details in a series of
correlations between physical and moral properties which
establish the basic moral polarities. Benson (1991, 138) also
stresses the fact that – in Conrad especially – the description of
physical reality is much more functional than just being the
backdrop to the action; it is fundamental to a faithful account of
human moral and spiritual experience. Narrative and descriptive
techniques then combine with thematics to form the intriguing
interplay between form and content which is such a distinctive
Conradian trait.

The implied notions of mystery and a menacing threat in the
letter (9 Dec. 1897) accentuate one of the most basic themes in his
work, namely that of isolation and provide an essential link with
general impressionist practice. Conrad's heroes are, for various
reasons, all isolated from the rest of mankind and find themselves in a strange and mysterious relationship with their environment, which is more often than not, violent and threatening. The
isolation of the individual is furthermore one of the logical
consequences of impressionism. Walter Pater states as much in
his celebrated conclusion to *The Renaissance*:

Experience, already reduced to a group of impressions, is ringed round for each of us by that thick wall of personality through which no real voice has ever pierced on its way to us, or from us to that which we can only conjecture to without thought. (247)

The Nigger, with its world of imminent death, fear and destruction of man and ship and the inability of the characters to translate their impressions into clear and firm knowledge and insight clearly originated in the same mind which produced these letters.

Conrad's mastery of rendering an exotic and mysterious atmosphere which found its first manifestation in *Almayer's Folly* and *An Outcast of the Islands* develops even more in the pervasive atmosphere and highly visualized detail of *The Nigger*. Here Conrad experimented with a number of impressionist techniques, thereby creating a text filled with colours, shapes, and sounds, and translates into language the texture and graphicity of painting. There is the drastic narrowing and widening of spatial perspective, the use of a dwarfing perspective, the stress on the beginning of a narrative, the use of atmospheric perspective, the accumulation of visual and aural detail, the use of adjectives, the repetition of key motifs, the chiaroscuro of light and dark and its concomitant symbolism.

The use of setting in the novel functions on various levels, the combined effect of which is to create the unique atmosphere. Conrad uses setting to create a semblance of realism for the reader by providing descriptions of observable phenomena or a location. He sometimes uses it to "frame" the narrative, or to enclose the action at a specific time in the narrative. Very often it is used to add a metaphoric energy to its mechanical function by infusing it with strong sensory images to affect the atmosphere and mood of the tales.

Schwarz (22), in a discussion of the transformation of the English novel during the period 1890-1930, compares the function of setting in the modern English novel with that in the works of Van Gogh, Matisse, and Picasso. This analogy is also applicable to Conrad, as setting in his work also becomes foreground, and the physical conditions under which the imagined world functions become a "moral labyrinth which the characters are unable to negotiate and which not only shapes their destiny but also subsumes them."[8] In contrast to Victorian fiction which depended on the mastery of space and the linearity of an unfolding narrative, setting in Modernist fiction undermines the notion that space and time can be mastered by anyone, including the author.

A number of points raised by Schwarz can be applied to *The Nigger*. The use of descriptive passages at crucial points in the narrative have a dual function: they can either be a mere pictorial description of a scene or of natural phenomena used to foreground the sense of beauty or corruption and provide a spatial dimension to the action, or they can be a brooding spirit filling the whole nervous energy of the story, conceptualized in metaphorical terms to describe persons or situations in visual terms (Curle, 66; Faris, 308-9).

While the narrative in *The Nigger* is fairly straightforward and linear, it is made up of a rapid succession of word pictures which present the men, the officers and James Wait either singly or in groups; they find themselves in the forecastle and on deck, forward, amidships and on the poop. There are frequent descriptions of the ship as it would have appeared to a distant observer – pictures of the sea as it appeared from the ship, of particular parts of the ship as seen from other parts on board, and of the land as it disappears from sight. We also have vignettes of the characters in thought about themselves, of the men as they appeared to the officers and vice-versa. There are conversations and the cacophony of excited voices shouting fragments of speech. It is important to note that in *The Nigger* we already find, albeit in rudimentary form, Conrad's first attempts to portray the characters from the outside as well as from the inside: the "outside" pictures of the characters reinforce and complement the "inside" pictures created by the unknown narrator by adding more color or shading the picture as, for instance, in the case of the mysterious James Wait.

The evocation and description of atmosphere also has a narrative function. The alternation between descriptive passages with a brooding or retrospective nature force the reader – in the words of Henry James – to create "stopping places" in the novella which foreground the preceding action, thereby necessitating a more "objective" examination and evaluation of the preceding action.[9] In this regard the ontological realities assist the epistemological processes of the reader. Just as Monet's paintings of the cathedral in Rouen can be read as a narrative, so the use of atmospheric descriptions in Conrad can be seen to have a narrative function, providing the reader with breaks in the narrative which may force him to reassess the implication of the action which has preceded the atmospheric description.

The dramatic opening paragraph of *The Nigger* not only corresponds with Ford's *règle generale*[10] but also reinforces the central symbolic polarity already established in the title:

> MR. BAKER, chief mate of the ship *Narcissus,* stepped in one stride out of his lighted cabin into the darkness of the quarter-deck...Above his head, on the break of the poop, the night-watchman rang a double stroke. (3)

Conrad's insistence on making his readers hear, feel and see is evident. There is an active sequence of sensations involved here: visual, "lighted cabin" vs. "darkness of the quarter-deck," but also kinetic ("in one stride") and aural: "rang a double stroke." This opening passage also introduces the basic black vs. white contrast which gathers more and more associations as the novella progresses. Two examples are particularly important: both the ship and her crew are linked to darkness, emphasizing the strong effect of evil deeds and invisible dangers, which in turn, underscores the notions of doubt and chaos so present in the lives of the crew. When the ship leaves the harbor, the *Narcissus* is described as

> an enormous and aquatic black beetle, surprised by the light, overwhelmed by the sunshine, trying to escape with ineffectual effort into the distant gloom of the land. She left a lingering smudge of smoke on the sky, and two vanishing trails of foam on the water. On the place where she had stopped a round black patch of soot remained, undulating on the swell – an unclean mark on the creature's rest. (27)

The crew is also described as "a shadowy mob of heads visible above the blackness of starboard bulwarks" who only step "into the circle of light" (15-16) when Mr. Baker calls out their names.

The first significant atmospheric passage which combines a number of impressionist techniques and characteristics also has specific spatial and colour implications. It follows the opening sections of the tale in which the reader has been left with certain random impressions of the preparation of the *Narcissus* and some of the crew, narrated by an unknown narrator. The sheer strength of the impingement of the physical world on the human senses, developed much more during the storm[11] episode, is in itself indicative of the ontological dimension of Conrad's fictional world:[12]

> Outside the glare of the steaming forecastle the serene purity of the night enveloped the seamen with its soothing breath, with its tepid breath flowing under the stars that hung countless above the mastheads in a thing cloud of luminous dust. On the town side the blackness of the water was streaked with trails of light which undulated gently on slight ripples, similar to filaments that float rooted to the shore. Rows of other lights stood away in straight lines as if drawn up on parade between towering buildings; but on the other side of the harbour sombre hills arched high their black spines, on which, here and there, the point of a star resembled a spark fallen from the sky. Far off, Byculla way, the electric lamps at the dock gates shone on the end of lofty standards with a glow blinding and frigid like captive ghosts of some evil moons. Scattered all over the dark polish of the roadstead, the ships at anchor floated in perfect stillness under the feeble gleam of their riding-lights, looming up, opaque and bulky, like strange and monumental structures abandoned by men to an everlasting repose. (14-15)

There is a concentric perspective in this word-picture which also portrays a number of impressionist oppositions: the near vs. far, confined vs. open, and up vs. down oppositions all guide the reader's "eye" as his vision is extended from the forecastle, the hub of the action with its sounds and movement, to the "town side," on to "the other side of the harbour," and finally up towards the "sombre hills" to the "point of a star."

The passage creates the impression of silence and immobility in a way which strongly echoes that of the opening passages of

The Lagoon. The oppositional structure of – "Outside" vs.
"inside," "On the town side" vs. the "other side;" "Far off" vs.
the implied closeness of the speaker's vantage point – is
supported by what Watts (143) calls the "dwarfing perspective."
This perspective offers a reductive, or dwarfing view of human
activities and is in agreement with one of Benson's (1991, 138)
basic tenets – that for Conrad, "a description, and by implication
an explanation, of physical reality is fundamental to a faithful
account of human moral and spiritual experience."

The reader is led to this point of stasis in the narrative via the
excitement and tension of the first few pages, and the sudden
change from a narrative into a descriptive mode underscores
another recurrent aspect of Conrad's technique, namely that his
spatial descriptions are in a sense always related to aspects of
time and temporal arrangement. A strong visual impression is
often, as here, intensified because it lasts only for a short while,
taking the form of a sudden insight, or with a gathering together
of ideas and impressions developed up to that point in the
narrative. Descriptive passages in Conrad are strongly linked
with the slackening of narrative progression.

The passage is in stark contrast with the hustle and excitement
aboard the *Narcissus* described and punctuated by short truncated sentences and phrases at the beginning of the novella:

> The two forecastle lamps were turned up high, and shed an intense hard
> glare...white collars, undone, stuck out on each side of red faces; big
> arms in white sleeves gesticulated; the growling voices hummed steady
> amongst bursts of laughter and hoarse calls. "Here, sonny, take that
> bunk!...Don't you do it!...What's your last ship?...I know her...Three
> years ago, in Puget Sound...This here berth leaks, I tell you!...Come
> on, give us a chance to swing that chest!... (4-5)

The linguistic categories represented in these passages confirm
the strong visual focus and set the pattern for the rest of the
novella. There are no fewer than seventeen words and phrases
with a visual connotation such as "glare," "stars," "luminous
dust." Lucas (125) calls these epithetic adjectives and adverbials,
the main function of which seems to be to provide optional

information which – if omitted – would not change the sense of the description in a fundamental way. Translated into a painting metaphor, one could liken the function of these visual categories to touches of a painter's brush to heighten the colours, to intensify the impression, to make the reader "see." The impressionist notion of "separate fleeting impressions" (Stowell, 14) is enhanced further by the connotations of relativity and subjectivity suggested by words such as "glare," "stars," "luminous dust" and "trails of light."

The end of the first chapter uses the favourite Conradian technique of presenting a sketch of a character – glimpsed very briefly and intensely – so that his visual appearance remains vivid in the mind's eye while his inner nature remains impenetrable.[13] In the following description of Singleton, Conrad succeeds in describing an imaginary space which moves the mind's eye out to what Faris (313) calls the "luminous activity" of the sea and sky and offers an interesting example of the impressionist fusion between concrete and abstract. Colour, light and darkness become the symbol of time, of "now" vs. "then:"

> Singleton stood at the door with his face to the *light* and his back to the *darkness*. And alone in the *dim emptiness* of the sleeping *forecastle* he appeared *bigger, colossal,* very old; old as Father Time himself, who should have come there into this place as quiet as a sepulchre to contemplate with patient eyes the short victory of sleep, the consoler. Yet he was only a child of time, a lonely relic of a devoured and forgotten generation. (24; my italics)[14]

In this passage the character is depicted against a background of light in a way not dissimilar to the Impressionist painters' use of light and shade. The interrelationship between narrative and descriptive passages is particularly striking. There are three different, but related, focuses. The first falls on the character, Singleton. The second on a contained space, the ship. The viewer/reader's gaze is then extended progressively farther and farther into a space occupied by abstract areas of time, darkness and light. A second important element pertains to Conrad's use of abstract and fluid concepts such as light and darkness. While this is not so obvious initially, a second reading will reveal that this passage deals with comprehension and communication: it confronts the reader with an unknown narrator's vision, a transparent film through which the reader sees and traces the movement of the character in space and time as the character moves in and out of focus through the narrator's descriptions.

Thirdly, granted that Conrad's atmosphere is the point of departure of this thesis, the visual connotations emphasize the ontological presence of these passages. Gould, an early reviewer of *Victory,* compared the movement to abstraction in the works of Turner and Conrad, and concludes that

> Mr. Conrad is here no more that a character-delineator (as in the sense in which Thackeray is, say, or Meredith), than Turner was a portrait painter. As in Turner, the human figures are pathetic and fugitive against *lurid* and *fulginous* spaces. (In Sherry, 300; my italics)

Singleton's world – in the words of Conrad – "spring[s] up on every side – till at last the picture is seen through the crafty tracery of words, like a building through leaves, both distinct- -and hidden. Light and gloom...wave before our eyes in the stir of sentences" (*CL,* 1, 331). The passage restricts the reader's visual impressions to fragmentary glimpses of objects, people, forms, and movement. These objects constitute the bare fragments of the Conradian universe – space, darkness, motion, atmosphere and mystery.

Finally, the descriptive passages in Chapter One also form what Lothe (89) regards as a structural frame around the climax of the chapter, the introduction of James Wait, thereby creating a "snapshot" or – in Iserian terms – a *Gestalt* on which the reader has to superimpose the subsequent impressions created in the rest of the novella.

To conlude, Impressionism, despite its neglect, is a crucial precursor of Modernism. Many of the characteristics of Modernism are explicitly impressionist in form, function and effect, as can be noted especially in its visual aspects, which carry ontological as well as epistemological implications. A reading of Conrad's impressionism which focuses only on the epistemological aspects – as the majority of readings mentioned earlier have done – will of necessity remain partly blinded. Only an approach which gives the rightful place to the ontological – and more basic – level of experience and perception, as this reading of *The Nigger* has hopefully illustrated – can truly be said to adhere to Conrad's famous – or what many critics feel to be notorious – creed stated in its "Preface," "My task which I am trying to achieve is, by the power of the written word to make you hear, to make you feel – it is, before all, to make you see" (xiii).[15]

NOTES

1. The use of the concept "movement" with regard to Impressionism is problematic and should be clarified at the outset. Impressionism as such was never really a "movement" in the sense of a consciously organized grouping of artists united, say, by an explicit manifesto. The practitioners should rather be seen as Stowell (14) describes them, as "a disparate breed" who shared some basic assumptions. The term "movement" will be used in this sense, and will be considered as a more or less discrete historical mode with distinctive stylistic patterns and devices, rather than merely a loose stylistic tendency, or a phenomenon rooted in a strong social and artistic organization.

2. The transitional role played by Impressionism is eloquently summarized by Stowell (14-15): "[I]mpressionism anticipated the most cherished qualities of modernism: the primacy of phenomenological perception, the atomization of a subjectively perceived reality, the acceptance of chance in a world so complex and unknowable as to render causality impotent, the necessity to come to terms with reality through the process of induction."

3. Kronegger (24) comments on this problem of definition as follows: "As soon as the term fell into the hands of the literary critics, it was distorted, defining impressionism as a literary movement in terms of the evolution or antithesis of an existing movement. It is an acknowledged literary movement in Danish, German and British literature, whereas in French and American literature, impressionism is one of those elusive terms which writers use as vaguely and variously as they use imagism, symbolism, stream of consciousness, decadent literature." This view is also echoed by Armstrong (1983, 245) when he comments: "The term 'impression' is an elastic construct which has been invoked by widely divergent theories of knowledge in philosophy, criticism, and art – from David Hume's skeptical empiricism to Walter Pater's ethic of artistic cultivation to the perceptual primitivism of the French Impressionist painters."

4. The need for a more precise definition is also underscored by Armstrong (1987, 5) when he states that only the context of the application will decide which of the multiplicity of meanings will be the most functional as a hermeneutic tool.

5. The following present a sample of the kinds of statement being made about Conrad's impressionism: "It is true that Conrad remained an Impressionist all his life and his novels and tales remain a living testament of his adherence to this ideal" (Yaseen 169); "[Conrad's] achievement...lies in relating an ironic, existential vision of exposure to an impressionistic mode of rendering experience" (Bradbury and McFarlane 616); "Nevertheless, it is unlikely that Conrad either thought of himself as an impressionist or was even significantly influenced by the impressionist movement" (Watt 179); "after celebrating the previous period's new emphasis on impressions, James, Conrad, and Proust reconstituted the whole concept of the word 'impression' in such a way as to deny the chief claims made for it by the 'impressionists'" (Hay 1988, 374).

6. Indeed, one of the most intriguing aspects of Conrad's position as a writer straddling the nineteenth and twentieth centuries has been the tendency of various scholars to appropriate him for a particular movement or school. He has at various times been labelled a Romantic, a Realist, a Symbolist, a Romantic-Realist and an Impressionist. Most of these claims were based on implicit agreement about the assumptions underlying the particular movement or "school" with which they wished to associate Conrad, and paid special attention to what in his oeuvre qualified him for membership. This cannot be said about the many divergent claims made for Conrad as an Impressionist.

7. The working titles for the novel all have a strong spatial focus. In the MS he originally called it *The Nigger of the "Narcissus,"* but in sending it to the publisher he suggested *"The Forecastle. A Tale of Ship and Men,"* but changed the Forecastle to *"Nigger"* a few days later. Its first appearance in print was in the *New Review,* under the title, *The Nigger of the "Narcissus" – A Tale of the Forecastle.* It was only in its second book edition (1898) that the final subtitle was changed to *A Tale of the Sea* (Najder, 205).

8. Cf. Benson's (1991, 140) statement: "This atmospheric immersion and physical disorientation are inseparable from the moral disorientation that accompanies them."

9. Iser's description of the reading process in *The Act of Reading* (21) provides a perspective on the reader's interaction with a novel which is particularly relevant to understanding the processes involved in the reading of impressionist texts. The novel does not point to a referential reality, but represents a pattern, of a "structured indication to guide the imagination of the reader" (9). This pattern is incomplete and full of "gaps," "blanks" or "indeterminacies" which the reader must "fill in," thereby constructing a *Gestalt* of the novel by linking the various perspectives (1978, 16).

10. Ford commented on the importance of openings in *A Personal Remembrance*: "Openings for us, as for most writers, were matters of great importance, but probably we more than most writers realized of what primary importance they are. A real short story must open with a breathless sentence; a long short story may begin with some leisurely phrases. At any rate the opening paragraph of book or story should be of the tempo of the whole performance. That is the regle generale. Moreover, the reader's attention must be gripped by that first paragraph. So our ideal novel must begin either with a dramatic scene or with a note that should suggest the whole book" (171).

11. See also *Typhoon* and *The Rescue* in this regard.

12. Ontology is used in the sense of how the world is, while epistemology is about whether and how we can know this. The distinction is necessarily arbitrary.

13. Cedric Watts describes this technique as an empirical hyperbole: "[T]he observer's fidelity to the immediate testimony of his senses entails the subordination or exclusion of conventional notions of the function, role or order of what is observed. Experience becomes at once vivid and recalcitrant" (141).

14. The relation between Symbolism and Impressionism is emphasized by Symons (1898, 858-859) in a way which is also applicable to this passage: "The Impressionist in literature as in painting, would flash upon you in a new, sudden way so exact an image of what you have just seen, just as you have seen it...The Symbolist in this new, sudden way, would flash upon you the 'soul' of that which can be apprehended only by the soul – the finer sense of things unseen, the deeper meaning of things evident."

15. Part of the research for this paper was conducted at the British Library; Birkbeck College Library, University of London; and the Polish Library, London. Permission to use these libraries and the assistance rendered is hereby gratefully acknowledged, as is the financial assistance of the Potchefstroom University for Christian Higher Education which enabled me to conduct the research, and the financial assistance of the Department of National Education which enabled me to attend the conference.

I would also like to thank the following colleagues whose comments on sections or earlier drafts of this paper greatly clarified my thinking on the topic. The views expressed, however, are my own, as are any misinterpretations and any other errors in thinking and judgment: Professors Laurence Wright (Rhodes University); Paul Armstrong (University of Oregon); Jakob Lothe (University of Bergen); and Ivo Vidan (University of Zagreb). Professor Donald Benson (University of Iowa) not only commented on sections of the paper but also kindly supplied me with material unobtainable in South Africa, while Professor Laurence Davies (Dartmouth College) graciously allowed me access to unpublished material. Owen Knowles (University of Hull) also provided useful advice in the revision of this paper.

WORKS CITED

Anderson L. *Bennett, Wells, and Conrad: Narrative in Transition*. London: Macmillan, 1988.

Armstrong P. B. "The Hermeneutics of Literary Impressionism: Interpretation and Reality in James, Conrad and Ford," *Centennial Review*, 27 (1983), 244-69.

Amstrong P. B. *The Challenge of Bewilderment in James, Conrad and Ford*. Ithaca: Cornell University Press, 1987.

Bender T. K. "Conrad and Literary Impressionism," *Conradiana*, 10 (1978), 211-224.

Benson D. R. "Impressionist Painting and the Problem of Conrad's Atmosphere," *Mosaic*, 22 (1989), 29-40.

Benson D. R. "Constructing an Ethereal Cosmos: Late Classical Physics and *Lord Jim*," *Conradiana*, 23 (1991), 133-150.

Bradbury M. and McFarlane J. eds. *Modernism: A Guide to European Literature, 1890-1930*. Harmondsworth: Penguin, 1976.

Brown C. S. "Symposium in Literary Impressionism," in *Yearbook of Comparative and General Literature*, 17, 80-6.

Cuddon J. A. *A Dictionary of Literary Terms*. Rev. Ed. London: André Deutsch, 1979.

Curle R. *Joseph Conrad: A Study*. Garden City: Doubleday, 1914.

Davies L. R. B. *Cunninghame Graham and the Concept of Impressionism*. Unpublished thesis, University of Sussex, 1972.

Delbanco N. *Group Portrait: Conrad, Crane, Ford, Wells and James*. New York: Morrow, 1982.

Farris B. "The 'Dehumanization' of the Arts: JMW Turner, Joseph Conrad and the Advent of Modernism," *Comparative Literature*, 41 (1989), 305-26.

Fraser G. *Interweaving Patterns in the Work of Joseph Conrad*. Ann Arbor, Mi.: UMI Research Press, 1988.

Ford F. M. *Joseph Conrad: A Personal Remembrance*. London: Duckworth, 1924.

Garnett E. Unsigned Article, *Academy*, 15 October 1989, 82-83, Sherry N. ed. *Conrad: The Critical Heritage*. London: Routledge and Kegan Paul, 1973, pp. 104-8.

Gould G. Unsigned Review of *Victory*, Sherry N. ed. *Conrad: The Critical Heritage*. London: Routledge and Kegan Paul, 1973, pp. 299-301.

Hay E. Knapp. "Joseph Conrad and Impressionism," *Journal of Aesthetics and Art Criticism*, 34 (1975), 134-44.

Hay E. Knapp. "A Conrad Quintet: Review Article," *Modern Philology*, 79 (1981), 179-87.

Hay E. Knapp. "Proust, James, Conrad and Impressionism," *Style*, 22 (1988), 368-81.

Higdon D. L. "Current Conrad Bibliography (1987-1988)," *Conradiana*, 22 (1990), 67-80.

Hillis Miller J. *Poets of Reality: Six Twentieth Century Writers.* Cambridge Mass.: Harvard University Press, 1966.

Iser W. *The Act of Reading: A Theory of Aesthetic Response.* Baltimore: Johns Hopkins University Press, 1978.

Johnson B. "Conrad's Impressionism and Watt's 'Delayed Decoding'," Murfin R. C. ed. *Conrad Revisited: Essays for the Eighties.* Alabama: University of Alabama Press, 1985, pp. 51-70.

Krajka W. *"Lord Jim.* An Impressionistic Novel?" *Folia Societas Scientiarium Lublinensis,* 26 (1984), 55-62.

Kronegger M. E. *Literary Impressionism.* New Haven: College and University Press, 1973.

Lothe J. *Conrad's Narrative Method.* Oxford: Clarendon Press, 1989.

Lotman J. *The Structure of the Artistic Text,* tr. R. Vroon. Ann Arbor: Michigan Slavic Contributions.

Lucas M. A. "Conrad's Adjectival Eccentricity," *Style,* 25 (1991), 123-50.

Moser T. C. *The Life and Fiction of Ford Madox Ford.* Princeton: Princeton University Press, 1980.

Murfin R. C. ed. *Conrad Revisited: Essays for the Eighties.* Alabama: University of Alabama Press, 1985.

Nagel J. *Stephen Crane and Literary Impressionism.* London: Pennsylvania University Press, 1980.

Najder Z. *Joseph Conrad: A Chronicle.* New Brunswick N.J.: Rutgers University Press, 1983.

"Narcissus." *Webster's Third New International Dictionary.* 1966 ed.

Nettels E. "Conrad and Stephen Crane," *Conradiana,* 10 (1978), 267-83.

Paruolo E. "Reality and Consciousness: Impressionism in Conrad," *L'Epoque Conradienne,* (1986), 75-84.

Pater W. *The Renaissance.* London: Macmillan, 1890.

Pavel T. G. *Fictional Worlds.* Cambridge, Mass.: Harvard University Press, 1986.

Schwarz D. R. *The Transformation of the English Novel, 1890-1930.* New York: St. Martin's Press, 1989.

Stowell H. P. *Literary Impressionism: James and Chekov.* Athens, Georgia: University of Georgia Press, 1980.

Symons A. "The Decadent Movement in Literature," *Harper's New Monthly Magazine,* 87 (1898), 858-9.

Symons A. *Notes on Joseph Conrad.* London: Meyers, 1925.

Watt I. *Conrad in the Nineteenth Century.* London: Chatto and Windus, 1980.

Watts C. "Conrad's Absurdist Techniques: A Terminology," *Conradiana,* 9 (1977), 141-8.

Yaseen M. *Joseph Conrad's Theory of Fiction.* Aligarh: Asia Publishing House, 1970.

Richard Ambrosini,
University of Rome,
Rome, Italy

Conrad's "Paper Boats"

At the beginning of 1924, Conrad was asked by his American publisher, F. N. Doubleday, to write a preface for a collection of his short stories, *The Shorter Tales of Joseph Conrad.* In April, a few months before his death, the author set out to provide a key to his shorter fiction, by using that figurative alliance of writing and sailing which he had already used to vindicate the continuity of his life in *A Personal Record.* But this time his revisitation of the early years – the ones in which "I launched my first paper boats in the days of my literary childhood" – took a different direction, and he tried instead to explain those "lofty ambitions of well-meaning beginners" which grounded his early works. "Much time has passed, since," he writes:

> and I can assure my readers that I have never felt more humble than I do to-day while I sit tracing these words, and that I see now, more clearly than ever before, that indeed those were but paper boats, freighted with a grown-up child's dreams and launched innocently upon that terrible sea that, unlike the honest salt water of my early life, knows no hope of changing horizons but lies within the circle of an Eternal Shadow. (*LE,* 142-3)

I suggest that Conrad's 1924 comments are a clear indication that the writer up to the end of his career was fully aware of the convictions that directed the evolution of his work, and that these comments can provide a perspective on those ideas which he articulated through the narrative voice of Marlow in the works written at the turn of the century.

My hypothesis is, first, that his "dream" was that he could create a suggestively impressionistic language which would have given universal effectiveness to his writing, by enabling him to express that universal content deposited in the subjectivity of

41

personal experiences. This "dream" was first communicated to his readers in the 1897 "Preface" to *The Nigger of the "Narcissus,"* in which the author set out his view of the poetic potentialities of prose language. In addition I suggest that this ideal proved unrealizable only after he carried out, tested, and eventually re-defined this "dream" in *Heart of Darkness* and *Lord Jim*, his "paper boats." Of all the formal experimentations, authorial self-questioning and figurative language to be found in these two tales, I will limit myself in this paper to only a few examples of how Conrad used Marlow to articulate the discoveries he was making about his medium in the act of writing.

In the first line of the "Preface," Conrad acknowledges that an ideal craftsmanship is required to enlarge the potentialities of prose language: "A work that aspires, however humbly, to the condition of art should carry its justification in every line" (*NN,* vii). After having launched the piece by addressing the aesthetic dimension of his view of fiction, however, he sets the artist's social responsibility in the foreground. In the paragraphs which follow, the author explains why his artistic prose should not be obscure by suggesting that the effectiveness of the art form he is striving for is based on the universality of its appeal. But the moral justification of a novel is not enough to make it universally effective and, at the beginning of the fourth paragraph, an echo of the first line sets the initial question in the foreground again: "Fiction – if it at all aspires to be art – appeals to temperament" (ix). This qualification of the opening sentence anticipates his own answer to that question: an artistic prose can be created only through a "care for the shape and ring of sentences" (ix). And the reward for the novelist is nothing less than bringing "to play for an evanescent instant...the light of magic suggestiveness...over the commonplace surface of words" (ix). Conrad could express his newly found awareness of the potentialities of fiction in the "Preface" because in its rhetorical structure he managed to shape his particular formulation of the artist's task by articulating both a moral and an aesthetic discourse. That he could make plain the interrelation between these two aspects of his artistic ideal proved that it was possible to convey his personal view.

The parallel discourse he had devised to enunciate his "dream" in the "Preface" was then used by Conrad to adapt his novel forms to the communication of his personal appeal. The distortions of the fictional language's linearity in the early Marlow tales, in fact, are the result of Conrad's articulating his moral and aesthetic concerns in a fictional context by interweaving rhetorical commentaries and fictional language. It was in particular the writing/sailing metaphor structured around Marlow, the imaginative sea captain aware of the dangers lurking below the surface of the sea, that enabled Conrad to construct a personal novel form. The internal narrator's preoccupation with the inexpressible side of experience dramatizes the author's groping for words, his quest for a poetically effective prose. In trying to remain faithful to his memory, Marlow's moral concerns become a questioning of the very possibility for the writer of communicating his past experiences. Conrad can thus make explicit the theoretical dimension of his own struggle to transform his memories into visual impressions, through his internal narrator's addresses to his audience.

Only with Marlow's appearance in *Youth* does the narrative frame Conrad first used in *Karain* become a rhetorical structure allowing the author to articulate a meta-commentary on the theoretical issues he is confronting in his writing. As a result, in *Heart of Darkness* and *Lord Jim* Marlow's interventions are in fact glosses on discoveries the author was making about his medium while writing. Two well-known passages in *Heart of Darkness* stand out in the tale's critical discourse as Conrad's most explicit attempt to actualize his "dream" by building into the fictional language an intellectual drama intended to draw attention to the suggestively impressionistic language through a clearly outlined reading model.

Marlow's function is made clear near the beginning of the story, when he warns his audience, "I don't want to bother you much with what happened to me personally;" but they must know the events of the story "to understand the effect of it" (*YS*, 51) on him. Conrad's narrative strategy is aimed precisely at conveying this effect. To do so he interweaves the *story* of "what happened" to Marlow and the *tale* of the effect those events had on him. Through an impressionistic account of Marlow's experience in the Dark Continent, Conrad makes the reader "hear...feel" and "*see*" (*NN*, x) scenes and characters from the past. But his internal narrator is aiming at a different kind of accuracy, which is pointed out in the first duet between Marlow and the frame narrator. For Marlow, in fact, "the meaning of an episode was not inside like a kernel but outside, enveloping the tale which brought it out only as a glow brings out a haze, in the likeness of one of these misty halos that sometimes are made visible by the spectral illumination of moonshine" (*YS*, 48). Critical commentaries on this passage have usually centered attention on the physical juxtaposition of "inside" and "outside," as if the pivotal term were "episode," whereas Conrad's emphasis falls on the word "tale." It is the tale, in fact, that brings out the episode's meaning, "as a glow brings out a haze." The telling, rather than the event itself, generates meaning and – the frame narrator warns his readers – one must not concentrate on Marlow's account of the events in which he is protagonist, but rather on the distortions which the re-creation of his subjective experience produces on the narrative. The "meaning" of the episode lies in the traces of how he experienced those events.

Conrad plays on the illusory quality of an impressionistic re-creation of memory to discuss the question which orders the tale's critical discourse: how to write (and read) a story? The solution which runs through the exchanges between narrator and listeners is a mirror-effect between impressionistic language and the re-creation of subjective experience. This mirror-effect dramatizes in the text the difficulty of translating the memory of visual and aural sensations into words.

A striking description of these theoretical overtones is contained in the writer's 1917 "Author's Note" to *Youth: A Narrative, and Two Other Stories*. In *Heart of Darkness*, Conrad explains, experience is "pushed a little...beyond the actual facts of the case for the perfectly legitimate, I believe, purpose of bringing it home to the minds and bosoms of the readers." "That sombre theme," he adds, "had to be given a sinister resonance, a tonality of its own, a continued vibration that, I hoped, would hang in the air and dwell on the ear after the last note had been struck" (*YS*, xi).

Conrad makes explicit these concerns in the text at the end of the scene in which Marlow lies to the Station manager's spy – the "brickmaker" – about his belonging to the same group as Kurtz. Why does Marlow lie for Kurtz? The argument set up in the long scene with the brickmaker, "this papier-maché Mephistopheles" (81), emphasizes the abstract quality of the attraction Marlow feels for Kurtz. "I could see a little ivory coming out from there," Marlow recalls, "and I had heard Mr. Kurtz was in there. I had heard enough about it, too – God knows! Yet somehow it didn't bring any image with it – no more than if I had been told an angel or a fiend was in there" (81). The relevance of Marlow's not having seen Kurtz at this point is central for the narrative strategy underlying the voyage toward Kurtz, which becomes apparent when Conrad sets the narrative frame's function in the foreground in this passage in order to emphasize the theoretical issues he will be tackling in the tale.

Marlow explains his white lie with the notion that "it somehow would be of help to that Kurtz whom at the time I did not see – you understand." What should his listeners understand? He widens the scope of "seeing" apparently to explain what he means: "He was just a word for me. I did not see the man in the name any more than you do. Do you see him? Do you see the story? Do you see anything?" (82). In having Marlow voice this appeal – which is a far more troubled formulation of Conrad's 1897 definition of his desire "to make you hear, to make you feel – it is, before all, to make you *see*" (*NN*, x) – the author is dramatizing his own doubts about being able to communicate with his readers.

The meta-narrative quality of the passage is confirmed by the narrator's comparing the re-creation of his past to a dream. "It seems to me," Marlow tells his listeners, "I am trying to tell you a dream – making a vain attempt, because no relation of a dream can convey the dream-sensation" (*YS*, 82). This is not simply another of Conrad's frequent revisitations of the Calderonian *la vida es sueño*. The central word in Marlow's appeal to his listeners is not "dream," but "dream-sensation." Conrad elaborates on this distinction in the paragraph which follows: "No, it is impossible; it is impossible to convey the life-sensation of any given epoch of one's existence – that which makes its truth, its meaning – its subtle and penetrating essence. It is impossible. We live, as we dream – alone" (82).

The questions Marlow raises are of central importance for an understanding of the conflicting difficulties Conrad found in expressing the personal experiences he worked into his fiction. Conrad's childhood and early youth had been totally alien to that of his English readers: he could never really count on an identification between his linguistic associations and those of his audience. This is why his use of his personal memories leads to a sequence of irreconcilable dualities. On the one hand, his memory was all that was left of his community, and integrating the expression of his memories was a commitment to that community. On the other hand, his reminiscences had to be translated into English words to be expressed in a communicable form. The aesthetics of fiction which he had enunciated in 1897 represent the clearest indication of the solution he attempted: in order to create a literary language which could transcend his alienness from his audience without repudiating his own cultural identity he would try to achieve the "condition of art" (*NN*, vii).

In the paragraph following the "life-sensation" passage Conrad reverts to using an "aside" of the frame narrator to share his doubts and hopes with his readers. After the frame narrator has interjected – "He paused again as if reflecting" – Marlow picks up the "seeing" theme which had launched his meditations: "Of course in this you fellows see more than I could then. You see me, whom you know." The frame narrator introduces at this point in the narrative his longest remark. He recalls, at first, that "It had become so pitch dark that we listeners could hardly see one another" (*YS*, 83). Why does the listener comment in this way? The apparently rambling digression suddenly tightens:

> It had become so pitch dark that we listeners could hardly see one
> another. For a long time already he, sitting apart, had been no more to
> us than a voice. There was not a word from anybody. The others might
> have been asleep, but I was awake. I listened, I listened on the watch for
> the sentence, for the word, that would give me the clue to the faint
> uneasiness inspired by this narrative that seemed to shape itself without
> human lips in the heavy night-air of the river. (83)

This passage confirms the role Conrad assigned to the frame
narrator in the duets with Marlow in the first pages of *Heart of
Darkness*. Here, the frame narrator is bringing out, as if he were
a litmus paper, the intellectual and emotional effect sought by
the author. In the increasing darkness he may be losing those
bearings which supported his comfortable notion of history, but
at this point in the narrative he has a very clear notion of what
could provide him with a "clue" to the irrational feeling
generated by the tale: a sentence, or a word. Thus, in this
definitive formulation of the reading model envisaged in the
"nutshell" passage, Marlow's "you fellows see more than I could
then" (83) is converted into the listener's realization that only
particularly suggestive words can bring out the meaning of the
story, "as a glow brings out a haze" (48). That "continued
vibration" of the theme's "sinister resonance" (xi) which Conrad
refers to in his 1917 "Author's Note" echoes in the perplexed
language of Marlow's revisitation of his past.

In *Lord Jim*, throughout Marlow's oral narrative, Conrad has
his internal narrator interpret the protagonist's figurative language to translate the expression of a subjective experience into
a statement of its universality. The resulting interpretation, on
the narrator's part, leads to the author's most extended attempt
to apply the model for an artistic fiction envisaged in the
"Preface" to *The Nigger*. But with the shift between Marlow's
inquiry into the *Patna* case and the Patusan romance Conrad
appears to rely on the effectiveness of particular narrative
structures rather than on a strategy based on a linguistic effect.
This shift signals the writer's gradual realization, in the act of
writing, that the artistic ideal which had shaped his commitment
to authorship was an illusion, a"dream."

A clear indication of the meta-fictional significance of Marlow's interpretation of Jim's figurative expressions is given by a particular theme recurring in the chapters that close, respectively, the omniscient narration (chapter 4) and the Patusan section (chapter 35), and the chapter that opens Marlow's written account (chapter 36): the theme of the radical conflict between the expression/interpretation circuit activated by Marlow's involvement in shaping Jim's fate on one hand, and the "language of facts" on the other. Thus, in moving from an impersonal narration to an oral narrative then to a written account, the themes emodied in Jim's figure are synthesized at the end of each segment with the author's discourse in theoretical problems which the following segment's narrative form appears more appropriate to solve.

In the courtroom scene in chapter 4 Conrad makes Marlow's function clear before having him speak. The magistrates ask Jim "pointed questions" and he, trying "to tell honestly the truth of his experience," finds himself using figurative language: "he said, speaking of the ship: 'She went over whatever it was as easy as a snake crawling over a stick'." The impersonal narrator comments that the "illustration was good," but "the questions were aiming at facts" (28). Jim, however, is seeking an explanation, not facts: "They wanted facts. Facts! They demanded facts from him, as if facts could explain anything!" (29).

Jim is willing to face the shame and humiliation of the witness-box because through the explanation of his act, he hopes to reconcile himself – as well as his audience – to the obscure motives which impelled his desertion: "After his first feeling of revolt he had come round to the view that only a meticulous precision of statement would bring out the true horror behind the appalling face of things" (30). But can the precise words he is seeking express what his imagination had seen? Can the gap between objectivity and subjectivity be bridged by the language which grounds the interhuman conventions he has broken? Jim's attempt cannot be communicated, but already Jim's presence in the witness-box demonstrates that he is hanging on to what could save his ideal self-image from the facts of his existential shipwreck. His efforts to explain are but an attempt to establish a "truth" – that is, something he can share with his audience. But the distance between words and intention becomes too great:

> He wanted to go on talking for truth's sake, perhaps for his own sake also; and while his utterance was deliberate, his mind positively flew round and round the serried circle of facts that had surged up all about him to cut him off from the rest of his kind... This awful activity of mind made him hesitate at times in his speech. (31)

Shortly after this passage Jim notices Marlow. The omniscient narrator points out an intuition of Jim's: "This fellow...looks at me as though he could see somebody or something past my shoulder" (33). The unexpressed object of Jim's words – "something else besides" (31) – finds a place in the world in the "interested" glance of the stranger sitting in the courtroom. The mechanism which superintends the passage from the omniscient narration (in its extreme form of reported thought) to Marlow's yarn is basically a reflection of what Jim wishes to put into words in the captain's sympathetic response.

A few lines after Marlow's first appearance, Jim starts to doubt "whether he would ever again speak out as long as he lived" (33). It is at this point that Conrad explicitly sets up a juxtaposition of Jim's problems with language and the narrative which follows:

> The sound of his own truthful statements confirmed his deliberate opinion that speech was of no use to him any longer. That man there seemed to be aware of his hopeless difficulty. Jim looked at him, then turned away resolutely, as after a final parting. (33)

The "final parting" is such, first of all, on a narrational level. From now on, no omniscient narrator will relate Jim's thoughts. It will be Marlow's interpretation of the young man's utterances that will dramatize and carry on Jim's doubts about language.

The most explicit instances of this use of Marlow occur during the night talk on the verandah of the Malabar Hotel. When Jim's story reaches the fatal moment before his jump, Marlow looks at the young man holding his head in his hands and comments: "These were things he could not explain to the court – and not even to me; but I would have been little fitted for the reception of his confidences had I not been able at times to understand the pauses between the words" (105). Marlow is not boasting of a supernatural perceptiveness. With this comment, Conrad sets in motion the function he has assigned to his internal narrator. Throughout his inquiry into the moral overtones of the *Patna* case, Marlow will unravel Jim's figurative expressions by echoing them through a suggestively impressionistic language.

This technique finds its most thorough application during Marlow's account of the four castaways adrift at night after their desertion. At one point, Jim "muttered something about the sunrise being of a kind that foretells a calm day" (122). These words have a marked effect on the experienced seaman Marlow, who comments upon them in what seems at first a Master's characteristically paternalistic way: "You know that sailor habit of referring to the weather in every connection" (122). As it turns out, however, this comment introduces Marlow's participation in the scene's rendering:

> And on my side his few mumbled words were enough to make me see the lower limb of the sun clearing the line of the horizon, the tremble of a vast ripple running over all the visible expanse of the sea, as if the waters had shuddered, giving birth to the globe of light, while the last puff of the breeze would stir the air in a sigh of relief. (122-3)

Jim's mutter has been translated into an evocative representation.

Marlow's inquiry into the *Patna* case reaches its culmination when he finds a first sympathetic response to his interpretation of Jim's case in Stein's readiness to recognize the reality of Jim's illusions. At the end of the scene in Stein's study, while he is accompanying Marlow to his room, the German adventurer--scholar repeats once again, "He is romantic – romantic...And that is very bad – very bad...Very good, too." Marlow does not have much patience left for Stein's perplexing musings and interrputs him: "But *is* he?" His friend's reply brings out a possible ambiguity in Marlow's question: "Evident! What is it that by inward pain makes him know himself? What is it that for you and me makes him – exist?" (216). When Marlow tells Stein that he is at least as much a romantic as Jim, his German friend answers "Well – I exist, too" (217). Marlow's realization that Jim is real, and "exists" for him precisely because he is romantic, is a significant stage in his interpretation of the young man's personality. After relating that Stein has finally found a "practical remedy" for Jim – i.e. Patusan – Marlow returns to the issue of Jim's existence with a question which revives for a moment the discussion in Stein's study: "And what business had he to be romantic?" He stops and tells his listeners:

> I am telling you so much about my own instinctive feelings and bemused reflections because there remains so little to be told of him. He existed for me, and after all it is only through me that he exists for you. I've led him out by the hand; I have paraded him before you. Were my commonplace fears unjust? I won't say – not even now. You may be able to tell better, since the proverb has it that the onlookers see most of the game. (224)

In the romantic tale the narrator's "feelings" and "reflections" will no longer guide the reader in the slow uncovering of his own coming to terms with the problem of Jim. The young man has been provided with a stage on which to act out his own play and, as Marlow tells Jim, "it would be for the outside world as though he had never existed:" "Never existed – that's it, by Jove!" is Jim's enthusiastic comment (232).

On a meta-narrative level, by presenting Patusan as the result of Marlow's interpretation of Jim's case, Conrad makes clear that only a fictional world can create that „suspension of disbelief" which makes a fictional character exist. Conrad makes it immediately clear that Patusan's dimension outside western history is apt for the unconventional romance he is creating: everything Jim will achieve among the people of the village, "love, honour, men's confidence" is fit material "for a heroic tale; only our minds are struck by the externals of such a success, and to Jim's successes there were no externals" (226). If Jim had become a hero to his own community, the distinction between illusion and reality established during Marlow's inquiry would have been blurred. Jim is significant for Marlow because the way in which he lives his situation questions the relationship between principles and reality. He has been judged and found guilty for a fact he cannot dispose of, and yet goes on believing in, and suffering for, the very ideal which that fact belies. If Jim had been able to do so in an environment familiar to Marlow's audience, he would have become a hero – that is, he would have re-asserted a coincidence between reality and illusion.

The Patusan fiction-within-the-fiction, however, rather than fulfilling the self-projection which underlies Marlow's interpretation of Jim's case, signals Conrad's relinquishing of an involved narrator voicing the author's reflection on fiction and foretells the change in settings and narrative techniques after *Lord Jim*. The light under which Marlow sees Jim at the end will be the moral viaticum which will transform the captain into a narrator. In saying goodbye, Jim says to Marlow "I must go on, go on for ever holding up my end, to feel sure that nothing can touch me. I must stick to their belief in me to feel safe and to – to...to keep in touch with...you, for instance" (334). Marlow, who is going back to the "impeccable world" (331), is humbled by Jim's words: "I felt a gratitude, an affection, for that straggler whose eyes had singled me out, keeping my place in the ranks of an insignificant multitude" (334). Jim's "singling out" in the courtroom had launched Marlow's involvement, but here the narrator seems to be referring to an enlargement of Jim's appeal. Through Marlow, Jim will try to keep in touch with the whole "multitude" in which he could not keep his place. Now, at the end of the fiction-within-the-fiction, Jim is demonstrating how he has put into practice those ideals which Stein and Marlow had perceived in his internal conflict.

The words Jim utters at the very last, "as if he had found a formula – 'I shall be faithful'" (334), constitute for Marlow a clear moral victory. Marlow is quick in picking up the connection between the light these words cast on Jim and that interpretation of his personality he had reached at the end of his inquiry only with Stein's help: "Ah! he was romantic, romantic," he comments, and adds: "I recalled some words of Stein's...'In the destructive element immerse!...To follow the dream, and again to follow the dream – and so – always – *usque ad finem...*' He was romantic, but none the less true" (334). Marlow is made to be as explicit as possible in establishing the extent to which Jim has fulfilled in Patusan the two older men's interpretation of his case. Jim's faithfulness to the ideals he shares with his mentors makes him true and real in Marlow's eyes, because he appears to have lived out the potentialities they had detected in him.

If *Lord Jim* had ended at this point, one could have concluded that Marlow serves to voice Conrad's own convictions. But this is not the case, and Marlow's standing out so obtrusively only leads to Conrad's preparing a unique denouement: the internal narrator's point of view was based on his own illusions. These pages are the end of Marlow's three-hundred-page-long yarn. When Marlow resumes his narrative, Conrad will show him in the light of a puzzled witness without a final answer.

The most telling aspect of this shift in Marlow's role at this point is the way Conrad does not have him offer any comment about Jim's mysterious behavior at the very end. Both men know this will be the last time they meet, and Jim, almost as an afterthought, asks Marlow, "Will you be going home again soon?" Marlow replies, "In a year or so if I live," at which Jim unexpectedly shouts after him:

> "Tell them..." he began. I signed to the men to cease rowing, and waited in wonder. Tell who? The half-submerged sun faced him; I could see its red gleam in his eyes that look dumbly at me..."No – nothing," he said, and with a slight wave of his hand motioned the boat away. (335)

Marlow goes on to describe the sunset, and his yarn ends without his having commented on Jim's words. Jim's unvoiced appeal evokes the same agony he had been feeling while standing in the witness-box. He is unable up to the very end to translate his feelings into words. But at this point Marlow is satisfied with what he has heard and seen: Jim will be faithful; and even though he remains enigmatic, it is with this assurance that Marlow can go back – and it is with the same feeling, of course, that he narrates Jim's story.

Only in his letter to the privileged man will Marlow offer the comment he had abstained from when he originally related the beach scene. The formal investiture the narrator had apparently dismissed at the end of the Patusan tale has been accepted, now that he knows that Jim was not able to voice his appeal, not even at the end. Marlow reminds his reader of Jim's final appeal, a "Tell them...;" then he adds: "That was all then – and there shall be nothing more; there shall be no message, unless such as each of us can interpret for himself from the language of facts, that are so often more enigmatic than the craftiest arrangement of words" (340). The circle opened at the end of the first narrative segment comes to a close at this point. Marlow, the only one among the onlookers of Jim's ritual sacrifice in the courtroom who could articulate a language able to move beyond the factual aspect of the jump, steps back. He can only interpret along with the readers the enigmatic language of facts. It is not in his power to explain this language with a narrative meta--language.

The language of facts had been deconstructed by Marlow, at first in an attempt to illuminate the universality of Jim's case. The "crafty arrangement of words" in the Patusan tale had gone one step further than the analytical investigation into the causes of Jim's jump. On the basis of their interpretation of the ugly fact –Jim's jump – Stein and Marlow had decided that Jim's illusory self-image had to be given some confirmation in actuality. Theirs was an attempt to set up a fiction which could build an alternative reality, based on potentiality rather than specific determination, by giving Jim the opportunity to live out his ideal conception of himself. Jim's acting out his potential character would have confirmed the validity of their own interpretation. What had been figured as "illusion" throughout the analytical portion of Marlow's narrative had come true in Patusan and Marlow could feel satisfied at the end of the "romance:" the crafty arrangement of words which had re-created his interpretation had been a success. Jim's achievements and ideal faithfulness had turned into a fact.

Jim's death, however, puts an end to the illusory projection which had guided Marlow's story-telling, and the narrative becomes ostensibly a written chronicle. Marlow will now relate the facts without developing an antithesis to the historical verdict. The hermeneutical architecture of Stein and Marlow has collapsed, and the story-teller can no longer arrange words into a fiction, or throw at his philistine audience the implications of a word or an event. From now on Marlow will write as though he "had been an eye witness," begging forgiveness because his "information was fragmentary." In writing his account he has simply "fitted the pieces together, and there is enough of them to make an intelligible picture" (343).

The emphasis Conrad gives to the narrative shift does not point out a change, but an absence, in the surface of the written account that follows. There will no longer be a story of events configuring a fictional world, an illusory stage for human values not necessarily related to the language of facts. Conrad gives this absence an importance quite disproportionate to the difference in fictional language between oral and written narrative. The fact is that Marlow is being used to point out the lesson his creator has learned in the process of writing his last "paper boat." Though fiction shares with reality the minimal common denominator of words, the possibility it expresses cannot sustain an alternative to the merciless logic of actuality – Marlow's dramatic handing down of the burden as interpreter of the "language of facts," then, foreshadows Conrad's relinquishing of a central consciousness as narrative medium.

Jim's death and the elegiac passing on to the written chronicle marks the end of that artistic "dream" which freights Conrad's "paper boats." The tension which Conrad dramatizes in *Lord Jim's* story-telling – through Marlow's emotional involvement and his attempt to make illusions become reality on a fictional stage – reflects the end of a corresponding illusion on the author's part: that he could create his intended effect by articulating a suggestive language decodable through a rhetorical commentary which would make possible a direct line of communication between author and reader.

By putting Marlow temporarily aside, however, Conrad was not capitulating to more conventional novel forms. It was precisely the author's ongoing quest for an original novel form that brought about a readjustment in that balance between form and language which he had conceived in the initial formulation of his artistic ideal. Once Conrad relinquished the metaphorical possibilities offered by his narrator, he came to rely on the distortions created by narrative structure for the referentiality of his fictional worlds. The result was a series of experiments in genre which replaced Conrad's earlier experiments with language. From *Nostromo* on, through *The Secret Agent, Under Western Eyes* and *Chance,* he applied the narrative techniques elaborated in his "paper boats" to dislocate the meaning of stories which ostensibly respected sub-generic contexts. Viewed from the perspective of the writer's last comments on his art, the transformations of his narrative forms appear to be as many attempts to remain faithful to his early ideal.

Anthony Fothergill,
University of Exeter,
Exeter, England

The Poetics of Particulars: Pronouns, Punctuation and Ideology in *Heart of Darkness*

A slight admission may be in order at the outset. Owing to a typing error on my part, my title now appears as "The Poetics of Particulars: Pronouns, Punctuation and Ideology in *Heart of Darkness.*" Overlooking two particulars – a consonant and a vowel, "I" and "i" – meant that I forever dislodged the word "politics" from the intended title, "The Politics of Particulars."

I mention this not for reasons of Razumov-like self-confession, nor because it alters one iota what I will say! I could of course have passed silently over this mistake. But I realized that inadvertently my error was a trace of what in fact my paper seeks to address: the symptomatic slippages, the smallest features of grammatical or lexical detail – pronouns, punctuation marks, conjunctions – which, I wish to argue, can be read as traces, whether unconscious or not, which bear ideological significance.

If this interest has any theoretical value, and I think it does, it lies in countering a prevailing view that for a reading (or a theory) to be ideologically critical it must eschew close formal analysis. In this view, close reading is itself ideologically suspect – universalizing, ahistorical, (male) middle-class, and middle-aged.[1] It analyses formal textual qualities, and – so the argument goes – questions of form mean sterile formalism. It is this position that I would challenge by discussing the poetics – and politics – of particulars.

Conradians much more experienced than I, particularly editors, will already be familiar with textual errors or slippages in Conrad's works, which in some cases have been silently corrected. Close textual scrutiny will have revealed, if not outright mistakes, then idiosyncratic formulations, stylistic details, sites of what I will call "textual turbulence," which perhaps at most merit passing mention. Attention has recently been drawn, for example, to an aberrant little adjective at the beginning of *Nostromo,* where the anonymous (and insofar as there is one, authoritative) narrator of the opening pages refers to The Isabels, in the present tense, as "uninhabited." No doubt "uninhabited" is, ideologically speaking, more innocent here than the "uninhabited" which Shakespeare uses of Caliban's island. But it is technically still a problem, though only technically. For although all of us are reasonably attentive readers, I'm sure we are not all budding Genettes, obsessively tracking down with the assiduity of Inspector Heat every analeptic, or proleptic, anachrony in the order of narrative. Surely we tend to overlook the fact that, in the narrator's present, The Isabels are *not* uninhabited: logically (chronologically), the lighthouse, which features so significantly in the last third of the novel, would already have been built and the island thus already peopled. But it would rather have spoilt the reader's fun to have known this at the narrative outset. The drama of Nostromo's secret nocturnal visits to his silver would have been overlit, as it were, by our proleptic knowledge of future building developments. The demands of narrative focus always override strict logic. Which is why Shakespeare's Bohemia has a coastline; why Emma Bovary's eyes are variously described as brown, deep black, and blue; and why in *The New Testament,* Matthew's gospel offers a genealogy for Jesus stretching in intricate detail from Joseph all the way back to Abraham – when, at least as rumour has it, Joseph wasn't Jesus's father anyway.

If we notice the slip-up, we overlook it, just as we probably will have overlooked (at least until Avrom Fleishman reminded us of it) a more interesting narrative turbulence in the paratext to *Under Western Eyes.* I'm thinking of the epigraph below Conrad's title. It is unusual to the point of creating a real vertigo of textual disruption. For it quotes the words of Miss Haldin to the English teacher of languages: "I would take liberty from any hand as a hungry man would snatch a piece of bread." I have likened the effect to vertigo, but that does not quite do justice to the kind of giddying oscillation the reader feels trying to reconcile two different levels of textual reality, that of the fictional world of Razumov and Miss Haldin, and that of our real world of the paratext, Genette's word for those preliminary pages of a work – with its names of publisher, printer, author, title, and date, and maybe its preface or introduction – all standing in the vestibule, as it were, of this house of fiction, but definitely outside the rooms. When a fictional character takes her place on the title page of a novel, which is temporally and logically prior to her own coming into existence within its pages, funny things start to happen. That's a space normally reserved for the historically real but usually illustrious dead. With Miss Haldin on the title page, we begin to experience the destabilizing dynamic of Wittgenstein's duck/rabbit or, a closer analogy, the giddiness produced by an Escher drawing.

I do not know if there is a rhetorical term for this turbulent turn. I'm not sure the Greeks had a word for it, because I'm not sure that it would have been thinkable for them. "Trope," literally "turn," is useful but has probably lost its etymological power. Genette's "paratext" does not fully engage with the oscillation of inside and outside. "Parabasis," from the Greek *parabainou,* "to go aside, to step forward," might help. It's used of ancient Greek comedy, when the chorus would address the audience in the poet's name, in a way unconnected to the action of the drama. This, like Brecht's *gestus* and *Verfremdungseffekt,* has something of the effect of rupture, dislocation, which is part of this aesthetic. Certainly the prefix "para-" (at least as J. Hillis Miller has helpfully defined it) conveys the sense of oscillation between, crossing the boundaries of, two spaces or configurations allowing the outside in, and the inside out.[2] Whatever term we may come up with, what intrigues me about the example of Miss Haldin's epigraph is precisely this articulation of two textual realities: and by "articulation" (etymologically, "joint") I mean both connectedness *and* separation. I think the effect goes beyond what Fleishman alludes to as a literary device by which the author of a novel, Conrad, claims that he is not an inventor but only the conveyor of an authoritative document written by another. This device, according to Fleish-man, testifies to the document's truthfulness and the ontological reality of its characters. But ontological security is the last thing that is assured by such inverted parabasis, in which a fictional Miss Haldin steps out of the represented fictional world of speech/orality and into the text as epigraphic script. For we also note that she misquotes herself, so to speak. What she actually says in the novel (if the word "actually" has any reliable meaning left) is, "I would take liberty from any hand as a hungry man would snatch *at* a piece of bread" (135; my emphasis). "At." An error? Why is "at" omitted from the epigraph? Is it misquoting her? Or is she, with a turn Borges would have approved of, misquoting herself from the epigraph?

However, I am not much interested in designating this as a slip or unconscious error, one which (unfortunately, in my view) has been silently corrected by some editors. What I am chiefly intrigued by here is how this tiny preposition destabilizes both the main text and paratext, both the spoken and the written. It is not only that the addition of the preposition "at" transforms, indeed almost completely contradicts, the meaning of an other-wise identical sentence. It is that this turbulence occurs in a text which has as its main thematic burden the reliability – or otherwise – of words, their translatability, their transportability. It is a novel which tests the truth status of the spoken, the unspoken, and the written; and what people for their own purposes read into other people's assumed or actual utterances. In other words, this slightest of particulars bears traces of the political and ideological arguments which the novel explores.

And that brings me to my main text, *Heart of Darkness*, and three such similar sites of turbulence. One is a shift of personal pronoun form "we"/"you" to "I;" another is the modest conjunction "and;" and the third is a fortuitous semi-colon. To repeat, I do not want to cite these instances as errors (only one of them may be). Nor am I interested particularly in arbitrating their conscious or unconscious presence in the work. For one thing, I do not have privileged access to what Conrad was thinking of or thought he was thinking of, nor what he was not thinking of – although I suppose I would like to think that my three instances are examples of what in a letter to Cunninghame Graham he called those secondary notions producing "some little effect," with which the idea of the story was so wrapped up that even Cunninghame Graham would miss it.[3]

Each is a moment, indeed a turning-point, when the written speaks, when the reader may become aware of the written text breaking through the oral world of Marlow's telling. These turbulences, though trivial in themselves, can be seen as symptoms. They "speak" to issues more central even than the meaning of Kurtz's cry. They articulate crucial insights into the major thematic preoccupations of the work: the possibility of critical self-knowledge; the chances of conveying this knowledge to a known community of listeners; the complicity of this same community in imperialist activities to which it is blind. As turning-points, hovering between the written and the spoken moment, they also signal the juncture of Conrad's double--imagined audience – the listeners to a tale aboard the *Nellie* and the reader of the text. But they do so in such a way that only the reader (not the listener and not Marlow the teller) can know. For Marlow isn't aware that he is also written. The text does indeed tell more than Marlow could see then.

As literal or metaphorical turning-points, each instance embodies what is, of course, a fundamental figure in Conrad's imagination. Limits, thresholds, liminal states, are all crucial motifs in Conrad. And I think we would do well to recall that a crux moment in Marlow's relationship to Kurtz, indeed a moment which arguably motivates the whole tale, is just such a literal turning-point. Marlow, kicking his heels at the Central Station and getting pretty fed up with most of the talk of his fellow Europeans (including incidentally talk of this man Kurtz) happens to overhear snippets of conversation between the manager and his uncle. It is a very fragmented narrative – about "that man" – but Marlow, responsive reader of narratives if ever there was one, fills in all the narrative gaps and for the first time, suddenly, *sees* Kurtz. He *pictures* him turning away in his dugout, turning his back on the Central Station. It is really a double turn: for this getting inside a story triggers Marlow's subsequent search for the voice which he imagines or needs to imagine will somehow speak to him of the incomprehensible darkness.

My first example of stylistic turbulence occurs soon after Marlow sets off for Kurtz's Inner Station. Appropriately enough, Marlow is piloting his boat through barely navigable waters (92-4). The turn is the rapid shift in pronouns from "we" or the generalized and sliding "you" to an insistently, almost hysterically, repeated "I," all within a few lines. This same configuration of shifting personal pronouns is, I think, reiterated in all significant particulars within a couple of pages (95-7), a fact that tends to add to rather than lessen its significance as an ideological symptom. For purposes of quotable brevity and to highlight what I discern as a pattern, I will, to some extent, conflate the two passages. In both passages, just as "we"/"you" yields to the insistent "I," the narrative is suddenly fractured by a further turn, the intrusion of the "you" audience on the *Nellie*.

Marlow describes "going up that river" towards Kurtz's Inner Station with manager, pilgrims, and fine cannibal crew on board, as if "travelling back to the earliest beginnings of the world" (92):

> We penetrated deeper and deeper into the heart of darkness. It was very quiet there.... We were wanderers on prehistoric earth, on an earth that wore the aspect of an unknown planet. We could have fancied ourselves the first of men taking possession of an accursed inheritance, to be subdued at the cost of profound anguish and of excessive toil.... We were cut off from the comprehension of our surroundings; we glided past like phantoms, wondering and secretly appalled...We could not understand because we were too far and could not remember, because we were travelling in the night of first ages. (95-6)

This prehistoric world with its howling, drum-beating, "primitive" inhabitants gives cause for deep and complex thought on the relationship it bears to the European civilized bourgeois world embodied, in brief, by those aboard the *Nellie*, with Marlow the amateur archeologist of the European male mind.

How do the shifting pronouns trace these thematic moves? In the course of the writing, the "we" of the passage quoted can easily modulate into the public, generalized "you." Nothing too surprising there. But the deictic "you" pronoun is very flexible, and Conrad exploits its floating imprecise reference to full advantage. Actually, on close inspection, it seems to me that the shift from "we" to "you" tends characteristically to occur with the increasing sense that "we" are no longer quite in control of events. The surroundings in all their incomprehensible strangeness start to overwhelm when the object of "our" travelling gaze and of "our" penetration starts to look back at us. Then, when the wilderness becomes an agency felt to be threatening the subject, "you" tends to take over as a pronoun.

> you lost your way on that river as you would in a desert...till you thought...yourself bewitched and cut off for ever from everything you had known once – somewhere – far away – in another existence perhaps.... It looked at you with a vengeful aspect. (93)

Because „you" can be both public and plural, private and singular, subject and object, the reader can no longer be too sure who the referent is, who is doing what to whom.

But of course it's not all oppressive. "It made you feel very small, very lost, and yet it was not altogether depressing, that feeling" (95). Indeed, it is the troubling attractiveness of this African Other which is most fascinating to Marlow.

> what thrilled you was just the thought of their humanity – like yours – the thought of your remote kinship with this wild and passionate uproar. Ugly. Yes, it was ugly enough; but if you were man enough you would admit to yourself that there was in you just the faintest trace of a response to the terrible frankness of that noise. (96)

Then at the precise moment when the psychic turbulence of this introspection reaches its height, when critical self-knowledge is bursting in upon him, Marlow represses the fascinating threat by retreating into his work, and the pronominal slippage resolves itself into an incessantly repeated "I."

> I got used to it afterwards; I did not see it any more; I had no time. I had
> to keep guessing at the channel; I had to discern, mostly by inspiration,
> the signs of hidden banks; I watched for sunken stones; I was learning to
> clap my teeth smartly before my heart flew out when I shaved by a fluke
> some infernal sly old snag...I had to keep a look-out for the signs of
> dead wood. (93)

And, as I said, at just this turn, the narrative level is fractured by
the intrusion of Marlow's narrating situation into the narrated
space. At the peak of the pronominal confusion, or at the
moment of breakdown, if you prefer, "you" suddenly attaches
itself to Marlow's listeners on board the *Nellie*: "You performing
on your respective tightropes," he says – and the world of
London, his immediate audience, breaks in: "Try to be civil,
Marlow." In the second passage, the movement is the same,
although the intrusion of his London audience is implicit:

> Of course, a fool, what with sheer fright and fine sentiments is always
> safe. Who's that grunting? You wonder I didn't go ashore for a howl
> and a dance? Well no – I didn't. Fine sentiments, you say? Fine
> sentiments, be hanged! I had no time...I had to mess about with
> white-lead...I had to watch the steering. (97)

And with this dislocation, we return, again, to the insistent "I."
    Bearing in mind all these wandering pronouns, my main
question is on one level rather simple. Who is this "we?" And in
the pressured turn from "we" to "you" to "I," what ideological
tracks are being covered? What affiliations is Marlow assuming,
and why do they founder? Who is the implied communality of
the "we?" Indeed, does it exist at all? My suggestion is that little
words are called upon to do big ideological work.
    "We" is in a way a rhetorical sleight-of-hand. It asserts
plurality and shared perceptions – "we were wanderers on
prehistoric earth;" "we fancied ourselves the first men." But
everything we know about Marlow's fellow-travellers contradicts the notion that Marlow is here representing their
thoughts or fancies. Whether or not they all share a taste for pink
pyjamas (and unfortunately the text fails to mention the color of

Marlow's), I strongly doubt that the manager and other pilgrims could ever think what Marlow represents them/"us" as thinking. They are incapable of feeling a kinship with the inhabitants of the "prehistoric" space, a term that would not in any case have occurred to them. These can only be Marlow's perceptions, ones which carry, of course, their own ideological and racist charge. Indeed, their subsequent actions make it clear that most of this collective "we" – that is, the other white European males, for the "fine cannibals" are left out of account – regard the incomprehensible surroundings as good only for rifle practice.

Under the differentiating and fragmenting pressure of Marlow's own quality of thought, the collective "we" is therefore soon internalized into an ambivalent "you," which in turn becomes increasingly private and singular, until the "I" makes explicit its own isolated alienation both from the would-be community and from the bewitching surroundings.

And if that "we" dissolves under its own contradictions, so too (as a coherent collective) does the narrative community. As soon as the deictic, floating "you" gets clearly attached to them – "You do your tricks very well" – *this* white European male "we" is likewise exposed as a fragile community. With the possible exception of the framing narrator, they are no more able than the pilgrims to position themselves imaginatively to comprehend Marlow's way of looking – as their resisting, disassociating interjections reveal. No wonder Marlow retreats into the protective isolation of the "I."

And should the reader be surprised? The "we" of the steamer and the "we" of the *Nellie* are surely two ends of the same sort of colonial enterprise. We remember the very anonymity of Marlow's audience, reduced to their professional identities as Director of Companies (note the plural – this is no simple shopkeeper), Lawyer, Accountant. I'll return to accountants later. What the anonymous narrator is, we do not know, but the implied affection for the others might let us number him among this bourgeois group. "Each [is] moored with two good addresses – a butcher round one corner – a policeman round the other." And then we recall the almost surreal moment when, chasing into the jungle after Kurtz, Marlow has an imagistic flash which is potent with political meaning:

> I had some imbecile thoughts. The knitting old woman with the cat obtruded herself upon my memory as a most improper person to be sitting at the other end of such an affair. (142)

One end of colonialism is the grove of death and the other is offices in London and Brussels. Imperialism, or colonialism, works most efficiently at arm's length, mainly out of sight. But at this moment of pronominal turbulence, Marlow implicates his own listeners, at least in their professional capacities, as also sitting at the other end of the imperialist affair with all the contradictions in it that Marlow's narration is revealing. It's not a comfortable position to be made aware of, so they resist it: they are blind to their complicity, as socially and ideologically they have to be. So the "we" collapses. They are auditors who cannot hear, and they turn away. But the reader can register this turn in the particulars of pronouns.

Let me now turn to the humble copula and subtle semi-colon for my last two turbulent particulars. Both are cruxes, turning--points in the narrative. Both articulate the juncture of spoken and written; and, in so doing, both construe a reader who perhaps reads against the grain, whose formation is an ideological effect of Conrad's written text, which counterpoints Marlow's spoken tale.

So first to the humble copula. Very close to the beginning of the tale come Marlow's first words: "'And this, also,' said Marlow suddenly, 'has been one of the dark places of the earth'" (48). After the framing narrator's glowing words about the Thames and British imperial endeavour, this parataxis abruptly signals the turn into Marlow's narrative, in effect the originating threshold of the whole story. And with his words, the very first actually uttered in the novel, Marlow undercuts for the reader the rhetorical sentiments and ideological thrust of the preceding paragraphs – the framing narrator's eulogy to the Thames and the glorious history it has witnessed and serviced. Two points about this turn I find particularly interesting. First, rather remarkably, the framing narrator's words of historic grandeur, to which Marlow's are a sort of dialogic counter-discourse, themselves anticipate almost verbatim phrases from Conrad's later essay on the Thames, "London's River."[4] Or, to put it another way, Conrad not only later plagiarizes himself, but in doing so, bizarrely chooses a passage which his own narrative has effectively subverted.

The second and for present purposes more intriguing point is the little unobtrusive word "and" with which Marlow intervenes. As gentle skimmers (as Beckett called readers), we might miss it under the impact of what follows. It is after all an extraordinary enough entry: a jolting reversal to the glorified tale of trade and empire and its implicit ideology of Victorian progress which the framing narrator has unproblematically offered. But why "*and* this also?" It's as if Marlow were just a partner in mid-conversation, replying to the narrator, modyfing the previous sentiment. Or – had read the eulogy in the previous paragraph. Which is, in a way, my point. Significantly, as *readers* we hardly have any difficulty with Marlow's conjunction, for it marks a continuity with, if disassociation from, the remarks in the foregoing paragraph. But paragraphs are part of the writerly text not the oral tale, and they have not been "remarks" as such. Marlow's entry into the narrative occupies the borderline between the written and the spoken, while eliding it; it flags the undecided (possibly undecidable) but crucial zone between the heard and the read.

"And:" that little word, like Miss Haldin's "at," can produce giddiness at the borderline. Perhaps Conrad himself was made slightly giddy. At any rate, he was not always consistent, for he has Marlow later refer to the narrator's thoughts as if spoken ("You say knights"). But the narrator makes quite clear how all on board have been lulled into silent meditation at the closing of the day. Surely the framing narrator's "remarks," as it were, are representations of his thoughts. Certainly the literary quality of his rhetoric does not suggest to me the casually spoken word. So Marlow is not responding to an utterance, though it may at first glance seem so to us as readers. The appearance of continuity can exist only at the level of the written, not the spoken (as, I suspect, any attempt to dramatize the whole for television would reveal). The dialogic continuity exists on your page. But not on your *Nellie*. Unless, of course, Marlow is telepathic. Or, so shared is the men's sense of community and common assumption, that they *know* what others are thinking and would say and can commune in silent dialogue. But Marlow's intervention itself contradicts the cosy notion that they are all of one mind. In effect at this point Conrad construes two audiences. By making it possible for a reader to see Marlow's words as being in dialogue with what's gone before, Conrad creates the conditions for him or her to register what the audience on the boat cannot hear. Neither literally nor metaphorically can *they* hear where Marlow is coming from, nor can they hear the subverting ironies, the critical revisions to the dominant ideological tendency of what has preceded. Only the reader can "hear."

Of course, it may well be that we read over the turbulence of written and oral which "and" represents and fail to notice the writerly sleight-of-hand because we (and Conrad?) have a vested interest in continuity and comfortable assumptions about the known speech community. But if so, we do it at the very moment when the text explores and contests shared values, community understanding, and social continuity – the politics of defining the group.

Now, from the implied politics of the copula, let me finally turn to the politics of punctuation marks: to be precise, two subtle semi-colons. My first turbulence, the peripatetic personal pronoun, only indirectly addressed the question of Conrad's two audiences, the listener/reader, in exposing the contradictions in the notion of a collective. My second, the surreptitious copulative "and," muddied the waters at just this boundary between the written and the spoken and pointed to the ideological strains within this transaction. My third example has, I think, all the virtues of precision while, as written sign, it is visible to a reader but not audible to a listening community.

It is an instance which addresses absolutely head-on the

question of Marlow's own ideological allegiance and his stance vis à vis European imperialism, its potentially justificatory work ethic, and its barbarity. All are obviously crucial themes in the novel. Is Marlow (and by implication Conrad?) a colonialist or an anti-colonialist? I think Conrad's punctuation marks answer the question quite categorically – by coming down right in the middle. To be blunt, and particular, Conrad's semi-colons trace Marlow's semi-colonialism.

The contradictions in Marlow's position have been well rehearsed by Conradian critics. On the one hand, he ridicules what he construes as his aunt's jingoism. He is scathing about all "the rot let loose in print" justifying colonial expansion; the waste and futility of war and exploitation; the culpable ignorance of those in the sepulchral city. Above all, perhaps, he expresses disgust at the brutalizing of the chain-gang – but expresses it, symptomatically enough, by turning away: only to be confronted by imperialism's left-overs in the grove of death. But at the same time he appears to approve of all the red bits on the map, representing the vast British colonial presence in Africa: "good to see at any time because one knows that some real work is done in there" (55) – words, surely, to bring joy to the ears of those on the *Nellie*. He seems to believe in a redeeming "idea at the back of it" all. And not *all* the participants in the philanthropic civilizing process seem corrupt. I have discussed in detail elsewhere what I take to be the nature of Marlow's position and how far we can read out of it assumptions about Conrad's politics.[5] Let me just draw attention to one particular, that involving the immaculate accountant – as I said, I had a bill to settle with accountants – who has proven a disruptive element in most critical arguments.

From an anti-colonial viewpoint he can be seen as instrumental in the machinery of government and exploitative production, a vital cog in the wheels of bureaucracy and torture. He accounts for the smooth workings of genocide. On the other hand, we have Marlow's attitude towards him. There's Marlow, no *ingénue* and not, we would think (pink pyjamas or no) a stickler for fashion, showing baffling respect for, of all people, this

bizarre epitome of sartorial elegance, this "miracle" of efficiency, the immaculate Chief-Accountant. He keeps his books clean,
however "distracting" may be the groans of invalid, dying
agents, stuck inconveniently outside his office, however loud the
"frightful row," "the uncouth babble" (Marlow's words) of
slave-labour African carriers (69). (Is his the sort of efficiency
praiseworthy for keeping the trains running on time, despite
recalcitrant passengers?) How are we meant to understand this?
What insight does Marlow have into this contradiction?

At an absolutely literal turning-point, Conrad, I think, gives
us the answer to at least the second question. Standing at the
threshold of the accountant's office, just as he is leaving, turning
(once again) from one site of the machinery of colonization only
to be confronted by another; turning, too, to leave for the Central
Station, Marlow looks back. He sees behind him the accountant,
whose own retraining scheme for the under-employed has, not
without inconvenience to himself, given a native woman the
blessed task of starching his collars. What else Marlow sees and
how Conrad represents his seeing, the passage will reveal with
particular precision:

> He [the accountant] turned to his work. The noise outside had ceased,
> and presently in going out I stopped at the door. In the steady buzz of
> flies the homeward-bound agent was lying flushed and insensible; the
> other, bent over his books, was making correct entries of perfectly
> correct transactions; and fifty feet below the doorstep I could see the
> still tree-tops of the grove of death.
> Next day I left the station at last, with a caravan of sixty men, for
> a two-hundred-mile tramp. (70)

Seeing is understanding here, for semi-colons are only readable,
not audible. They can be read as political traces/glosses,
available to Conrad's readers, but not directly to Marlow's
audience on the *Nellie*. Furthermore, they are strictly speaking
a writerly trace of Conrad – a placing by him of Marlow, who is
an effect of the writing but certainly not ontologically in control
of the punctuation which articulates him. The written/oral turn
is met once again, and in a politically potent way, as Marlow
himself is literally at the threshold.

Let me spell out what I take to be the political implications of the wonderfully precise punctuation. At a syntactical level the three clauses, referring to the immaculate accountant, the irritating sick agent, and the current inhabitants of the grove of death, are articulated by semi-colons. Gramatically this signals, indeed insists upon, a sort of connectedness between the elements in the sentence without making explicit, maybe without determining, what the nature of this connection is. Read as a political trace, the semi-colon is a precise notation of Marlow's relation to both sides of the colonial coin. For it insists upon a connection betwen accountancy and two forms of barbarism without dictating the precise nature of this connection. Standing in the doorway, at the threshold, Marlow mediates betwen the two faces of colonialism. He can see – and thus try to convey to his audience – the link which the accountant neither literally nor ideologically can see, can afford to see. And which his statistics, some of whom are dying in the grove, are perhaps beyond seeing now. The semi-colon is, I think, a perfect written particular to represent Marlow's own hovering between the administrator and the barbarity he enables. The semi-colon doesn't assert causality, doesn't theorize economic, political, human links. It just proposes them, senses them. It renders visible – and leaves the reader to contemplate – the connections. Marlow's semi--colonialism does not, cannot, fully resolve the contradictions of his position. And furthermore, as it is the text which registers it and allows us to read it, the semi-colons are an articulation which is also inaudible to Marlow's immediate audience, both literally and ideologically.

To conclude, let me return to the "we" of the opening: Conrad's audience. We all know what doubts and hesitations Conrad suffered in writing his major works. He could not take his audience for granted. But was this a wholly bad thing? Put it another way: what of interest would he have been able to say if this bourgeois audience had been able to take him for granted, as "one of us?" If his aesthetic programme, as famously espoused in the "Preface" to The Nigger of the "Narcissus," is "to make you see" – not, note, to let you see, but to make you see – the

imperative suggests an effort, a labour. His very foregrounding
of Marlow's act of narration, and the turbulences which register
the interface of speakable and unspeakable, audible and inaudible, both confirm, I think, the centrality of the problem of
how we, as readers, position ourselves. With whom do we
affilliate? With whom are we being aligned – and how? To turn
an earlier question this time against myself: who is this "we"
anyway? In my urgency to make other differentiations, have
I reduced the readers of *Heart of Darkness* to a convenient
homogeneity of historical period, gender, and social class, and
cultural identity?

These questions in a way bring me back to my opening
remarks about the politics of close reading. Maybe here we can
adopt Conrad's marvellously rich figure of the turn – which this
close reading has explored – in our own reading praxis. If reading
against the grain troubles the smooth surfaces of Conrad's work
to open up, by means of trivial details, new political complexities, perhaps we should trouble the surface, also, of our own
readings. In a dialectical turn, we could direct ourselves to a close
reading of our close reading. We might then take seriously
a passing comment that Marlow makes. In the middle of his
meditation on the Romans' invasion of Britain, he simply adds,
"If we may believe what we read" (49). Read simply, that's an
easy cliché. My suggestion is that Conrad's writing practice,
both at the most minute and at the grandest thematic level,
seriously asks us to commit ourselves to the labour of transfor-
ming this from an easy cliché into a critical, political reading
practice for ourselves. We might then gloss it thus: what is it that
I need to believe, that I am prepared to believe, that I am being
asked to believe, in order to believe what I read?

NOTES

1. See, for instance, John Barrell's comments on close reading in the first chapter of *Poetry, Language and Politics.*

2. "'Para' is a double antithetical prefix signifying at once proximity and distance, similarity and difference, interiority and exteriority, something inside a domestic economy and at the same time outside it, something simultaneously this side of a boundary line, threshold, or margin, and also beyond it, equivalent in status and also secondary or subsidiary, submissive, as of guest to host, slave to master. A thing in 'para,' moreover, is not only simultaneously on both sides of the boundary line between inside and out. It is also the boundary itself, the screen which is a permeable membrane connecting inside and outside. It confuses them with one another, allowing the outside in, making the inside out, dividing them and joining them. It also forms an ambiguous transition between one and the other. Though a given word in 'para' may seem to choose univocally one of these possibilities, the other meanings are always there as a shimmering in the word which makes it refuse to stay still in a sentence." (Miller, 219)

3. See Conrad's letter to R. Cunninghame Graham, 8 February 1899, in *Collected Letters,* 2: 157-8.

4. Conrad's essay appeared in *London Magazine* in July, 1906. A slightly revised version of this, known as *The Faithful River,* was one of the essays in *The Mirror of the Sea.*

5. See particularly Chapter 4 of my *Heart of Darkness.*

WORKS CITED

Barrell J. *Poetry, Language and Politics.* Manchester: Manchester U.P., 1988.

Fleishman A. "Speech and Writing in *Under Western Eyes," Joseph Conrad: A Commemoration,* Sherry N. ed., London: Macmillan, 1976, 118-28.

Fothergill A. *"Heart of Darkness."* Open Guides to Literature, Milton Keynes: Open University Press, 1989.

Genette G. "Introduction to the Paratext," *New Literary History,* 22 (1991), 261-72.

Miller J. Hillis. "The Critic as Host," *Deconstruction and Criticism,* Bloom H. et. al. ed., London: Routledge, Kegan Paul, 1976, 217-53.

Phil Joffe,
University of Natal,
Durban, South Africa

Africa and Joseph Conrad's *Heart of Darkness*: The "bloody racist" (?) as Demystifier of Imperialism

Addressing Chinua Achebe's objections to *Heart of Darkness* is an essential task for any teacher of undergraduates in South Africa, a country which has a colonial history which, for at least the past 43 years has taken the racially obsessive shape of the Apartheid system. On the campus of a liberal university where opposition to the officially-sanctioned racial inequalities of the government in power is a fundamental principle, one teaches undergraduates from hugely differing socio-econonic, educational and cultural backgrounds. *Heart of Darkness*, as one of the most profound fictional renderings of Europe's attitudes to the African continent at the beginning of the twentieth century provokes students and teachers into an investigation and analysis of inherited conceptual categories and contemporary assumptions concerning the self and the other. Because Conrad's text interrogates not only issues such as the European imperialist thrust into Africa after Bismarck's 1884 Berlin conference spurred the scramble for the continent, but also those psychological mechanisms which characterize our attempts to relate to others, it generates deconstructive processes which are salutary. *Heart of Darkness*, as the title suggests, combines a concern with Europe's political and economic invasion of Africa, a geographical location, and an exploration of the hinterland of the human psyche, a metaphysical location.

Achebe's indictment has been thoroughly catalogued. Crucially, he believes that "white racism against Africa is such a normal way of thinking that the manifestations go completely undetected."[1] He writes of the need "in Western psychology to set Africa up as a foil to Europe, as a place of negatives at once remote/and vaguely familiar, in comparison with which Europe's own state of spiritual grace will be manifest." Achebe asserts that Conrad contributes to the "dehumanization of Africa and Africans" so that "the very humanity of black people is called in question." *Heart of Darkness* is read as "an offensive and deplorable book" and its author described as clearly "a bloody racist." In addition, Achebe notes that while "Conrad saw and condemned the evil of imperial exploitation," he "was strangely unaware of the racism on which it sharpened its iron tooth." Achebe's is an impassioned polemical argument and a number of commentators over the years have responded, Cedric Watts's 1983 piece in the *Yearbook of English Studies* being one of the most "eloquent and measured defence(s) of Conrad's position."[2]

As a teacher discussing *Heart of Darkness* with numbers of black South African students who all suffer directly the consequences of racial categorizations and inequalities, I wish here to offer some of the argument generated in class discussion, to add to the body of material which recognizes the complexity of Conrad's text which, while it might be implicated in the discourse of colonialism, is firmly and critically opposed to the racist obfuscations characteristically associated with the former.

To begin, one needs to objectify the term "racism." Todorov defines it as "a type of behaviour which consists in the display of contempt or aggressiveness toward other people on account of physical differences (other than those of sex) between them and oneself."[3] Gareth Cornwell notes further that racism is "a particular instance of that response to human difference which interprets and reproduces otherness as dichotomous opposition to self."[4] Racist behaviour, typically, manifests "an inability or refusal to recognize the full equivalent subjectivity of the other, and consequently exhibits a tendency to dehumanize and objectify that other"[5] so that dissimilarity is read as inferiority. In addition, investigators such as Fanon and Jan Mahomed[6] comment on the significance of cultural stereotypes in imperialist thinking wherein the cultural other is defined in terms of polarized oppositions so that the "binary opposition to which racism reduces the self-other relationship is inevitably...hierarchical,"[7] the European colonizer always seeing himself as naturally superior. My argument is that the major thrust of Conrad's text, through the tale that Marlow tells, recounted by his companion aboard the *Nellie,* the frame narrator of *Heart of Darkness*, is to refute these racist imperatives and to deconstruct the imperialist mode of thought which characterizes the language of race, one in which "particular skin colour appears to stand in metonymical relation to a constellation of traits, physical, behavioural, intellectual, (and) moral...."[8] Cornwell suggests that skin-colour differences have always been perceived through "the perceptual filter of traditional Western ethico--religious black/white symbolism," and that the myth of the sons of Ham has, from the beginning, been "localized in Africa."[9]

The persisting stereotypes we continue to associate with Africa arise from the popular tradition of the adventure romance. This genre developed especially in the late nineteenth century in response to the newly awakened interest in the African continent stimulated by the romanticizing of the journeys of the militant explorers, Mungo Park, Livingstone, Stanley and others. Colonial romances such as *King Solomon's Mines* (1885) and *She* (1887) by H. Rider Haggard, one of the most widely read of late Victorian imperialist writers, or later, *Prester John* (1910) by John Buchan, helped to reinforce the dominant ideologies of their times by teaching their readers to see Africa as the dark continent, mysterious, romantic, dangerous, peopled by inferior savages, primitive and centuries behind Europeans in social and moral evolution, but consumed by instincts and passions which the civilized Europeans are more able to control. Fanon's view is that "the real Other for the white man is and will continue to be the black man...For the majority of white men the Negro represents the sexual instinct (in its raw state). The Negro is the incarnation of a genital potency beyond all moralities and prohibitions."[10] Be this as it may, into the mythological cosmos of Africa arrive the whites supported by the superior attributes of their European culture. They confront the test of the wilderness and succeed always in proving their superiority.

Popular poet, Kipling, without irony, reinforces the stereo-

type of the racial and cultural supremacy of the white imperialist
and the ingratitude of those he seeks to nurture in his call to

Take up the White Man's burden-
And reap his old reward:
The blame of those ye better
The hate of those ye guard-
The cry of hosts ye humour
(Ah, slowly!) towards the light:-
"Why brought ye us from bondage,
Our loved Egyptian night?"

Contemporary popular writing of this nature continues to
reinforce such notions as the "natural" master-servant relationship between white and black and the dangerous lack of restraint
and gratitude suffered by the former in the romances of authors
such as Wilbur Smith.

   Heart of Darkness is a much more complicated matter.
Conrad's own experiences in the Congo in 1890 as an employee
of the *Société Anonyme Belge pour le Commerce du Haut Congo*
are transmuted into a carefully considered work of fiction. Like
Marlow, Conrad had felt the glamorous desire to explore that
"mighty big river" (52) which appeared on the maps which
fascinated him in his childhood. As a result of this venture,
however, the disillusioned Conrad, in the last year of his life,
wrote of his "distasteful knowledge of the vilest scramble for loot
that ever disfigured the history of human conscience and
geographical exploration" (*Geography and Some Explorers*
[1924]). Marlow, in recounting his tale to his companions aboard
the cruising yawl, the *Nellie,* opens significantly, with his
conviction that "the conquest of the earth, which mostly means
the taking it away from those who have a different complexion
or slightly flatter noses than ourselves, is not a pretty thing"
(50-1), suggesting that Marlow does not himself subscribe to that
form of racism which shows contempt for the other on account
of physical differences. Ian Watt's judgement of the book as "the
most powerful literary indictment of imperialism"[11] is confirmed throughout the text and Conrad has Marlow bear witness to

the effects of the imperialist venture in Africa as he moves on his journey from station to station, up the river, deeper into the interior. He becomes acquainted with "a flabby, pretending, weak-eyed devil of a rapacious and pitiless folly" (65) asserted in all the activities of the company. "A taint of imbecile rapacity" (76) blows through the squalid practices of those ironically named "pilgrims" who seek only their own enrichment regardless of the cost to the continent or its peoples. For the prize of ivory, trashy trade goods, "ghastly glazed calico that made you shudder only to look at it, glass beads value about a penny a quart, confounded spotted cotton handkerchiefs" (84) are offered, or with the superior weaponry of a Kurtz who comes with "thunder and lightning" (128), the ironical "thunderbolts of that pitiful Jupiter" (134), the countryside is "raided" and its riches plundered.

Heart of Darkness reveals not just the wide gap between the official doctrines of colonialism's aspirations and its actual practices, the truth about those "bearers of a spark from the sacred fire" (47) whose actions prove them to be merely "sordid buccaneers" (87). It furnishes us also with a telling analysis of the obfuscations fundamental to the mechanics of imperialism. Because biological notions such as natural selection and survival of the fittest were translated into the social Darwinism of influential thinkers such as Herbert Spencer, the competitive economic expansion of the European powers came to be justified on "natural" evolutionary grounds. Thus, by technological advantage Europe's domination of the colonies was seen as proof of the former's fitness not only to survive but to rule, evidence of its inherent racial superiority. To cloak the often coercive brutality of the system imperialism necessarily relied on the creation of what Jeremy Hawthorn calls "linguistic duplicities;"[12] behind such words as civilization and enlightenment. *Heart of Darkness* reveals barbarism, exploitation and death.

Thomas Pynchon in his novel *Gravity's Rainbow* suggests graphically that the colonies were not simply created to meet imperialism's need for cheap labour and overseas markets:

Colonies are much, much more. Colonies are the outhouses of the
European soul, where a fellow can let his pants down and relax, enjoy
the smell of his own shit. Where he can fall on his slender prey roaring as
loud as he feels like, and guzzle her blood with open joy. Eh? Where he
can just wallow and rut and let himself go in a softness, a receptive
darkness of limbs, of hair as wooly as the hair on his own forbidden
genitals. Where the poppy, and cannibals and coca grow full and green,
and not to the colours and style of death, as do ergot and agaric, the
blight and fungus native to Europe. Christian Europe was always
death...death and repression. Out and down in the colonies, life can be
indulged, life and sensuality in all its forms, with no harm done to the
Metropolis, nothing to soil those cathedrals, white marble statues
["whited sepulchre" (41)], noble thoughts...No word ever gets back.
The silences down here are vast enough to absorb all behaviour, no
matter how dirty, how animal it gets.[13]

Conrad's Kurtz prefigures the truth of these perceptions.
Released from restraint, he capitulates to all those illegitimate
desires which late nineteenth-century Christian, western European culture strictly represses. The colonial penetration of
Africa separates him from the controlling scrutiny of the
metropolitan culture and allows him the freedom to indulge
himself. He turns for release from his sexually chaste Intended,
entombed in her sarcophagus-like home in a street of houses "as
still and decorous as a well-kept alley in a cemetery" (155) to the
"wild and gorgeous" black woman, "savage and superb,
wild-eyed and magnificent" (135-6). (In his evocation of her,
Marlow relies on the clichés of colonial romance fiction, similar
to those found in *She*.) However, Kurtz's psychotic hatred of
those whom he dominates and exploits and to whom he is
illegitimately bonded is expressed both in the written words,
"exterminate all the brutes!" (118) (as the potential leader of an
extreme party, Kurtz is an ominously accurate prophecy of the
Hitlers to come in the twentieth century), and in all those
activities which Marlow can only hint at, in which the rampant
ego seeks further and more extreme gratification until it loses
itself in orgies of self-deification.

Kurtz confirms the conspiratorial brickmaker's assertion that
"Anything – anything can be done in this country" (91). He raids

the country, takes what he wants and, as the Russian harlequin explains, "there was nothing on earth to prevent him killing whom he jolly well pleased" (128). Kurtz's greed, like imperialism's, knows no limit. Marlow has a vision of him "opening his mouth voraciously, as if to devour all the earth with all its mankind" (155). The cannibal allusion is apt; in contradistinction to the totally unrestrained Kurtz, the flower of civilized Europe, Conrad offers Marlow's crew of twenty starving cannibal tribesmen. Their restraint represents truly civilized behaviour. They meet their contractual obligations to their indifferent employers, resisting the pressing temptations to vanish into the jungle or overpower the five Europeans on board to satisfy their extreme hunger. The subject of Kurtz's "noble and lofty expression" is always my ivory, "my Intended, my station, my career, my ideas" (147). Behind the "unfulfilled ideals" of both imperialism and Kurtz hover only "unimplemented intentions"[14] and the gratifying of desires institutionally restrained back "home" in Europe where the individual faces sufficient social pressure to conform to accepted notions of behaviour. Marlow laconically explains that at home one is surrounded by "kind neighbours ready to cheer you or to fall on you;" one is forced into line, to step "delicately between the butcher and the policeman, in the holy terror of scandal and gallows and lunatic asylums" (116). Colonialism frees the individual European from such pressures; in Africa, away from the eyes of neighbours, butcher and policeman, Kurtz and Marlow and the others are put to the test.

Achebe accuses Conrad of using Africa merely as "setting and backdrop which eliminates the Africans as human factor;" he believes, therefore, that the "real question is the dehumanization of Africa and Africans." While the novel *is* concerned, essentially, with the colonizers and the debilitating effects of their practices on themselves, Conrad does take care to present Marlow as a cultural relativist, unlike any of the other Europeans, able to acknowledge a shared humanity with the blacks who people his profoundly disturbing continent. This cultural relativism acts to contravert the readers' impressions of racist attitudes to Africans which would deny them their "full equivalent subjectivity" or suggest that their differences automatically represented inferiority. When Marlow begins his tale with the words "And this also...has been one of the dark places of the earth" (48), Conrad indicates his narrator's historical appreciation of how the early Roman invaders must have responded to what they perceived as the savagery of the British wilderness. When he chooses to end *Heart of Darkness* with the anonymous frame narrator's awakened perception that the chartered and domesticated Thames itself "seemed to lead into the heart of an immense darkness" (162), the reader gathers a final illustration of Conrad's faith that civilization in any culture, at any historical moment, depends on human restraint, in that "obscure, back-breaking business" (117) of keeping alive and active a "deliberate belief" (97) in moral standards of behaviour which practice too often proves to be illusory.

Readers note how Marlow turns with positive relief to the boat "paddled by black fellows" (61) as they cleave the surf off the African coast after he has witnessed the French man-of-war's absurd firing into the vast continent:

> They shouted, sang; their bodies streamed with perspiration; they had faces like grotesque masks – these chaps; but they had bone, muscle, a wild vitality, an intense energy of movement, that was as natural and true as the surf along their coast. They wanted no excuse for being there. (61)

The voice of the surf is "natural and true" because in a novella that treats all kinds of language from pure noise (such as the surf) through breath, whispers, babble, jabber, technical language, speech, and eloquence, the surf is untained by language/speech. Marlow, the bluff Englishman, acknowledges the physical unfamiliarity of Africans – faces like "grotesque masks" (Conrad anticipates Achebe's citing of the importance of African masks for inspiring the cubist creations of Picasso?), but his major insistence is on his human fellowship with these men who represent in their activities a useful and natural purpose; they are "chaps," good "fellows" functionally in harmony with their environment, and as Anthony Fothergill,[15] in his excellent Open University guide to reading the novel attests, they are not in their right place as racial stereotypes but because of a cultural legitimacy unshared by the European invaders who are the ones truly out of place. When Marlow notes the depopulated terrain he traverses, he confirms his relativistic tolerance:

> Well, if a lot of mysterious niggers armed with all kinds of fearful weapons suddenly took to travelling on the road between Deal and Gravesend, catching the yokels right and left to carry heavy loads for them, I fancy every farm and cottage thereabouts would get empty very soon. (70)

Fothergill notes that Marlow's role in the text is to offer "a radical critique of [the] processes [of African colonization] while at the same time revealing the contradictions in his own status."[16] Concomitant with Marlow's unthinking use of the patronizingly ugly nomenclature for blacks current at this time, is Conrad's revelation of the increasingly contradictory position in which Marlow finds himself, rejecting Western imperialism's conceptions of the African other, thereby becoming more marginalized and isolated. Marlow can listen to the "tremor of far off drums" and perceive in them, perhaps, "as profound a meaning as the sound of bells in a Christian country" (71). When he enlists the twenty cannibals as crewmen he can describe them as "Fine fellows – cannibals – in their place. They were men one could work with, and I am grateful to them" (94), whereas, in all his varied confrontations with European agents of the trading company Marlow consistently expresses his disgust at the hypocrisies inherent in the functioning of the system he uncomfortably serves.

Throughout the text Conrad resists any form od dualistic discourse "in terms of which what is white and European is the privileged point of reference against which the deviance /corruption/ degeneracy of what is black and non-European can be measured (and found to be freakish/unhealthy/bestial)."[17] The rapacious Eldorado Expedition, European "pilgrims" seeking ivory, is swallowed up by the patient wilderness and Marlow

comments ironically, "Long afterwards the news came that all
the donkeys were dead. I know nothing as to the fate of the less
valuable animals" (92). It is just such ironical distancing which
characterizes Conrad's handling of all his material, Marlow
included, prompting Achebe's plaint that Conrad "neglects to
hint however subtly or tentatively at an alternative frame of
reference by which we may judge the actions and opinions of his
characters." Achebe believes that Marlow must be identified
with Conrad so that Marlow's lapses, his occasional sliding into
representing some of the more suspect socio-cultural views of his
time, is laid at the feet of his creator. In discussion, my students
tend to recognize the multiple levels of ironic discourse in *Heart
of Darkness*, seeing with Fothergill that Conrad still offers "a
discourse of actions" which supply the reader with "a critical
viewpoint on Marlow's discourse of language"[18] so that they
register the ambivalencies and contradictions in Marlow's
discourse without concluding that Conrad has a racist agenda.

The "adjectival insistence" that Leavis and Achebe feel to be
a weakness, Marlow's struggle for words to approximate his
struggle to comprehend his experiences, is actually an essential
element in the book's meaning. *Heart of Darkness* manifests
Conrad's modernist perception of the inadequacies of language.
Marlow's journey to find Kurtz is a quest for meaning which
encourages the reader to seek beneath the surface for further
meanings. All Conrad's defamiliarizing techniques are directed
towards forcing the reader to explore the resonances the text
creates. Authorial omnipotence is replaced by submerging
Marlow's narration within another subjective narration; the
landscape of Africa is both mythic and surreal; the host of
grotesque, often ironic characters are generalized with the use of
type names such as the accountant, the brickmaker, the manager, and finally, in the insistent imagery of black and white, light
and dark, found throughout the text, western civilization's
conventional categories are subverted, questioned and often
reversed.

The simple moral antitheses invested in the basic tenets of
colonial thinking in which white and black represent good and

evil, purity and debasement, truth and ignorance, the beautiful and the atrocious, are constantly called into question. Black Africa and its peoples are not merely seen as the dark locus of barbaric, morally depraved forces corrupting the integrity and decency of white Europe. White is shown as sepulchred death and black as vital energy; the immaculately white-clad tailor's dummy of an accountant, slave to the white ivory all pursue, is cruelly indifferent to the dying, just as it is a white-haired secretary who opens the office doors leading into the darkness of the trading company's activities. The Intended is the white girl placed in a sombre, black setting, while we notice the black woman's sexual energy and passionate loyalty to Kurtz, and so on, with almost every page of the text manifesting the complexities of this primary dichotomy of iconography.

The book, I have suggested, is concerned with the effects of colonization on the invaders of Africa. As Marlow travels up the river the wilderness becomes the externalized objective correlative of all the atavistic appetites and forces which inhabit the human soul. "Going up that river was like travelling back to the earliest beginnings of the world" (92). Marlow fancies himself and the other colonizers as "wanderers on prehistoric earth" (95), the "first of men taking possession of an accursed inheritance, to be subdued at the cost of profound anguish and of excessive toil" (95). As he explains, "the mind of man is capable of anything – because everything is in it, all the past as well as all the future" (96). Marlow's journey takes on, then, the resonances of a mythic return of western man to some imagined, shared primal condition from which Europe has supposedly advanced over the centuries with struggle and hard-earned progress. Lurking within all of us are the residues of primitive passions (the equivalent of the Freudian id forces), in existence since the dawn of humanity.

For Conrad, sharing many of the somewhat pessimistic notions concerning the human soul current in the philosophical thinking at the close of the nineteenth century, civilization depends, in essence, on the repression of these atavistic desires, on the fundamental dynamism of restraint. As we move with

Marlow deeper into the wilderness, from station to station, the barriers erected by the invading Europeans against the menace of these primeval forces are shown to erode. The Central Station is enclosed only on three sides by "a crazy fence of rushes" with a neglected gap as "all the gate it had" (72), and Kurtz's Inner Station has "no enclosure or fence of any kind" (121), the wilderness having taken full possession.

Through Marlow's narrative, in its ambiguous conceptualization of Africa, Conrad exhibits something of the limitations of the imperialist imagination. The Europeans arrive, bearing the darkness already within the hearts of each individual, but Africa, it is suggested, is also a special environment. It is one in which the spirit of place, the inscrutable, "great and invincible" (76) forces of the wilderness wait, brooding with a "vengeful aspect" (93), ready to claim the souls of the invaders. While it is hinted that these instinctive forces are potentially liberating – they contain "truth stripped of its cloak of time" (97) – to the Europeans, whose repression of them has been too severe, the release of restraint will expose pitilessly only "human weakness" (127), and awaken "forgotten and brutal instincts" and "monstrous passions" (144). The natives are accepted as entirely natural in their more "primitive" behaviour, but they are perceived as "prehistoric man" (96), believed to be centuries behind Europeans in evolutionary growth. Marlow accepts, with a thrill, the thought of his "remote kinship" with these people, ironically noting that they "were not inhuman" (96), just as he acknowledges the "claim of distant kinship" (119) with his dead helmsman. He confesses that what kept him from going ashore "for a howl and a dance" (97) was only the imposed task of keeping the tin-pot steamer afloat. Marlow seems to subscribe to the view that, because of its technological advances, Europe is the more developed, yet younger brother of a humanity, shared with Africa. While this is patronizing, it is not necessarily racist and Marlow does not share the other Europeans' dehumanizing perceptions of the Africans.

Marlow notes that in Europe "we are accustomed to look upon the shackled form of a conquered monster" – the instinctive life is tamed and domesticated – but in the Africa he explores, "you could look at a thing monstrous and free" (96). Kurtz confronts the wilderness (initially through language), but, supported by the freedom from restraint his imperial position provides, and without the sanctions of public opinion to curb his actions, the hollowness of the pretensions of European superiority is exposed. Kurtz lacks all restraint; the wilderness caresses him, loves him, embraces him, seals "his soul to its own" (115); the wilderness finds him out early, whispers things about himself which echo loudly because "he was hollow at the core" (131). The fate of Kurtz, the rotten flower of civilized Europe, suggests, then, the emptiness of the latter's illusion of evolutionary superiority and, also, the tenuous nature of the defences available against reversion to egoistic savagery.

Heart of Darkness, finally, focuses on Marlow and the alternative he evinces. He clings insistently to his devotion, not to the egoistic self, but as already mentioned, to that "obscure, back-breaking business" (117) of keeping alive and active a "deliberate belief" (97) in certain selfless standards of behaviour which practice does often prove to be illusory. He finds the innate strength and the "capacity for faithfulness" (116) to notions of civilized behaviour which Kurtz lacks. Marlow has recognized the lessons of our age, that ours is not an ethical universe; at best, it is indifferent to humanity, at worst, malignant, and so we must actively assert significance and create standards of behaviour to which we must struggle to give allegiance. He confesses that life is often merely "that mysterious arrangement of merciless logic for a futile purpose," and that the most you can hope from it is some knowledge of yourself" (150). The importance of his quest to find Kurtz, the "enchanted princess" (106) of romance, is that in wrestling with the soul of Kurtz which has "stepped over the edge while I had been permitted to draw back my hesitating foot" (151), Marlow has been given the opportunity to look into his own soul and to discover important things about himself and, by implication, others. This element of the novel introduces us to one of the most ambiguous qualities of *Heart of Darkness*. The book investigates the institution of imperialism and offers a revelation of the complex effects this has on the colonizers, locating this analysis firmly within the parameters of an actual historical moment, and at the same time, it seeks to provide insights into an idealist conception of human nature which is, by implication, totally ahistorical and timeless.

This notwithstanding, Marlow comes to discover that he must assert through positive action, which may violate his ethic of honesty and compromise his stated belief in the detestation of lies, the need to support positive illusions of shared values which will enable those in the metropolitan society to live in some form of communal harmony. (The Africans already have this, violated only by the disruptions of the colonizers, as exampled in Conrad's description of the destruction of the village during a squabble over two black hens.) Marlow is the only figure to commit himself to values beyond the self. Approaching the home of the Intended, he has a vision of the vengeful rush of the "conquering darkness" and feels the need to keep this back "alone for the salvation of another soul" (156). Thus, just as Kurtz is buried "in a muddy hole" (150) after making his final pronouncement which Marlow is determined to see as "a moral victory" (151), not merely a "judgement upon the adventures of his soul on this earth" (150) but a wider one, embracing all humanity, penetrating "all the hearts that beat in the darkness" (151) so Marlow learns that we have to find ways to live in a world stinking of dead hippo, "and not be contaminated," by generating strength and faith enough to dig "unostentatious holes to bury the stuff in" (117).

The truth about Kurtz is too bleak a message for those like the women at home (though, not for Marlow's listeners or his readers, male and female). It is Marlow's belief that "we must help them to stay in that beautiful world of their own, lest ours gets worse" (115). This declaration should not be taken as a sign of Conrad's chauvinism but of Marlow's decision that he must bury certain stinking, contaminating truths, lest the world grow even worse. The novel ends with the full force of paradox. On the one hand, Marlow's final lie to the Intended reinforces the lies and evasions on which imperialism has been shown to depend; alternatively, it is an illustration of Marlow's return to sanity after his Gulliver-like misanthropic state in which he returns to the sepulchral city, loathing its inhabitants filching money from each other, dreaming their "insignificant and silly dreams" (152) and offensively intruding on him with their stupid ignorance of the true realities of existence. Instead, it is the latter, he finds, which require of him the saving lies which will enable the Intended, as it does others, to continue living with some purpose, balancing precariously on their "respective tightropes," performing those "monkey tricks" (94) which only the faith in created meanings can justify.

Heart of Darkness, finally, is Conrad's testimony to his stoical belief, despite so much evidence to the contrary in "the subtle but invincible conviction of solidarity that knits together the loneliness of innumerable hearts...the solidarity in mysterious origin, in toil, in joy, in hope, in uncertain fate – which binds men to each other and all mankind to the visible world" ("Preface," *NN*, viii).

NOTES

1. Ch. Achebe, "An Image of Africa: Racism in Conrad's *Heart of Darkness"*: *An Authoritative Text. Backgrounds and Sources. Criticism,* third edition (New York: W. W. Norton and Co., 1988), pp. 251-62. An amended version (1987) of the second Chancellor's Lecture at the University of Massachusetts, Amherst, February 18, 1975; later published in *The Massachusetts Review*, 18 (1977), pp. 782-94.

2. A. Fothergill, *Heart of Darkness* (Milton Keynes: Open University Press, 1989), p. 27.

3. T. Todorov, "'Race', Writing, and Culture," in *The Conquest of America: The Question of the Other,* trans. Richard Howard (New York: Harper and Row, 1984), p. 173.

4. G. Cornwell, "Race as Science, Race as Language: A Preliminary Enquiry into Origins," *Pretexts,* 1:1 (Winter 1989), p. 4.

5. *Ibid.,* p. 4.

6. See F. Fanon, *Black Skin, White Masks,* trans. Ch. L. Markman (London: Granada, 1968) and A. J. Mahomed, *Manichean Aesthetics: The Politics of Literature in Colonial Africa* (Amherst: University of Massachusetts Press, 1983).

7. Cornwell, p. 4.

8. *Ibid.,* p. 13.

9. *Ibid.,* p. 5.

10. Fanon, p. 125. As quoted in G. Finchams's lively article "Living Under the Sign of Contradiction: Self and Other in Conrad's *Heart of Darkness,"* *The English Academy Review,* 7 (December 1990), p. 3.

11. I. Watt, *Conrad in the Nineteenth Century* (London: Chatto and Windus, 1980), p. 161.

12. J. Hawthorn, *Joseph Conrad: Language and Fictional Self-Consciousness* (London: Edward Arnold, 1979), p. 25.

13. T. Pynchon, *Gravity's Rainbow* (London: Picador, 1975), p. 317.

14. Hawthorn, p. 32.

15. Fothergill, pp. 52-53.

16. Ibid., p. 58.

17. Cornwell, p. 8.

18. Fothergill, p. 56.

I am indebted also to insights offered by B. Parry, *Conrad and Imperialism: Ideological Boundaries and Visionary Frontiers* (London: Macmillan, 1983).

Tadeusz Rachwał and Tadeusz Sławek,
University of Silesia,
Katowice, Poland

D'abord l'à-bord: Conrad's Borrowed Home

I alluded to the peculiar atmosphere of his recent drawings.
"Yes," he said, "atmosphere is my style."
(Ruskin relating his conversation with Turner)

Pictures of nothing, and very like.
(Hazlitt on Turner's pictures)
It will perhaps be in the State of New Orleans or
Louisiana – countries are after all only a pretext.
(Schulz, *The Spring*)

"Boats are never far away when one is handling figures of rhetoric,"[1] says Derrida writing on the parergon of Kant's oeuvre, on the margin of philosophy. The movement through language is like a journey among the metaphors and metonymies of metaphysics, as pen is a shuttle whose movement to and fro upon the blankness of paper weaves the textual space, links the seemingly unrelated islands of meaning with one another, makes them correspond with each other, exchanges letters along the tracks or routes of *écriture*. The philosophical geography of semantics which Derrida suggests is based less on strictly cartographic measures, and more on certain suspicions of meaning which must remain secret. In *The Secret Sharer* Conrad offers his reading of such a geography:

> On the blue background of the high coast they [the islands] seem to float on silvery patches of calm water...unknown to trade, to travel, almost to geography, the manner of life they harbour is an unsolved secret. There must be villages...on the largest of them, and some communication with the world is probably kept up by native craft. (*TLS*, 133)

Shaped like a boat, his shuttle-pen handles figures of rhetoric, harbours nearby (boats are never far away) without invading their territory, but, rather, carrying their tropes elsewhere, disseminating them within the inter-space of text.

Boats are never far away when one is handling language. It is through language that we broaden our horizons, that we visit foreign lands, discover new shores. For Derrida style advances: "In the manner of *spur* of sorts. Like the prow, for example, of a sailing vessel, its *rostrum,* the projection of the ship which surges ahead to meet the sea's attack and cleave its hostile surface."[2] It is through language that we embark upon a journey leaving our home-shore behind, and we are bound to return only to different shores, to return no longer quite ourselves. "It is quite likely, as Homer has said," Foucault suggests,

> that the gods send disasters to men so that they can tell of them, and that in this possibility speech finds its infinite resourcefulness; it is quite likely that the approach of death – its sovereign gesture, its prominence within human memory – hollows out in the present and in existence the void toward which and from which we speak.[3]

We speak toward, and from, a certain emptiness, toward and from a nothing of non-language and non-event, from a hollow space from which we have departed, and toward which we, infinitely, return and simultaneously delay the return in language, through the language. It is quite likely that the Golden Age, when men lived securely without the laws or the judges, was the only time without language, the only age when no journey away from home was thinkable, when there was no dealing with figures of rhetoric, and thus no boats at hand. Then, Ovid tells us the story, "Never yet had any pine tree, cut down from its home on the mountains, been launched on ocean's waves, to visit foreign lands: men knew only their own shores."[4] The age of silver which replaced the age of gold made people sensitive to the outside, it actually made up a limit, a border between a thereness and a hereness, it produced two contiguous spaces for whose existence the idea of border, or limit, is indispensable.

The world has thus become a metonymic construct of sorts,

a construct in which the unfamiliar, windy world closely surrounded the familiar world of home (or cave) and simultaneously provided it, from the outside, with the space to be explored and domesticated. To domesticate is to make something "homely" or "*heimlich*," as Freud had it; and understanding, according to Hayden White, as a process of rendering the unfamiliar familiar, "can only be tropological in nature, for what is involved in the rendering of the unfamiliar into the familiar is a troping that is generally figurative."[5]

When one is handling (these) figures of rhetoric, when one is troping, boats are never far away. Positing understanding as troping, Hayden White does not only talk about the necessity of troping *in* understanding, but he also renders understanding as a rhetorical figure of bringing something (back?) home, as a figure of both conquest and return. In order to understand understanding one has to displace it, one has to mark it as an unknown, unfamiliar territory which is simultaneously bound to be brought to the sphere of familiarity, to the sphere of things already understood whose strangeness has been done away with.

Away from home and still ascribed to a home, bound to return, understanding "dwells in a borrowed home," in a home not far away, but not quite at home. "A borrowed home" is a metaphor which Cesar du Marsais uses as a metaphor for metaphor,[6] for a word used in a sense different from its *proper* sense, for a word not far away from that sense, for a word's foreword. In order to explain or explicate a metaphor, in order to *understand,* one has to bring words to their proper places, to "familiarize" the abundance of sense which one finds estranging or unfamiliar. A borrowed home of metaphor is thus also, figuratively, a ship or a boat, something which harbours not far away, but which cannot be brought home; something which can only be used to either go away or come close to a home: thus on board (of a boat or a ship) one is always already on the border, *d'abord l'à-bord,* on (the) bo(a)rder,[7] in a borrowed home between the home/land and the stormy seas. In *Freya of the Seven Isles* Conrad shows both his disbelief in the synonymity between the ship and home ("this brig was the home to be...the floating paradise which he was gradually fitting out like a yacht to save his life blissfully away in with Freya. Imbecile!") and a mocking disapproval of the protagonist's mooring his ship in front of his verandah rather than "tucking for the anchorage in a proper and seamanlike manner" (*TLS*, 152).

On board the *Nellie* anchored on the south bank of the Thames, between the land and the sea, but also between day and night, between now and then, and between here and there, Marlow begins his story: "And this also...has been one of the dark places of the earth" (*YS*, 48). "This" is a demonstrative pronoun, but the place it is supposedly pointing to *is* and *was* at the same time ("hundred years ago – the other day"); such a place cannot be simply demonstrated. Marlow does not use his "this" quite literally but, rather, in some sense other than its proper sense, he uses it, say, metaphorically. His "this" does not point to anything but only promises a demonstration and its function is very much the function of a preface, of the gesture of introduction which posits itself outside the main (demonstrating) text and says that "this" is in fact a "that" to be found "there," in what follows in the story. "Where is the pleasure of the text," asks Gary John Percesepe,

> [including the present text] to be found, if not in the pre-facio, the fore-play? Here we find, do we not, *Vorlast*, "preliminary pleasure" which [Hegel informs us] reaches satisfaction only at the end, the *climax* of the science. In a sense, then the preface for Hegel is stolen, forbidden pleasure – such pleasure [as we know] is the sweetest of all.[8]

The stolen pleasure, the illegal pleasure of Hegel's prefacing is improper because it does not lead to the climax and because it does not take place in the proper place. In *Phenomenology of Spirit* Hegel writes:

> To show that now is the time for philosophy to be raised to the status of Science would therefore be the justification of any effort that has this aim, for to do so would demonstrate the necessity of the aim, would indeed at the same time be the accomplishing of it.[9]

The prefatory demonstration of the necessity of the aim is thus conflated with its accomplishment and the stolen pleasure of prefacing is legalized as belonging to the proper field of "Science." Hegel is always already at home, in the proper place, although he sees this proper place and approaches it from the distant perspective of his prefaces. His *Vorlast* is simultaneously the accomplishment, and although the accomplishment does not take place, it justifies the prefatory announcements and, actually, the prefatory character of Hegel's oeuvre. Although Hegel is always away from the accomplishment he promises, he simultaneously presents or "pre-sends" the accomplishment, sees the land and says he is already at home. "Here [with Descartes]," he says in *Lectures on the History of Philosophy*, "we can say, we are at home, and like the mariner after long wanderings on tumultous seas, we can cry 'Land'."[10]

Unlike Marlow, Hegel does not quite realize that his "here" is also "there." Marlow is not an ordinary seaman. "Most seamen lead, if one may so express it, a sedentary life" and they never really depart from home because their minds, like Hegel's, are "of the stay-at-home order, and their home is always with them – the ship; and so is their country – the sea" (48). Most seamen needn't return anywhere as they are always here, at home, and their "this" points to things "veiled not by a sense of mystery but by a slightly disdainful ignorance" (48). Marlow, unlike those seamen, "was a wanderer, too" (48). Like other seamen he did spin yarns but his shuttle (a thing shaped like a boat) made the yarns into somehow different textures:

> The yarns of seamen have a direct simplicity, the whole meaning of which lies within the shell of a cracked nut. But Marlow was not typical (if his propensity to spin yarns be excepted), and to him the meaning of an episode was not inside like a kernel but outside, enveloping the tale which brought it out only as a glow brings out a haze, in the likeness of one of those misty halos that sometimes are made visible by the spectral illumination of moonshine. (48)

There is thus no kernel in Marlow's story, no heart (of darkness?) which one can show, display, explain, point to, reveal from behind the web or veil of a text. The meaning is already on the surface but the surface is not directly accessible to understanding because of its vagueness, because of the amorphic mistiness occupying the space always at a distance from the centre. The meaning is a story, the surface, "the veil of mystery," the envelope without which the message cannot be delivered. Without this story of meaning there is no meaning, though the meaning cannot be told by the story. There is thus a kind of madness in Marlow's story, the madness of the preface which invites, promises and introduces into the secret that there is no secret, to the secret which will lose the secrecy without this "introducing, introducing..." (57). The veil of mystery protects and veils at the same time, it protects, by veiling, the secret and thus actually brings the secret to life. Without this veil, let us repeat, there is no secret.

Nietzsche, using a similar rhetoric of veiling, will introduce the theme of history here:

> But every people, even every man, who wants to become *ripe* needs such an enveloping madness, such a protective and veiling cloud; now, however, we hate ripening as such because history is honoured above life.[11]

History is, for Nietzsche, a discourse that kills life, a discourse which desires to be factual and scientific; an operation performed upon bare facts neatly locked in nutshells to be cracked in the manner most seamen spin yarns in Conrad's story. Such bare facts are lifeless, they are in fact barren. "Every living thing," says Nietzsche,

> needs to be surrounded by an atmosphere, a mysterious circle of mist: if one condemns a religion, an art, a genius to orbit as a star without an atmosphere: then one should not wonder about its rapidly becoming withered, hard and barren. This is just how it is with all things great indeed, "which without some madness ne'er succeed..."[12]

History brings things home, history leads a sedentary life and propagates this barren kind of life by unveiling things, by confining them to what it thinks they are, by domesticating them. All things great stay away from home, they madly dance and pirouette on the margins of scientific books, away from Hegel's accomplishment, in the misty madness which veils them and protects their living mystery, their unaccomplishment.

Accomplishment breeds pestilence. All things great live, like metaphors, in a borrowed home, on (the) bo(a)rder. Like Marlow they are both seamen and wanderers pursuing their own shadows, the atmosphere of "mist(ery)," "introducing, introducing continuously to the unknown." Without that introducing there is only the bare and barren heart of immense darkness. As if in the act of double criticism against the belief that a story can have its heart of darkness and against Conrad's presentation of the problem of his famous story, Bruno Schulz finds the heart (which was to mark the end of stories) already populated with tales:

> Give me your hand, take another step: we are at the roots now, and at once everything becomes dark, spicy, and tangled like in the depth of a forest. There is a smell of turf and tree rot; roots wander about, entwined, full with juices that rise as if sucked up by pumps. We are on the nether side, at the lining of things, in gloom stitched with phosphorescence. There is a lot of movement and traffic, pulp and rot, tribes and generations, a brood of bibles and illiads multiplied a thousand times! Wanderings and tumults, the tangle and hubbub of history! That road leads no further. We are here at the very bottom, in the dark foundations, among the Mothers. Here are the bottomless infernos, the hopeless Ossianic spaces, all those lamentable Nibelungs. Here are the great breeding grounds of history, factories of plots, hazy smoking rooms of fables and tales.[13]

Nietzsche's life and Marlow's stories take place on the margin, between Hegel's work accomplished and the absolute outside, within the space traditionally reserved for a commentary. Although there seems to be a world of difference between prefacing and commenting, the space the two kinds of writing occupy is almost the same. Both are and are not the same text, the same book, both belong to the text, both are, as in Hegel, paradoxical things. If there is some madness in prefacing, there seems to be even more in the commentary, at least in Foucault's reading of it:

> By a paradox which it always displaces but never escapes, the commentary must say for the first time what had, nonetheless, already been said, and must tirelessly repeat what had, however, never been said.[14]

The commentary, like the preface, serves the purpose of confirming the accomplishment of the main text. It repeats anew, in different words, what has been already accomplished, points to the accomplished ideas, rephrases them, epitomizes, and so on. In this respect the commentary functions like a preface: it announces the truth of the father text and, simultaneously, as a marginal kind of writing, renounces and denounces its own textuality, its status of an original text. Saying the same in different words, the commentary also "repeats" what the text does not say, that is, supplements (yet another marginal kind of writing) its imperfections, something "silently articulated" by the text, and yet lacking verbal actualization.

The division into primary and secondary texts, into creative and original writings and the texts which only comment or gloss is by no means given once and for all. "Plenty of major texts," says Foucault, "become blurred and disappear, and sometimes commentaries move into the primary position."[15] What constitutes the condition for the existence of human discourses is not how texts have been classified and differentiated, but the "principle of differentiation...continuously put back in play."[16] Discourses of truth, discourses which follow in the wake of what Foucault calls "will to truth," desire to eradicate the principle of differentiation and take the division into central and marginal, primary and secondary, for granted. They, in fact, search for an unquestionable centre from which, or around which, a profusion of repetitive commentaries is produced, but which can still exist independently of the marginal. Hegel's home is reached regardless of the prefatory status of his writing. Seekers of this kind of truth are never away from home, and in Conrad's phrasing they are seamen but not wanderers. They seek something already found. The wanderers, like Marlow or Nietzsche, on the other hand, realize the paradox that "'home' is needed and can be imagined only when it is dispossessed and left behind: we cannot know, despite reassurances, whether we will reach the land, whether we are really in sight of land at all."[17] In Nietzsche's philosophy the wanderer is one who subjects the land of the Derridian operation of *sous rature*:

> We have left the land and have embarked. We have burned our bridges behind us – indeed, we have gone farther and destroyed the land behind us.[18]

A wanderer's position is always *d'abord l'à-bord,* away from the centre, from truth, from accomplishment, and thus his task, his teleology, is always inconclusive. The wanderer is always away from home, even if, like Captain B. from Conrad's *The Mirror of the Sea,* he is sitting in his drawing-room surrounded by armchairs, cushions and other familiar objects. We shall thus never learn the what, the where, the when of Marlow's introductory "this" and his story will envelope this "this" in other events, with other places, other times; we are "fated...to hear about one of Marlow's inconclusive experiences," to quote the narrator's commentary on Marlow's narrative (51). For this reason Conrad's title, *Heart of Darkness,* is, as it were, titular. The accomplished heart exists only in the name while the story takes us on board a ship travelling through different shades of darkness, through the ATMOSPHERE of darkness, through Marlow's commentary which only signals the existence of the main text, but never reveals it, "introducing, introducing...."

The problem of the analyst of atmosphere, like Marlow, Conrad or Nietzsche, is that he always runs the risk of either positing the marginal sphere of his interest as central and thus falling prey to the will to truth, or of being accused, like Turner's paintings in the epigram, of being an analyst of nothing. Yet, Nietzsche's "life," for instance, is a "category" which does not efface the centre; it only calls it dead when considered in itself, outside the reach of the principle of differentiation. So too

Marlow warns us that his destination, the place towards which he will wander is "Dead in the centre" (56), he warns us that the route which leads towards that centre is always already marked by a death. "And the river was there – fascinating – deadly – like a snake. Ough!" (56). What fascinates Marlow is thus the parergon, and not the ergon, the task accomplished; the deadly atmosphere, and not death. With such a bias life and death are no longer opposite terms, but a sphere of mutual contamination where neither life nor death occupies the central position. If Marlow's story can be read as life's commentary upon death, then death, the seeming main text, also comments upon life and on its margin makes the wanderer's life/journey "deadly." And it is in this deadly atmosphere where, as in Derrida's dangerous supplement, man dangerously dwells.

A foreplay of the play of the centre and margin in *Heart of Darkness* is Marlow's visit to the Company's offices in Brussels. Having crossed the Channel Marlow arrives "in the city that always makes me think of a whited sepulchre. Prejudice no doubt" (55). Marlow's prejudiced eye sees more than what shows itself to it, he sees the city as already deadly, thus rendering it as an introduction to his voyage towards darkness (in the wake of darkness) of which the city is ominously reminiscent: streets in "deep shadow," "a dead silence." There is also "grass sprouting between the stones" (55), rehearsing the vision of grass growing up through Captain Fresleven's ribs (54). Marlow has no problems finding his way to the colonial centre, to the company's offices: "It was the biggest thing in the town, and everybody I met was full of it" (55). The building, the centre, is both outside and inside, visible and invisible at the same time. The town hypocritically says it has no mysterious secrets, it posits the centre as easily accessible through "innumerable windows," and "immense double doors standing ponderously ajar." Yet, Marlow's prejudiced eye notices venetian blinds in the windows and his passage to the central office, to the director's room, is incessantly delayed. It turns out that the centre is guarded by another door, by two women knitting black wool and, eventually, it turns out that the centre is a vague memory of words vaguely murmured by a great man in the biggest building in the city and an invitation to further voyage. There is, in fact, no secret, but Marlow is made to sign "some document. I believe I undertook amongst other things not to disclose any trade secrets. Well I am not going to" (56).

If the secret is, as Foucault pharses it, that there is no secret then Marlow in a way does disclose this paradox. If anything, the secret is a story, a tale told by a wanderer pursuing a shadow, by a seaman knitting yarns into texts which signify nothing. It is this signification of nothing that makes nothing a significant "secret of the trade," that posits nothing beyond signification. To "signify nothing" is not to signify at all, to be insignificant, and in the sphere of any exchange (of ideas, for instance) it has no value. In order that there is an exchange, a trade, the nothing must be hidden behind a venetian blind, behind a pall of black wool as a secretive object which can be conquered (be it a heart, a truth or a Congo) and brought home or changed into a place where one feels at home.

The key "home" on the computer keyboard sends the cursor to the beginning of the line, to where it started its movement through the line of some text. Yet this home is no longer its own; it is already occupied by a letter or by an invisible "space." If anywhere, the cursor dwells in a borrowed home. It is at home only before there is a text, and the moment someone begins a text, a story, the return back home becomes an illusion, and the word "home" (on the computer key, for instance) a rhetorical figure. Boats, as we know, are never far away when one is handling figures of rhetoric. In the course of writing, the cursor, be it also a pen or a quill, is always already away from home, in the sphere of style, in the sphere of the misty atmosphere which, as Hazlitt rightly noticed, is a picture of nothing, and very like, "a storm full of sound and fury" in whose centre there is a nothing, a ship, for instance, or a "steam boat off a harbour's mouth making signals in shallow water, and going by the lead" (the rubric with which Turner's "Snowstorm" was shown in London's National Gallery in 1842).

"Guarding the door of Darkness" (57) there is "the horror" of an endless (and pointless) prefacing, of the position off a harbour's mouth which is the position of one who tells stories, who writes, who signifies nothing only "introducing, introducing...."

NOTES

1. J. Derrida, *The Truth in Painting,* trans. G. Bennington and J. McLeod (Chicago and London: University of Chicago Press, 1987), p. 54.

2. J. Derrida, *Spurs, Nietzsche's Styles,* trans. B. Harlow (Chicago: University of Chicago Press, 1979), p. 39.

3. M. Foucault, "Language to Infinity," in D. F. Bouchard, ed., *Michel Foucault, Language, Counter-Memory, Practice. Selected Essays and Interviews,* trans. D. F. Bouchard and S. Simon (Oxford: Blackwell, 1977), p. 53.

4. Ovid, *Metamorphoses,* trans. M. M. Innes (Penguin Books 1974), p. 31.

5. H. White, *Tropics of Discourse. Essays in Cultural Criticism* (Baltimore and London: Johns Hopkins University Press, 1987), p. 4.

6. J. Derrida, "White Mythology," trans. F. T. C. Moore, *New Literary History,* 4 (Winter 1974), p. 53.

7. J. Derrida, *The Truth in Painting,* p. 54.

8. G. J. Percesepe, *Future(s) of Philosophy. The Marginal Thinking of Jacques Derrida* (New York, Bern, Frankfurt-am-Main, Paris: Peter Lang, 1989), p. 1.

9. G. W. F. Hegel, *Phenomenology of Spirit,* trans. A. V. Miller (Oxford: O.U.P., 1977), p. 4.

10. Quoted in: R. Flores, *The Rhetoric of Doubtful Authority* (Ithaca and London: Cornell University Press, 1984), p. 27.

11. F. Nietzsche, *On the Advantage and Disadvantage of History for Life,* trans. P. Preuss (Indianapolis and Cambridge: Hackett Publishing Company, 1980), p. 41.

12. *Ibid.* p. 40.

13. B. Schulz, *Sanatorium Under the Sign of the Hourglass,* trans. C. Wieniewska (Picador, 1980), p. 43.

14. M. Foucault, "The Order of Discourse," R. Young ed., *Untying the Text. A Post-Structuralist Reader* (Boston, London and Henley: Routledge and Kegan Paul, 1981), p. 58.

15. *Ibid.* p. 57.

16. *Ibid.* p. 57.

17. R. Flores, *The Rhetoric of Doubtful Authority,* p. 28.

18. F. Nietzsche, *The Gay Science,* trans. W. Kaufman (New York: Random Books, 1974), p. 180.

Adam Gillon,
State University of New York,
New Paltz, USA

Adapting Conrad to Film: *Dark Country*

The release of Francis Coppola's *Apocalypse Now* sparked a lively discussion in the press, with critics basically divided into two camps: one that shared Vincent Canby's view that Coppola "vaporized"[1] Conrad, and the other that favored Gerald Morgan's opinion that Coppola "has given a special twist and a higher intensity to Conrad's famous story *Heart of Darkness*."[2] I wavered between the two and ultimately settled on the only logical compromise, suggested by Raymond T. Brebach: "Francis Coppola's *Apocalypse Now* is not a film *of Heart of Darkness*, but a film *after* or *inspired by* Conrad's novella. Coppola of course has the right to adapt freely, and it would be a mistake to belabor him simply for not following Conrad more closely."[3] Yet it is difficult for Brebach and other Conrad lovers not to fault Coppola for changing Marlow's character and thereby upsetting "one of the important balances in the story."[4]

I fully understood Coppola's predicament when I began working on my own screenplay *inspired by Heart of Darkness* rather than *adapted from* Conrad's novella. How could the original Marlow be transported to the gory battlefield of Vietnam without undergoing a sea change? How could *any* character in the story remain the same, given the utterly different setting and historical time? As Julia Whitsitt points out in "No Choice of Nightmares: Coppola's Willard vs. Conrad's Marlow," Willard is tortured by Col. Kurtz and he "has only the choice of killing Kurtz or being killed by him; he is inextricably caught in the conflict between the dehumanization of the war machine and the inhumanity of Kurtz's idiosyncratic violence."[5]

I also toyed with the idea of placing *my* Marlow in a similar apocalyptic setting – that of World War II. He would command a destroyer, and the film would open with a spectacular shot of

103

his ship sailing into the becalmed waters of New York Harbor. At the close of the day, sitting on deck, smoking his pipe and drinking whiskey with a group of listeners, he would tell his story, against the backdrop of the giant city that never sleeps, hardly offering the serenity or the brooding gloom of Conrad's vision of London. And, as the sun would sink on the West Side, Marlow could make his initial dramatic comment, referring to New York: "And this also has been one of the dark places on the earth." He would be thinking of the conquest of the New World, which was not that different from the white man's conquest of Africa.

And his tale would be of the darkness that fell upon Europe and the horrors of the Holocaust. I saw Kurtz as a commander of a Nazi concentration camp, with his Intended as one of the inmates. Conrad's dark vision evoked grim and painful memories. To me, his perception of inhumanity and horror meant a vision of my own mother, machine-gunned along with some thirty thousand other women, children and men, and then buried, many of them alive, in a huge trench that once was a moat of a medieval castle. This enormous grave heaved and groaned for many hours. If I were to translate *Heart of Darkness* into a contemporary cinematic story, my Marlow's mission would be to bring Kurtz to justice. I tried to imagine what Kurtz's reaction would be if he recognized his fianceé at a roll-call or at some bestial act of torture? I wondered what her response would be? Conrad's ironic ending, like so many similar scenes in *Under Western Eyes,* provided good reading. But I doubted that such a scene, in which every word counted, could be re-enacted on the screen. Besides, I confess that not being particularly enamored of the Intended, I really wanted to create another kind of woman, who would be able to face the truth about her lover and herself. Which, of course, demanded a totally different ending.

I wrote a brief treatment of the film along these lines. Several weeks later, after reading it a few times, I realized that I was imitating Coppola by trying to show the whole world as a place of darkness, merely exchanging his Vietnam scene for my

Nazi-occupied Europe. The treatment played havoc with Conrad's conception of the principal characters. My film would not vaporize Conrad – it would destroy him altogether.

I abandoned the enterprise until the Thirteenth Annual Meeting of the Joseph Conrad Society in 1987, for which I had suggested the topic: "Conrad and Film." Robert L. Carringer's paper, "Orson Welles's Unmade *Heart of Darkness* Film" rekindled my interest in the project. Ian Watt took a dim view of Welles's first adaptation treatment. In his witty response to Carringer, he ridiculed Welles's "devastating" six-stage river surrounded by the jungle. Welles was not satisfied with Conrad's elaborate and richly adjectival descriptions of the river. Said Carringer: "As his first step toward adapting Conrad's story, he is *re-imagining it in visual terms,* at this point without any regard for the practical and technical exigencies of filmmaking."

Welles intended not only to re-imagine the story but also to adapt its narrative technique to that of the cinema, so that "the story would have been told entirely through the point of view of Marlow as the eyes of the camera. Marlow's status as first--person observer would occasionally be cued by the lighting of his pipe protruding into the foreground of the camera field or by his reflection in windows or other mirroring surfaces...Observational first person storytelling of this sort is perhaps the most cumbersome of all filmic modes of narration." Despite this criticism, Carringer concluded that Welles's fragment had considerable stature when it was compared with "the flatulent pomposity of *Apocalypse Now* and the limpid inanity of the Richard Brooks version of *Lord Jim.*"

Professor Carringer was kind enough to send me Welles's 17-page fragment and further information about Welles's project in the Mercury Theatre archive at Lilly Library, Bloomington, Indiana, and in Carringer's book, *Making of Citizen Kane.* What struck me most about Welles's treatment was the extent to which he relied on Conrad's text by describing his vision of the river, and the suggestion that he needed two boats, one to be used for navigation in Everglades, Florida, and the other in a studio. Then, there was a casual mention of a white girl in one of the stations reached by Marlow.

Suddenly, I knew that I no longer wanted to delve into Welles's abortive treatment and the vast amount of material on the *Heart of Darkness* project. There was a boat, a white girl and a mixed crew of whites and natives, going up a jungle river. No, this wasn't going to be another *African Queen,* though I wish I could have written such a delightful script and secured such an incomparable pair of actors as Katherine Hepburn and Humphrey Bogart. I remembered Oliver Stone's admission that there was a lot of himself in *Midnight Express* which he adapted for the screen. "The character in the book isn't the way he's portrayed in the film. The real Billy Hayes is quite different. I romanticized him. I used my own experience in jail. I'd been thrown in jail when I came back from Vietnam. It was a feeling of terror. I used my experience and met the character halfway."[6]

I too was willing to meet my characters halfway while re-imagining them, as Welles suggested, in a story which must be told in moving pictures, a story which must be dramatic. The more I examined Conrad's text the more I became aware of its limitations as an action-adventure drama. While the passage of a steamboat along a jungle river could be visually exciting, there is very little action aboard the *Roi de Belges,* except for the attack of the natives and the removal of some snags. My Marlow would not be telling a story – he would be one of the principal characters involved in action and in the plot.

I was not happy with the reasons Conrad's Marlow offers for his decision to seek the position of captain of a river boat: a child's dream and a need for a job seemed not dramatic enough. I needed a more compelling reason for Marlow to go into the heart of the African continent. I thought of another character, with whom I, like Conrad, could fully identify: Lord Jim. Marlow would harbor a dark secret, a memory of a transgression, a betrayal of duty. Like Jim he would be on the run, to hide from shame, and to seek an opportunity to redeem himself. Looking for Kurtz, he would find himself. Perhaps, in a non-Conradian twist, he might even get Kurtz's girl whom I pictured as carrying his child, and determined to claim him as her lawful husband. I saw her as a rich and spoiled young lady,

accompanied by a maid she called "Nanny" who would provide
a measure of comic relief. Once I got the two women aboard the
steamboat commanded by Marlow, I would have plenty of
complications and action. The die was cast. I had embarked on
an adventurous journey to a land I called "Dark Country."

Since a great deal of action would take place aboard the
steamboat, I needed a real model for my set. The available
photograph of the *Roi de Belges* was inadequate. So I began to
look for steamboats up and down the Hudson River, from
Kingston to New York, but could find no vessel to serve my
need. A trip to New York Library solved the problem. I read
a number of books with drawings and photographs of steamboats that plied the rivers of Europe and Africa, and was able to
produce a composite model of the boat which I christened (with
an appropriate, sardonic grin) the *Lux*.

Then I set about inventing new names and identities for my
characters. Though I drew heavily on Conrad's text, I wanted to
imagine them in terms of my plot which departed from the
novella. Once I bestowed a local habitation and a name upon the
protagonists, they began to clamor for attention, and continued
doing so for almost a full year. I heard Carringer's paper on 28
December 1987. I registered the completed screenplay with
WGAE (Writers Guild of America East) on 7 December 1988.
The script was 138 pages long, and contained 419 scenes or full
shots.

The film begins with a Prologue, introducing a musical bridge
of heavy metal group, suggesting diabolical themes. William
Reston (my Marlow), aged ten, points to a blank spot on a map
of the world in his father's study. The stern father rebukes him
for dreaming. Next we see William aged twenty-five, in a merchant marine uniform, being lectured by his father in the manner
of old Polonius: "above all, be true. Be faithful to your
profession." "I will, father," William swears. The initial film
credits are faded in over a scene borrowed from *Lord Jim*. Like
Jim, Reston freezes in a moment of danger, then jumps off his
ship. We see him in court, listening to the verdict proclaiming his
disgrace. When he walks in the street, looking for the Conti-

nental Trading Society building, he is haunted by the words of
the Presiding Officer of the Commission of Inquiry: "You've
disgraced your uniform, Reston...You should have crawled into
the darkest hole on this earth, to hide your shame...."

I follow Conrad's text faithfully as Reston encounters the
company's secretary, the doctor and the knitting women. At the
same time, Cathy Morrison (the Intended) is buying gifts of
ivory for her fiancé, Jason (Kurtz) at the company store. Cathy
catches up with Reston as he is loading up the *Lux*, presenting
him with a letter from the company, authorizing her passage
aboard the steamboat. Though Reston is most reluctant to take
her aboard, he has no choice.

The pure-minded Cathy regards Jason as a saintly missionary.
Neither she nor Reston knows that Jason has turned into
a worshipper of Satan, and crowned himself King of Dark
Country. The presence of this beautiful young and rich woman
and her maid aboard the small begrimed steamboat stirs dark
passions in the hearts of the white crew: Peter, Borg and Tony.
Even before the *Lux* reaches the First Station, where Cathy
witnesses the white man's inhumanity to the black natives, the
three white ruffians that serve Reston are planning to attack, rob
and kill the women, after disposing of Reston and the three
native crew members, Mamba, Bulu and Chinoe. Petunia Dipps
(Nanny) overhears them and tells her mistress who then informs
Reston. The captain gives his revolver to Cathy for self-
-protection.

Reston and Cathy disembark at the First Station, followed by
other white crew members. While the appearance of the Station
Manager, whom I call Maurice Maurier, is in accordance with
Conrad's description of the incongruous dandy in the bush, his
character is drawn after Mr. Jones from *Victory*. I provided him
with a trio of henchmen (also inspired by this novel): Waldstein,
Cardoza and Hund, an ape-like muscle man and the enforcer of
Maurier's designs, eager to crush Reston's bones.

Maurier charms Nanny with his suave manner, but then he
kidnaps Cathy with Hund's assistance. Peter rescues her but
promptly begins to make advances to her. It is now Reston's turn

to save his maiden in distress. He brings the women back to the steamboat, but it offers little protection from Peter and his two ruffian buddies who smell blood and are ready for the kill.

There is a great deal of mayhem aboard the *Lux*. When the steamboat finally reaches the Inner Station, the only survivors are Cathy, Reston, Bulu and Chinoe. Siggy Freund (my equivalent of the bepatched Russian) reveals Jason's mad plans and explains the dangers of opposing his master. Reston and Cathy are taken prisoner by Jason's warriors. Without having seen her, Jason orders Cathy to be sacrificed on an altar. She is stripped naked and brought to Jason, seated on a throne, his native Queen at his side. When the veil is lifted off Cathy's face, she stammers in disbelief, "You?" She collapses and has a miscarriage. Jason decides to spare her life and make her his First Queen; he tries to persuade her to adopt his Satanic creed. He wants Reston to carry his offer of drug and ivory trade to Europe. He has grandiose dreams of becoming the richest and most powerful man in the world. The Black Queen asks Shaman, the medicine man, to give her a love potion for Jason. Shaman, who wants the throne for himself, gives her poison instead. The Queen administers it to Jason who gets very sick. Reston convinces Siggy to leave with him and Cathy who is beginning to see the difference between her former fiancé and Reston. The dying Jason is brought aboard the *Lux*. Jason dies and is buried on a small island in the river. But the Black Queen does not know it, and she wants her man back. She attacks the steamboat with warriors in three canoes, and succeeds in boarding the *Lux*. She manages to stab Reston when he defends Cathy. The steamboat survives the attack and chugs down the river, escaping the pursuing warriors. Reston has fainted from the loss of blood. Cathy nurses him. At dawn, he wakes after a nightmare. She puts her arms about him and kisses him tenderly.

This, briefly, is the synopsis of *Dark Country*. I have imagined Jason more in the likeness of a mad Jones in Guiana than Conrad's raving Kurtz. I have built the screenplay on the premise that with the exception of Reston and the three blacks, the white crew was villainous, as were most of the whites in the

First Station. I have attempted to *show* some horrors on the screen: the massacre of a peaceful village, the starving natives, the callousness of the white administrators, the ruthlessness and satanic practices of Jason, the dastardly violence of the white crew. But I have also tried to balance my film with the essentially positive nature of Reston and Cathy, who find love at the end.

I can hear the howls of some critics, charging, "This is pure *schmaltz*. This is a saccarine Hollywood ending." Maybe it is. But my characters, *inspired by* Conrad's *Heart of Darkness,* have the right to go their own, merry way. I fear that I shall never have to cry all the way to the bank. Especially if the prospective producers, directors and investors are apprised of the connection between *Dark Country* and Conrad's novella. Francis Coppola was careful not to stress this connection. As Gary Taylor remarked about the posters and newspaper advertisements for Kenneth Branagh's *Henry V,* "you will notice that Shakespeare's name is never mentioned. Ingratitude is monstrous, but the film's American distributors were no doubt correct in thinking that the name itself would, like a knell, affright the many-headed multitude and send the movie to an untimely grave. What's in a name? Several million dollars. You can quote me."[7]

So far, I have not tried to hide my indebtedness to Conrad when I sent the script to 21st Century Film Corporation, Aaron Spelling Productions and RKO Pictures-Pavilion Communications, Inc. The first two returned the script, pleading it was inconsistent with their needs. Gail M. Kearns, Creative Affairs of RKO-Pavilion, wrote: "Ted Hartley received your screenplay submission of *Dark Country* and it was read with much interest. Although we think an action-adventure film based on Conrad's *Heart of Darkness* is a thrilling prospect, this is not the kind of material we are looking for at this time...We hope you will consider us with other projects in the future."

Kendel-Grayson Productions, Inc., on the other hand, specifically asked for my filmic version of *Heart of Darkness.* Their letter of 19 July 1991 reads:

Thank you for your recent submissions including those based on Joseph Conrad. We have British acting clients who have expressed interest in the works of Conrad, and we will be preparing for you a more detailed letter in this connection regarding our entertainment of production of these items in the 1992-1993 period. I apologize for not having responded to your kindness in sending promptly the screenplay based on *Heart of Darkness* which we requested, and which I enjoyed immensely...Mr. Aymar of our firm has read your work, and has recommended the material to me. Cordially, Todd A. Grayson, President, Kendel-Grayson, Inc.

The virtue of adversity, says Bacon, is fortitude. The best way to deal with a situation like this is to find the right quotation to cheer oneself up. But David Mamet claims (quoted by Gary Taylor) that "We live in an illiterate country, and it is the fashion of these times to quote movies, not books."[8] Scarlet O'Hara's immortal words come to mind: "After all, tomorrow is another day." One must be patient and hope that, unlike so many Conradian tales, my continuing saga of adapting Conrad to film will have a happy ending. On second thought, perhaps I ought to quote from a book. As Natalia puts it in *Under Western Eyes*: "I believe that the future will be merciful to all of us...."

NOTES

This essay represents a section of Chapter Eleven of my forthcoming book, *Joseph Conrad: Comparative Essays,* to be published by Texas Tech University Press.

1. V. Canby, "Coppola Vaporizes Conrad," *The Dallas Morning News,* 9 August 1979, p. 1.
2. *Joseph Conrad Today,* 5: 2 (January 1989), p. 139. Culled from *Monday Magazine,* Victoria, Canada, 5 November 1979.
3. R. T. Brebach, "Marlow and Willard: A Note on *Apocalypse Now,"* *Joseph Conrad Today,* 5: 3, p. 147.
4. *Ibid.*
5. J. Whitsitt, "No Choice of Nightmares: Coppola's Willard vs. Conrad's Marlow," *Joseph Conrad Today,* 5: 3 (April 1980), p. 149.

6. Quoted by S. Field in *Selling a Screenplay: The Screenwriter's Guide to Hollywood* (New York: Bantam Doubleday Dell Publishing Group., A Dell Trade Paperback, 1989), p. 187.

7. G. Taylor, "Brush up Your Shakespeare," *The New York Times Book Review,* 22 July 1990, p. 28.

8. *Ibid.*

Jakob Lothe,
University of Bergen,
Bergen, Norway

Narrators and Characters in *Lord Jim*

It is an attractive feature of the humanities that a good observation – on, for instance, Conrad's *Lord Jim* – can remain useful much longer than in many other disciplines. Thus I shall begin this paper by referring to an early essay on *Lord Jim*; and I shall end by quoting from a review published in 1900 – the year in which the novel appeared. My focus throughout is on narrators and characters in *Lord Jim*, Conrad's first full-blown modernist novel and unquestionably one of his major works. It needs to be said that the brevity of the paper (which is based on an oral presentation of just half an hour) unavoidably entails a rather cursory treatment of complex issues.

My starting-point is a passage from Dorothy Van Ghent's study *The English Novel* from 1953. Considering Jim's desertion from the *Patna,* Van Ghent finds that it

> defines Conrad's method in this book, his use of reflector within reflector, point of view within point of view, cross-chronological juxtapositions of events and impressions. Conrad's technical "devices," in this case, represent much more than the word "device" suggests: they represent extreme ethical scrupulosity, even anxiety; for the truth about a man is at once too immense and too delicate to sustain any failure of carefulness in the examiner.[1]

Van Ghent then goes on to stress Conrad's need for Marlow as the main narrator in the novel. In this particular book, she claims, "*Marlow has to exist.*" And continuing, "For Jim's 'case' is not an absolute but a relative; it has a being only in relation to what men's minds can make of it. And Marlow provides the neccessary medium of an intelligent consciousness."[2]

These comments are, many would still agree, perceptive and persuasive. In actual fact they adumbrate several of the issues

113

explored by more recent criticism of *Lord Jim*. An example is the emphasis Van Ghent puts upon Conrad's "technical devices," but it is equally significant that she stresses the ethical dimension of the novel's thematics. Furthermore, although critical discourse has undergone radical changes since the fifties, there seems no reason to dissent from her high evaluation of Marlow – both as integral part of the thematics of *Lord Jim* and as a key device in the narrative strategy Conrad employs.

One obvious but important reason for Marlow's importance resides in his combined function as narrator and character. As Van Ghent puts it, Marlow provides the "medium of an intelligent consciousness." However, his significance and complexity as a character make him more than just a medium, and neither is he the only one. Broadly, his functions are diverse and multi-facted, integrated into – and indeed aiding Conrad to construe – a sophisticated narrative method. Thus it is only to be expected that references to Marlow tend to occur and recur in most discussions of *Lord Jim*. So they will here, but rather than focussing on Marlow directly I choose to comment on the functions of the third-person narrator, the French lieutenant, and the "privileged" reader.[3] All are interestingly related to Marlow, but they also carry their own narrative and thematic import.

In *Lord Jim* transitions are frequently blurred between narrator, narrative information, and character. The structural complexity of the novel is further augmented by the fact that as the narrators narrate they tend to interpret what they narrate. Gathering and passing on information about Jim they also try to understand him, his actions, and the reasons for their own interest in his fate. This applies particularly to Marlow as principal narrator, but in other ways too *Lord Jim* insists on a close relationship between narration, interpretation, and reading. We can suggest, referring to an interesting essay by J. Hillis Miller,[4] a division into five distinct yet related groups of interpreters in the novel. As it bears an obvious relation to the interplay of narrators and characters, this division needs briefly to be presented.

The first group is constituted by Jim, especially in his long conversation with Marlow in the hotel room after the trial. Now Jim's primary role is that of protagonist rather than narrator; he is as it were the enigmatic centre towards which the narrators' interpretative efforts are directed. Still, it is interesting to see how, in the hotel conversation, Jim makes a sincere, almost desperate attempt to interpret his experience by putting it into words addressed to Marlow. If, as I would suggest, there is a narrative element in Jim's attempt at self-interpretation here, then a curious connection is established between its incompleteness and the indeterminacy of the novel as a whole. This indeterminacy, which makes the thematics of *Lord Jim* more open and more ambiguous, is closely related to the interplay of narrators and characters. More specifically, it is also linked to the way in which Marlow's diverse function supplements and extends that of the third-person narrator, modifying the latter's views without openly contradicting them.

In the second group we have the contributions which the novel's minor characters make to an understanding of Jim. Again, these are characters more than narrators, but clearly their interpretative endeavours enhance the complexity of Jim as character; and they also provide relevant information which Marlow makes use of in his narrative.

The interpreters in the third group include such fascinating characters as Stein and the French lieutenant. Stein is surely one of the most intriguing characters in all Conrad. Marlow presents Stein as the person most capable of understanding, and possibly helping, Jim. But his diagnosis of Jim as "romantic" (212) is highly ambiguous; and the suggested remedy of Patusan proves eventually disastrous. Hillis Miller sees Stein either as "an unreliable narrator or a trustworthy commentator."[5] Although his function as a narrator is less apparent than that of the French lieutenant, there is a curious narrative potential or promise attached to Stein. It is suggested not only by his apparent insight into Jim's psyche, but also by the similarity between his spacious, gloomy house and the setting of Marlow's narrative (as it is established at the end of chapter 4).

Marlow is, no doubt, the novel's principal interpreter as well as its most important narrator. Technically, Marlow is a first--person narrator. Still, his narrative project and performance not only exceed those of most first-person narrators, but also incorporate elements that seem strangely authorial. This is another way of saying that Marlow's narrative function may approximate to functions Wayne C. Booth ascribes to the "implied author." This somewhat controversial concept, strongly defended by Seymour Chatman in his recent *Coming to Terms*,[6] is commonly understood as an image of the author issuing from his or her text, as the combined result of all its narrative strategies and literary qualities. Thus the implied author is an abstraction of the reader's – it is a construct we need in order to structure our understanding of the text, and specifically to identify unreliable or biased narration (the obvious example in the Conrad canon is *Under Western Eyes*: the title, which can be related to the implied author, implicitly comments on the restricted narrative perspective of the language teacher as first-person narrator). In *Lord Jim* both Marlow's narrative and that of the third-person narrator may variously take on an authorial appearance, but surely it does not follow that their functions as narrators can be equated with that of the implied author. While Marlow represents the fourth group or chain of interpreters, this third-person narrator constitutes the fifth.

In *Lord Jim*, then, narration and interpretation blend. As I have just suggested, there are interpretative elements in the third-person narrator's discourse as well. The centrality of Marlow seems to have diverted critical attention from this narrator of the novel's opening chapters, but I would argue that he too plays a necessary and highly productive role. Actually, it is more difficult than we might expect to reply to questions such as: who is the third-person narrator? What does he do that Marlow cannot, how is he related to Marlow and Jim, and what is his relation to Conrad? The last question needs, I would argue, to be included. Critical interest in the narrators of *Lord Jim* does not necessarily imply a devaluation of Conrad as writer. The narrator, or as here a combination of narrators, is Conrad's primary means of presenting and developing *Lord 'im* as a fictional text. We expect these narrators to perform certain structural and thematic functions; their use needs to be justified by the action they present and the thematic issues it activates. A narrator whose activity is unproductive easily impairs the literary quality of the work.

In *Lord Jim* the distinction between third-person and first--person narrators is clearly a necessary one. In order to suggest some partial answers to the questions just asked, a passage from Franz Stanzel's *Theory of Narrative* will be helpful. The contrast, says Stanzel,

> between an embodied narrator and a narrator without such bodily determination, that is to say, between a first-person narrator and an authorial third-person narrator, accounts for the most important difference in the motivation of the narrator to narrate. For an embodied narrator, this motivation is existential; it is directly connected with his practical experiences...For the third-person narrator, on the other hand, there is no existential compulsion to narrate.[7]

This broad, theoretical distinction is illuminating with regard to *Lord Jim*. No reader can doubt that Marlow's interest in Jim does have an existential dimension. It is manifested, for instance, in his growing interest in Jim's problem; and it is even more clearly evidenced by the time and energy he invests in his "case." That Marlow finds it hard to *explain* this interest not only initiates and prolongs his narrative, but also makes its existential aspect more apparent:

> Why I longed to go grubbing into the deplorable details of an occurrence which, after all, concerned me no more than as a member of an obscure body of men held together by a community of inglorious toil and by fidelity to a certain standard of conduct, I can't explain. You may call it an unhealthy curiosity if you like; but I have a distinct notion I wished to find something. (50)

Stanzel's accompanying observation, that the third-person narrator has no corresponding motivation to narrate, also seems valid in relation to *Lord Jim*. However, this more "negative" description – drawing attention to a quality missed rather than possessed – is rather vague. Some of this imprecision is reflected in the varying terms referring to the same device: "third-person," "impersonal," and "authorial" narrator. My reasons for preferring "third-person" are intimated below, but it needs to be remembered that there are critical problems associated with all these concepts (for instance, "authorial" may lead some readers to establish too close a connection between the narrator and Conrad).

In order briefly to describe the third-person narrator, I proceed from the point just made about the narrator as the author's primary means of presenting the fiction he or she creates. As the main alternative to first-person narration, the third-person narrator is a device more than a character, hovering as it were above the action instead of participating in it. The identity of this narrator is obscure, but he/she/it is often endowed with extraordinary powers. These powers may include knowledge of a character's thoughts and feelings. They also enable the narrator to make evaluative judgements which, though often authoritative, may seem distinctly personal (in a way which can make it problematic to use the term "impersonal narrator"). As a narrative device the third-person narrator needs to be related not only to the author, whose narrative instrument he is, but also to other narrators the text may include, its narratees and characters. Finally, in many cases (and certainly in *Lord Jim*), manipulation of the reader's response and understanding is one of the key functions the third-person narrator is made to perform.

Overall, *Lord Jim* gains very considerably from the insertion of a third-person narrator between Conrad as writer and Marlow as the main first-person narrator. One very productive effect is the widening of temporal and spatial perspective which the third-person narrative allows for – especially as the constitutive elements of this larger frame prove to be closely related to the later Marlow narrative. Moreover, the third-person narrator is also instrumental in establishing what Ian Watt, in his excellent *Conrad in the Nineteenth Century,* calls "the sylleptic quality of Conrad's narrative."[8] As Watt convincingly shows, "syllepsis, the rhetorical term for 'taking together,' seems appropriate to denote the way Conrad's complicated use of anachrony places the main emphasis on linking or bracketing events, rather than insisting on their original temporal separateness."[9] Thus the opening of the novel, with the third-person narrator's focus consistently on Jim, juxtaposes the presentation of Jim's appearance with a professional description of a water-clerk's duties, then going on to outline the connection between his incognito and the necessary hiding of "a fact" (4).

"Fact" is a key word in the novel, well discussed by Tony Tanner in his book on *Lord Jim.*[10] In an important sense, therefore, not just this particular word but much of the novel's opening are proleptic, anticipating central sections such as the jump from the *Patna* and the concerns of the inquiry. Clearly, it is easier to incorporate such anticipatory glimpses into a third-person description, particularly as it continues analeptically by providing selective but highly relevant information on Jim's background. It is noteworthy how Conrad exploits the flexibility of third-person narration here. A precondition for the flexibility is the narrator's omniscience, but although this omniscience can be pointed, the glimpses given of Jim's inner life are selective, the criterion of selection being the relevance of these imperfect views to the following Marlow narrative.

An example of this is the mention of Jim's *Conway* training. The *Conway* was a mercantile marine school ship, accepting her first cadets in Liverpool in 1859; and the narrator's reference to the élitist education it offered serves to enhance the gravity of Jim's later mistake. It is also significant that the episode selected from Jim's training period aboard the *Conway* is doubly proleptic: not just foreshadowing his jump from the *Patna* by revealing it as a form of repetitive action, it provides the reader with a crucial piece of background information which makes him or her more sceptical about Jim's defensive explanation of the jump. And, as this information is not shared by Marlow, it also makes the reader more critical of Marlow's sympathies and of the motivation for his narrative undertaking.

At this point I would like to return to Van Ghent's notion, in my introductory quotation, of Conrad's technical devices as representing "much more than the word 'device' suggests: they represent extreme ethical scrupulosity, even anxiety." If we go along with this well-made point, then it suggests a reason for using the term "third-person" narration about the opening of *Lord Jim*. For although the third-person narrator is not identified as a character at the diegetic level of action, still he is endowed with, stresses and in a sense even represents, personal qualities of the kind Van Ghent mentions. It does not follow that these qualities coalesce with those of the author, for a narrator is also a kind of mask – a distancing device enabling Conrad to speak more freely and eloquently – and clearly the thematics of *Lord Jim* are generated and shaped by the combined cont- ributions of all narrators and characters. Still, the authority of the third-person narrator is considerable. For instance, the kind of omniscience giving the narrator access to Jim's thoughts is supplemented by this comment: "The danger, when not seen, has the imperfect vagueness of human thought" (11) – a generalized statement whose validity the action of the novel affirms. That the statement might have been made by Marlow does not make it less significant, but provides an example of the numerous links that exist between the text's third-person and first-person narratives. I shall briefly comment on a couple of the most interesting of these connections.

Early in chapter 2 the third-person narrator characterizes Jim thus: "He was gentlemanly, steady, tractable, with a thorough knowledge of his duties; and in time, when yet very young, he became chief mate of a fine ship, without ever having been tested by those events of the sea that show in the light of day the inner worth of a man" (10). Obviously, the accuracy and narrative authority of this description become clearer as we read on, soon reaching the narrator's own account of Jim's test-like *Patna* experience.

Many readers will know of the importance of the test as a recurrent thematic element in Conrad. As H. M. Daleski has observed, the essence of the test in Conrad "is that it is always unexpected...in the Conradian universe...it is readiness, not ripeness, that is all."[11] Now the character in *Lord Jim* most eminently capable of passing the test, though significantly he does not himself use this particular word, is the French lieutenant. Thus this third-person description is not only related to Jim's approaching test aboard the *Patna*, but also to another character's very different response to it. On re-reading, it is striking how well the qualities praised by the third-person narrator seem personified in the character of the French lieutenant. This character, who also plays a narrative role as one of Marlow's informants, illustrates through his attitude and action a swift and practical response to the test, contrasting with Jim's much more hesitant attitude.

As one of the French officers who boarded the abandoned *Patna*, not only has the lieutenant come aboard the ship Jim left and stayed there for thirty hours while it was being towed to harbour. He has done so without hesitation and as the most obvious exercise of duty – probably also, as I am suggesting, without thinking of it as a "test." What he did was of course extremely dangerous. Only two years ago, incidentally, a ship immeasurably better equipped than the *Patna* suddenly sank while it was being towed to harbour in West Norway, and the two men aboard both drowned.

The lieutenant seems aware both of the danger and the accompanying possibility of fear, but his ability to resist the fear is at once greater and less problematic than Jim's. This is why he finds it difficult to follow Marlow in the latter's search for extenuating circumstances. When Marlow asks if "the honour," a main concept for the lieutenant and a key one in the novel as a whole,[12] "couldn't...reduce itself to not being found out?" (149), his curt response is that "This, monsieur, is too fine for me – much above me – I don't think about it." Marlow's question might seem dubiously subtle for the third-person narrator too. However, at this stage of the novel his functions are largely suspended, thus providing a slanting movement into Marlow's narrative perspective. It would seem, though, that Marlow's narrative authority is somewhat reduced, or at least cautiously questioned, by the lieutenant's unambiguous comments on Jim's "case." As a result, the interplay of first-person and third-person narration is strengthened; and, because Conrad succeeds in making the lieutenant's narrative consistent with his attitude as an officer, so is that of narrator and character.

As the characters of *Lord Jim* experience a pressure towards narration, so the reader of the novel becomes engaged in an interpretative process which also includes narrative elements. At this level too there is a connection between narrator and character. For the reader is also a character, though not a literary one. He or she is historically situated, operating within a particular *horizon,* to use Hans-Georg Gadamer's helpful term, influenced by what Jürgen Habermas has called fundamental *interests* related to sex, class, profession, and other factors brought into play as we read. It is striking how well *Lord Jim*, as a fiction, illustrates and thematizes these complex issues.

One interesting example is the relationship between Marlow's narratees and the "privileged man" (37), the anonymous character who receives the packet from Marlow. This privileged reader is introduced by the third-person narrator, who thus makes a re-appearance at this point. If part of his function here is to modify Marlow's first-person account (there is no indication of his contradicting it), this is done only implicitly, by reminding the reader that the novel contains a narrative instance supervening, and more knowledgeable than, its principal first-person narrator. However, the omniscience of the third-person narrator is less pointed now than it was in the early, pre-Marlow descriptions of Jim. His function at this late stage is essentially an editorial one, introducing the reader to the "privileged man" and outlining the contents of the packet. Implicit in the introduction, however, is a tacit invitation to compare the position of this character with that of Marlow's narratees. These are, we remember, largely silent; as this silence signals a meditative and broadly accepting attitude to Marlow's narrative, it becomes part of Conrad's manipulation of our response as readers. The privileged reader has also been one of Marlow's narratees. As Marlow ends his oral narrative,

> Each of them seemed to carry away his own impression, to carry it away
> with him like a secret; but there was only one man of all these listeners
> who was ever to hear the last word of the story. It came to him at home,
> more than two years later, and it came contained in a thick packet
> addressed in Marlow's upright and angular handwriting.
>
> The privileged man opened the packet, looked in, then, laying it
> down, went to the window. His rooms were in the highest flat of a lofty
> building, and his glance could travel afar beyond the clear panes
> of glass, as though he were looking out of the lantern of a lighthouse.
> (337)

As Jacques Derrida has demonstrated, there is a significant
difference between reading a text and listening to a story in
a given setting. A striking thing about the "privileged man" is
that he does *both*: not only has he been part of Marlow's pensive
audience on the verandah, he is now – after an anachronic reach
of two years – going to *read* the conclusion of a narrative which
has established itself as essentially *oral*.

There can be little doubt that the introduction of the
"privileged man" – or, the re-appearance of the narratee as
reader – constitutes one of the most striking, and certainly also
one of the most experimental, features of the narrative of *Lord
Jim*. Although its narrative and thematic implications cannot be
fully explored here, we can at least make a few prefatory
observations. One striking effect is to point, amazingly explicitly, to the connections that exist between *narrative and reading*.
As the third-person narrator indicates, the "privileged man" is
a kind of narratee also in the capacity of reader. However, while
the narratee is usually understood as the instance or agent
addressed by the narrator (implicitly or, as here, explicitly), the
reader is engaged in a rather different activity, responding to and
endeavouring to understand what is *written*. The shocking
nature of this shift is suggested by the extent to which it seems to
challenge – we could almost say "deconstruct" – the well-
-established convention of the novel which tells us that while the
narratee is inside the fiction, the reader is outside it. Although it
could be countered that the introduction of the privileged reader
is made less shocking by the careful, manipulatory way in which

the third-person narrator presents him, still he serves to indicate how radically experimental a novel *Lord Jim* is.

This comment blends into the next one to be made. I put it as a question: what are the thematic effects of this narrative shift from a *repeating oral* narrative (Marlow, we recall, would tell the story of Jim "many times" [33]) to a *single written* one? Does it signal a movement towards a definite understanding of Jim? Is the concluding view contained in the "thick packet" also conclusive? Perhaps to some extent, but some points made by Marlow in his written narrative seem to have a different effect. Consider the beginning of the final three paragraphs:

> And that's the end. He passes away under a cloud, inscrutable at heart, forgotten, unforgiven, and excessively romantic. (416)

If Jim is enigmatic to Marlow throughout, the thematics of *Lord Jim* remain open and highly complex for the reader – for the reader *of* the novel and possibly also for the privileged reader *in* it. It is striking to what extent the novel's narrative variation and thematic suggestiveness are related to the problem of repetition as it is presented here. As Reynold Humphries puts it in a thoughtful essay, the "interaction of repetition and post-ponement sums up perfectly the relationship of Marlow to his material, of any narrator to what he/she recounts, of the writer to the inevitable choice of where to begin – and where to end."[13] Returning to his sense of kinship with Jim, and to the privileged reader, Marlow's last reflections bring together his earlier contradictions and doubts; in this sense the end of the written narrative establishes a kind of link with the earlier oral one. As the reflections are not followed by any framing remarks made by the third-person narrator, Marlow's textual authority seems strengthened here at the end. On balance, though, we need the views and perspectives of not just his narrative, but also that of the third-person narrator. Although they do not combine to give us a "complete" picture of Jim, they supplement and enrich each other in an intriguing manner; their narrative interplay is very productive for the development of the novel's thematic ambiguity and complexity. Tentatively concluding, we must agree with the reviewer of *Lord Jim* who, as early as in the autumn of 1900, observed in the *New York Tribune* that "what the author has to say is absorbing, but even more so is the way in which he says it."[14]

NOTES

1. D. Van Ghent, *The English Novel: Form and Function* (New York: Harper and Row, 1961; first published by Rinehart and Company, 1953), p. 237. See also D. R. Schwarz, "'The Idea Embodied in the Cosmology:' The Significance of Dorothy Van Ghent," *Diacritics*, 8 (1978), pp. 72-83.

2. D. Van Ghent, pp. 237-8.

3. For a more extended discussion of Marlow see my *Conrad's Narrative Method* (Oxford: Clarendon Press, 1989; paperback edn. 1991), pp. 133-74.

4. J. Hillis Miller, "*Lord Jim*: Repetition as Subversion of Organic Form," ch. 2 of his *Fiction and Repetition: Seven English Novels* (Oxford: Blackwell, 1982), pp. 22-41.

5. J. Hills Miller, p. 33.

6. S. Chatman, "In Defence of the Implied Author," ch. 5 of his *Coming to Terms: The Rhetoric of Narrative in Fiction and Film* (Ithaca and London: Cornell University Press, 1990), pp. 74-89. Wayne C. Booth introduced the concept of the implied autor in *The Rhetoric of Fiction* (Chicago: University of Chicago Press, 1961; second edn. 1983).

7. F. K. Stanzel, *A Theory of Narrative* (Cambridge: C. U. P., 1983), p. 93.

8. I. Watt, *Conrad in the Nineteenth Century* (London: Chatto & Windus, 1980), p. 301.

9. J. Watt, p. 301.

10. T. Tanner, *Conrad: "Lord Jim"* (London: Edward Arnold, 1963), p. 18.

11. H. M. Daleski, *Joseph Conrad: The Way of Dispossession* (London: Faber and Faber, 1977), p. 81, cf. p. 80.

12. See Z. Najder, "*Lord Jim*: A Romantic Tragedy of Honor," *Conradiana*, 1 (1969), pp. 1-7.

13. R. Humphries, "The Reader in *Lord Jim*'," *Fabula*, 8 (1986), p. 63.

14. Unsigned review in the *New York Tribune*, 3 November 1900. Included in Thomas Moser's critical edition of *Lord Jim* (New York: Norton, 1968), pp. 359-60.

Robert Foulke,
Skidmore College,
Saratoga Springs, USA

From the Center to the Dangerous Hemisphere:
Heart of Darkness and *Typhoon*

Some of you may recall that wonderful passage in Faulkner's *As I Lay Dying* where Addie Bundren, now dead, speaks of words as rising in a thin line higher and higher in the sky while deeds go crawling along the earth. I view Conrad's rhetoric in the voyage fiction in much the same way, so I begin by examining what seamen do in their own context of action through the techniques and language of seamanship, then try to make some connection between those deeds and the rhetoric of an omniscient author or narrating voice.

First, to continue in a Faulknerian vein, let me note a few gaps and lacks in the argument. I have eliminated most of what might be said about the links between *Heart of Darkness* and *Typhoon* to concentrate on a few that have epistemological implications, and I have truncated what I might say about *Heart of Darkness* in order to concentrate on *Typhoon*. For example, I will not have time to develop parallels between the severely condensed voyage out of the heart of darkness and the missing transit through the dangerous hemisphere of the typhoon; between the blank center in the map of Africa and the calm eye of the typhoon; between the "unspeakable rites" at the inner station and the chaos in the hold of the *Nan-Shan*; between the functions of black *and* white (not black *vs.* white) imagery in each story; between Marlow's visit to the Intended and the three letters of the *Nan-Shan* officers; between Marlow's lie and MacWhirr's distribution of dollars; or between Kurtz's voice from the wilderness and MacWhirr's voice in the speaking tube. Finally, I quote from the text of *Typhoon* a bit more than this audience needs, but in a tale where transformations and reductions of the meaning of voice are crucial, I want it to be ringing in your ears.

127

I start with the suspicion that Conrad, who used seamanship as a symbol of moral order in *Heart of Darkness*, would be unlikely to glorify such a stupid seaman as MacWhirr just a few years later. The history of composition also suggests continuity rather than a shift in Conrad's preoccupations at the turn of the century. *Heart of Darkness* was underway in December, 1898 and completed in February, 1899; *Typhoon* was begun in September 1900 and finished in January 1901; and *Lord Jim* was completed and published between the two shorter masterpieces (Najder, 249-50, 265-6, 267). It is difficult to believe that Conrad became simplemindedly optimistic about the possibility of world order during this period. That skepticism is confirmed by the image of cosmic fury that dominates and articulates the structure of the story: Conrad brings the *Nan-Shan* through the first half of the typhoon into its eye but abandons altogether any attempt to describe the ship's transit through the second half. In the dangerous hemisphere of a typhoon, the winds generally coincide with the storm's direction of movement, increasing their velocity and destructive power. Like the heart of darkness, the dangerous hemisphere is beyond words.

Marlow's journey to the center of the continent of darkness, represented on maps as a blank white void, raises radical doubt about the connection of representation with experience, the word with the world. He chases the phantom of meaning in a spectral voice that is simultaneously "bewildering," "illuminating," "exalted," "contemptible," and "deceitful." Such oxymoronic insistence in a text deliberately overloaded with black-and--white imagery and with overballasted clusters of nouns and adjectives represents extremes of epistemological and ontological skepticism: as tale-teller, Marlow even asks his audience whether they see the man in the name or understand anything. Marlow finds his only sense of security in simpler forms of connection, like the rivets that will repair his ship or the instrumental use of language in an abandoned seamanship manual.

That deceptively simple language is less reassuring when it reappears in Captain Wilson's manual of storm strategy in

Typhoon. To understand the epistemology of *Typhoon*, we must define the nature and boundaries of its base language, the language of seamanship. That language works on two levels: it is always adequate to interpret what is happening to the ship but almost never to make human sense of the meaning of the typhoon. Themes of disconnection and doubt comparable to those in *Heart of Darkness* are elaborated in the cataclysmic sea world of *Typhoon*, which mirrors much of the imagery, structure, and preoccupations of the earlier story. The inescapable silence of the "brooding immensity" of the jungle is replaced by the incessant animal shrieks of the storm. *Typhoon* has no Kurtz to make a final pronouncement since MacWhirr does not see any meaning in the storm, much less articulate it as anything beyond a nasty bit of "dirty weather." For the reader, the story and the storm are isomorphic, a structure Conrad had also used in *Heart of Darkness*, but there the concentric spatiotemporal circles – London, Brussels, the Outer Station, with the Inner Station as center – serve as a physical and psychic geography for a quest with a beginning and an end. In *Typhoon* the structure is hemispherical, pivoting around and above the trapped ship, which is surrounded by raging seas, ragged clouds and shrieking winds conglomerated in an unnatural mixture of wrack and scud; sea and sky are no longer separable. Within this maelstrom the *Nan-Shan* is static, passively receiving the incomprehensible swells of an alien disturbance in the universe.

In spite of the constant, wild rolling and pitching of the ship, with waves breaking on deck, one after another, and the incessant whining of the wind, the form of the story is also static. It is spatial rather than temporal in mode. There is only one central situation – the ship in the midst of the intensity of the storm – containing a set of simultaneous but spatially separated scenes, each one independent of the other but linked to an unchanging setting. Like isolated rooms within a large house, each compartment in the ship has its own activity and theme. On the exposed wing of the bridge, huge boarding seas batter MacWhirr and Jukes apart and finally wash them together; in the wheelhouse, the determined helmsman struggles to hold course while the craven second mate cowers in the corner; in the darkness of the port alleyway, the deckhands lie about listlessly; in the coal bunker, the boatswain and Jukes struggle for a footing; in the stokehold, the second engineer and the donkeyman feed the boiler; in the engine-room, Rout and Beale turn valves that start and stop the propeller shaft; and in the 'tween decks, the raging coolies fight for their dollars and swarm up a ladder to break open the hatch that protects them from the fury above. Conrad describes the last scene as "the extraordinary complication brought into the ship's life at a moment of exceptional stress by the human element below her deck" ("Author's Note," *TS*, v).

With a few exceptions, all actions, like the motion of the *Nan-Shan* herself, are repetitive, for that is the peculiar horror of the storm: it does not stop. The most important exception to this endless cycle is Jukes's *Walpurgisnacht* in the 'tween decks with the coolies, and even that, in the ironic terms of the story, is essentially a repetition; to restow "cargo" that has broken loose is to stop one more batch of moving things that should be still, and thereby to hold on to the idea of the static structural integrity of the ship and provide yourself with visual assurance that she is not in fact breaking up in the storm. There are two nerve centers in the ship where repeated action is more than brute response or instinctive self-preservation. In the wheel-house Hackett is meeting each sea in the same way, making sure that the bow does not get knocked off the wind by a furious gust or a steep wave; he knows that one mistake may be fatal since there will be no way to damp the *Nan-Shan's* roll if she lies in the trough with seas coming in from abeam, and little chance of bringing her vow back head to wind again. Simultaneously, down below in the engine room Rout and Beale stop the shaft with each pitch downward to prevent cavitation (a runaway spinning of the propeller in air) that would destroy the drive shaft, and start it again as the bow rise to keep enough headway for steering into the wind and seas. Thus the very few acts of seamanship that do make sense in the midst of the typhoon are crucially important and endlessly repeated; other action is reduced to gestures of passive endurance and a few verbal formulae repeated by Rout and MacWhirr which serve as motifs within a setting that never changes.

The static, repetitive nature of the storm makes most action within it superfluous, apart from steering with care – a familiar but not always simple Conradian motif – and nursing the engine. The long vigil and subsequent collapse of Hackett resembles that of Singleton in the *Narcissus,* with one important difference: whereas Singleton waits helplessly at the wheel for thirty hours through the storm until it is possible to steer again, Hackett steers through every minute with intense concentration:

> The cords of his neck stood hard and lean, a dark patch lay in the hollow of his throat, and his face was still and sunken as in death...his head didn't budge on his neck, – like a stone head fixed to look one way from a column. (63, 65)

Although the context is totally different, the imagery here is clearly reminscent of the heads fixed to the poles of Kurtz's compond. Blinded by the shuttered windows of the wheelhouse and intent on nothing but the tiny patch of light within the binnacle, Hackett is steering a fixed course through a circular storm. The imagery here catches both the necessity and the anomaly of such steadfast human purpose within the whirling horrors of an unseen outside world:

> The little brass wheel in his hands had the appearance of a bright and fragile toy. ...The rudder might have been gone for all he knew, the fires out, the engines broken down, the ship ready to roll over like a corpse. He was anxious not to get muddled and lose control of her head, because the compass-card swung far both ways, wriggling on the pivot, and sometimes seemed to whirl right round. (63-4)

Comparison with the second-rate helmsman who abandons the wheel in *Heart of Darkness* will occur to most readers of Conrad, but one point of contrast˙reaches far beyond fidelity and infidelity: whereas Marlow's helmsman must avoid snags in a changing but well-defined river, Hackett, like Stevie ashore in

The Secret Agent, seeks his bearings in the midst of detached, whirling circles.

In the engine-room Beale, the third engineer, also "held between the palms of his hands the rim of a little black wheel projecting at the side of a big copper pipe" (67), turning it at Rout's command to try to contain the whirling vapours of the storm outside by keeping their own charge, the rotating shaft, from running wild. This effort takes place in the tomb-like engine room, last bastion of human purpose and order where connecting rods "like skeleton limbs" (69) still move crank heads with silent precision, insulated but not remote from the storm outside:

> A loud and wild resonance, made up of all the noises of the hurricane, dwelt in the still warmth of the air. There was in it the smell of hot metal, of oil, and a slight mist of steam. The blows of the sea seemed to traverse it in an unringing, stunning shock, from side to side. (68-9)

These three sentences give us the three senses that block out sight throughout the storm – hearing, smell, touch – in muted form here, buffered by the surrounding steel. But elsewhere the typhoon destroys the seaman's primary orientation to his world: sight. Only the binnacle light glows on the compass in the shuttered bridge, most of the other alleyways and compartments are dark, and on the exposed bridge seeing is totally impossible in air whizzing with wind and water. Both physically and metaphorically, the *Nan-Shan* is blindfolded, and she wallows in a darkness just as inimical to human purposes as the one Marlow discovers in the jungle.

Only in the engine-room and in the enclosed pilot house can work be done; elsewhere no action is possible. Thus the necessity for passivity becomes one of the most insidious trials of any storm, both in real experience and in the story. The crew lying about the darkened alleyway, the second mate curled up in the corner of the wheel house, the boatswain hearing but not seeing the lethal iron tool sliding by him in the coal bunker, and Jukes being washed and battered about the bridge – all feel the same helplessness before the unopposable physical power of wind and water. One of Conrad's early seaman-critics wrote that *Typhoon* "can only be appreciated to the full by those who have an intimate knowledge of the sea and its followers" (Cooper, 98). Although there is no direct evidence that Conrad had experienced a typhoon or hurricane at sea, he suggests that he had in describing the "physiognomy" of gales:

> In each of them there is a characteristic point at which the whole feeling seems contained in one single moment. Thus there is a certain four o'clock in the morning in the confused roar of a black and white world when coming on deck to take charge of my watch I received the instantaneous impression that the ship could not live for another hour in such a raging sea. (*MS*, 76)

This is, of course, exactly the conviction that MacWhirr records in his unread letter to his wife (even to the time, the beginning of the morning watch), ironically shared by the pusillanimous second mate who is sure no one on board will see another day, and carefully analyzed by Jukes in seamanlike terms:

> A dull conviction seized upon Jukes that there was nothing to be done. If the steering-gear did not give way, if the immense volumes of water did not burst the deck in or smash one of the hatches, if the engines did not give up, if way could be kept on the ship against this terrific wind, and she did not bury herself in one of these awful seas, of whose white crests alone, topping high above her bows, he could now and then get a sickening glimpse – then there was a chance of her coming out of it. Something within him seemed to turn over, bringing uppermost the feeling that the *Nan-Shan* was lost. "She's done for," he said to himself, with a surprising mental agitation, as though he had discovered an unexpected meaning in this thought. One of these things was bound to happen. Nothing could be remedied. The men on board did not count, and the ship could not last. This weather was too impossible. (45)

Thus the reader is given three distinct emotional reactions to the possible loss of the ship – MacWhirr's understated "I should hate to lose her," which stretches his capacity for language to the limit, the second mate's absolute, whining funk, and Jukes's intellectual conviction that the ship cannot survive, which drains him of will and makes him retreat into inaction and solipsism. ("Solomon" Rout, buried in the engine room and removed from direct contact with the storm, is far too busy to react to the emotional impact of the storm.) If we read *Typhoon* after *Heart of Darkness* and *Lord Jim,* we might ask who is going to perceive the full meaning of the typhoon. Put another way, why did Conrad recede into omniscient narration to build the epistemological structure of the typhoon theme? Since Rout and the second mate are out of it, why didn't Conrad let us see the storm through the eyes of MacWhirr or Jukes? Although our answers to such questions must be speculative, one grows from the assumption that no human perception could be fully adequate to measure the magnitude of the typhoon. Conrad plays with two extremes; he reveals both the hazards of ignorance in MacWhirr and those of imagination in Jukes, thus reverting to the psychological types of *The Nigger of the "Narcissus."*

If we look at MacWhirr more closely, we see that he cannot hold up all the weighty symbolism that has been loaded on his shoulders; he is a fit subject for Winnie Verloc's dictum that "things do not stand much looking into." In this instance Conrad's early seaman-critics are a better guide than their more learned followers. F. G. Cooper judges MacWhirr to be "stupid, dull-witted, and obstinate, doing what he considered his duty so far as his limited intelligence permitted him" (Cooper, 97). So far many academic critics would go along with Cooper, but they often take the next step and assume that these lacks are enough for a sea captain, that MacWhirr is adequate for his job. And here we must part ways, for seamanship is not as simple and clear-cut as all that, even on steamships or their diesel-powered replacements. Seamanship cannot be equated with the rule-governed conduct of MacWhirr any more than it can insulate more imaginative seamen, like Jukes or Jim, against the paralysis that grows from forseeing disasters not yet certain or even probable. Its power, like its range of application, is limited, and its certainties provide no basis for projecting order on the universe, but it is far from simple in its own domain.

In its broadest sense, seamanship encompasses everything one must know and do to move vessels safely from one port to another. It is a learned body of knowledge derived from past experience, applied physics, naval architecture, and marine engineering; it requires many specific skills in operating and maintaining machinery, handling boats, anchors, booms, winches, and using electronic equipment, as well as a working knowledge of tides, currents, wave formations, weather patterns, aids to navigations, and rules of the road. Above all, it is an art demanding foresight, initiative, the ability to improvize, a sense of proportion, and finely tuned judgment as men make ships cope with an unpredictable ocean. The practice of seamanship requires precision in the use of an extensive technical vocabulary, scrupulosity in the maintenance of hull, engines, and equipment, reliability in following established routines, alertness to changing conditions at sea, and readiness to cope with emergencies quickly and decisively. As the history of vessels lost at sea or wrecks along any coast graphically illustrates – as recently as the P&O ferry off Zeebrugge or the Greek cruise ship off Port Elisabeth – the sea is not yet nor ever will be tame. Conrad underscores the point in his vitriolic essays about the loss of the *Titanic* and in his meditation on the sinking of a Danish brig in the *The Mirror of the Sea*. And because the sea is neither totally predictable nor tolerant of human mistakes, the practice of seamanship is often complex, demanding imagination and discrimination more than adherence to fixed rules of procedure.

Conrad emphasizes MacWhirr's lack of all these qualities. Like blind Captain Whalley in *The End of the Tether*, he is unaware of the extent of his own limitations – a radical defect in his role as seaman – and his lack of imagination prevents him from seeing the ocean world that he must deal with as it really is. A man who lives in the present tense, he does not learn from past experience, seems incapable of anticipating what might happen, and even lacks interest in discovering the implications of immediate experience: "the past being to his mind done with, and the future not there yet, the more general actualities of the day required no comment – because facts can speak for themselves with overwhelming precision" (9). (For comment on this passage see Said, 115 and Daleski, 108-10.) Even when warned by the unusual fall of the barometer, that instrument which confirms "the wisdom of men...by the indifference of matter" (84), he hasn't the seaman's instinct to recognize the sure signs of the coming typhoon: "Omens were as nothing to him, and he was unable to discover the message of a prophecy till the fulfilment had brought it home to his very door" (86). Like the sheltered Count in Conrad's short story *Il Conde,* MacWhirr "had sailed over the surface of the oceans as some men go skimming over the years of existence to sink gently into a placid grave, ignorant of life to the last, without ever having been made to see all it may contain of perfidy, of violence, and of terror" (19).

In this single tag sentence – reminiscent of the line about Captain Allistoun's desire for nautical fame – we are given the essence of MacWhirr's ignorance, and for a seaman it is a far more debilitating flaw than ambition because it blocks any honest assessment of the relationship between knowledge and experience, either past or present. Such ignorance forstalls decisions by obscuring the need for action. We notice that MacWhirr does almost nothing throughout the typhoon, even by giving orders, which is the captain's normal mode of acting on board ship. He hasn't the foresight to order his ship to prepare for the storm; it is Jukes who stays on deck after his watch to see hatches battened down and ventilators covered while MacWhirr sleeps. MacWhirr refuses to order a course change prior to the onset of the storm, and he is not on the bridge to do so when the first gusts hit, so the ship is heading into the seas by pure accident; he does not direct the crucial acts of seamanship during the storm, like steering the best heading – not always directly into seas that are large and steep – and balancing the need for headway against the risks of cavitation and driving the ship under. Only once does MacWhirr direct these operations himself, when he moves the engine-order telegraph to full stop as the rogue wave approaches, and twice more he gives direct commands to Jukes, first to investigate the riot amongst the coolies, then to "pick up all the money" (73-75). It is interesting that these two verbal commands bracket the mechanical command of the telegraph and thus mark MacWhirr's one moment of direct response to the chaos enveloping his ship. For the rest of the storm, he, more than Jukes or anyone else but the second mate, is passive.

The needed command quality that Captain MacWhirr lacks is a sense of proportion, one that will allow him, at this extreme moment of stress in his ship's life, to quickly balance risks against gains. For a seaman that sense of proportion is a blend of remembered experience, book learning, judgments of the relative importance of facts and conditions, and imagined sequences of events. MacWhirr's weakness in all of these capacities is a constant motif of the story. He is, in all his thinking processes, a literalist and reductionist, and the text provides images of diminution to characterize these processes. His only response to taking command of a fine new ship is a complaint about faulty locks; he is amazed by the ability of others to talk for hours and distressed by the slightest playfulness in language, almost as if he were anticipating the rule-governed nature of computer languages; he cannot understand Jukes's emotional reaction to a symbol, the Siamese flag; he refuses to accept other men's experience with storms, whether related in conversation or written more formally in books; he takes risks without assessing consequences, like staying on the exposed wing of the bridge with Jukes unnecessarily when both might be washed overboard at any moment, leaving the ship in the hands of an incompetent second mate, or sending Jukes on hazardous ventures off the bridge to investigate the trouble below; and he judges the coal bill more important than the survival of his ship because he is unable to imagine what he cannot see before him:

> Had he been informed by an indisputable authority that the end of the world was to be accomplished by a catastrophic disturbance of the atmosphere, he would have assimilated the information under the simple idea of dirty weather, and no other, because he had no experience of cataclysms, and belief does not necessarily imply comprehension. (20)

He finally conceptualizes the severity of the typhoon and the possible loss of his ship only through finding his cabin in disarray.

MacWhirr's seamanship is a parody of that required by the situation, an empty form or meaningless ritual rather than the careful "storm strategy" demanded by ordinary seamanlike prudence; thorough knowledge of that strategy was required of all masters for Board of Trade certification. Descriptions of the structure and movement of tropical depressions (Atlantic hurricanes, Pacific typhoons, Indian Ocean cyclones) appeared in seamanship manulas throughout the latter half of the nineteenth century. Observations of circular storms go back to the eighteenth century, but formulation of the Law of Storms began with William Redfield, a New York naval architect, in 1831 and with Lieut.-Col. Reid of the Royal Engineers in 1838, who first deduced the rules of circulation and movement (Piddington, 3-6). In *The Sailor's Hornbook for the Law of Storms* (1848), Henry Piddington analyzes 47 typhoons in the China Sea from 1780 to 1845, including their tracks (northwest, west, and west by south), their rates of movement (7 to 24 mph), and their diameters (60 to 240 nautical miles), as well as anomalies (39-42, 58, 61). In his preface, Piddington states his intention to make this essential knowledge accessible to men like MacWhirr:

> To enable the plainest ship master, then, clearly to comprehend this science in all its bearings and uses, and as far as our present knowledge extends, is my first object; and on this account I have endeavoured to make the work as clear and as brief as possible. ...preferring the familiar terms of common sailor-language where I could use them as I think with better effect, to more scientific forms of expression. (i-ii)

Piddington is succinct in stating the application of the Law of Storms:

> [It] will afford the Seaman – FIRST, the best chance of avoiding the most violent and dangerous part of a hurricane, which is always near the centre of it; NEXT, the safest way of managing his vessel, if he is involved in one; and THIRDLY, the means of profiting by a storm! by sailing on a circular course round it, instead of upon a straight one through it, supposing always in this last case that he has sea-room. (6-7)

The value of this early work was recognized quickly and knowledge of it spread throughout the seagoing community. The 1894 edition of Alston's *Seamanship* lists seven works as references, ranging in date from Martin's *Rotatory Theory of Storms* of 1852 through the Admiralty's *Remarks on Revolving Storms* of 1883 (191-2). It admonishes masters in the path of a tropical depression to "make yourself all clear on the law of storms" and refers to the example of one who didn't: "The culpable disaster...resulted from disregard, or ignorance of these well-known laws, which, had they been attended to, would not only have enabled your friend to avoid all danger from the approaching storm, but would have taught him how to profit by it, and unhesitatingly to turn it to his own advantage" (190-1). The major concepts – "advancing semi-circles, left- and right--hand quadrants, the curves of the tracks, the probable bearing of the centre, the shifts of wind and the readings of the barometer" – all appear in the text of the story, and, in spite of the reaction of the bewildered MacWhirr, who becomes "contemptuously angry with such a lot of words and with so much advice, all head-work and supposition, without a glimmer of certitude," the principles of avoidance were well known and relatively simple (32-3). The objective was keeping clear of the right or dangerous semicircle of the advancing storm, where movement added velocity to already impossible winds.

Given the *Nan-Shan's* position in the China Sea north of the equator, the typhoon would have a counter-clockwise rotation of winds into the extreme low pressure of the eye, and its track would have been from east to west, with curving to the northwest caused by the coriolus force. That force, a side-effect of the rotation of the earth, also deflects the storm winds from their direct course towards the center. As the typhoon approaches the ship, then on a course of northeast with huge swells coming in from abeam (i.e., southeast), even without wind one could determine that the ship would cross its path. Therefore Jukes's suggestion that the course be temporarily changed four points or 45 degrees to due east, although jocularly put forward for the "comfort" of the "passengers" in the hold, would have been partly or wholly successful in getting the ship behind the storm track; its success would have hinged upon the ship's distance from the center and the total diameter of this particular typhoon, which might be as little as 60 or as much as 300 miles. That easy solution is dismissed by parody and ridicule in MacWhirr's contempt for Captain Wilson's storm strategy.

Later, when the wind comes in from the northeast, the rule of thumb for avoiding the worst of the storm is quite simple: first, in the northern hemisphere, determine the location of the center by putting your back to the wind and looking left eight points or 90 degrees; next, determine whether you are in the right semicircle or left semicircle of the storm by noting whether the wind is veering – i.e., changing in a clockwise direction – or backing – i.e., changing in a counter-clockwise direction; and finally, set a course with the wind four or five points (45 to 56 degrees) off the starboard bow if you are in the right semicircle, or the same bearing from dead astern on the port quarter if you are in the left semicircle, to head the ship away from the center towards the weaker fringes of the storm. (This is a paraphrase of the quite simple directions given in Alston, 192-4.) The theory can be explained in these few sentences, and masters were required to know it. Since MacWhirr would not countenance dodging behind the storm before the wind hit, and given the position of the *Nan-Shan* to the southwestward of the storm, i.e., in the path of the left or navigable semicircle, she should have changed her course to the south and east after the wind hit to get clear of the track, as far off the wind as she could manage and keep steering control. Because the *Nan-Shan* was kept headed directly into the wind and seas, she was drawn inevitably into the worst of the typhoon, the strongest winds and massive waves closest to the eye. And to get out she had to pass through the dangerous semicircle.

MacWhirr's philosophy of driving ships in a straight line – even though storms are circular – is the object of parody in his one long conversation. Like Allistoun of the *Narcissus,* another of Conrad's taciturn captains, MacWhirr is given a single soliloquy to reveal his *idée fixe*:

> All these rules for dodging breezes and circumventing the winds of
> heaven, Mr. Jukes, seem to me the maddest thing, when you come to
> look at it sensibly. ...About as queer as your extraordinary notion of
> dodging the ship head to sea, for I don't know how long, to make the
> Chinamen comfortable; whereas all we've got to do is to take them to
> Fu-chau, being timed to get there before noon on Friday. If the weather
> delays me – very well. There's your log-book to talk straight about the
> weather. But suppose I went swinging off my course and came in two
> days late, and they asked me: "Where have you been all that time,
> Captain?" What could I say to that? "Went around to dodge the bad
> weather," I would say. "It must've been dam' bad," they would say.
> "Don't know," I would have to say; "I've dodged clear of it." See that,
> Jukes? I have been thinking it out all this afternoon. (34)

Apart from the parody of MacWhirr's inability to understand
the importance of the law of storms, the monologue contains two
other indications that his vision of seamanship is seriously
flawed. The first is a matter of common practice and precedent
under maritime law. When MacWhirr worries about what
excuses he would make for not delivering the coolies on
schedule, he is thinking, rather imprecisely, about "deviation,"
which is stipulatively defined as a "voluntary departure, without
necessity, or any reasonable cause, from the regular and usual
course of the voyage assured;" for the purpose of marine
insurance, this "discharges the underwriters from the time of
deviation" (Steel, 133). But MacWhirr's afternoon of "thinking
it all out" has not got him to the essential point: "The ordinary
occasions by which a deviation is justified "include 'stress of
weather' and rely on the captain's good judgment...for there is
a liberty implied in every policy to do that which is absolutely
necessary for the preservation of the vessel and the lives of those
on board her" (Steel, 133).

In this light MacWhirr's refusal to deviate makes him
culpable, and the straight-line "steamship" philosophy that
motivates the decision is both unseamanlike and a breach of
trust for a captain charged with the safety of both ship and crew.
A notorious example of such brashness, cited by Piddington, is
nearly parallel to the story of the *Nan-Shan,* apart from the
happier ending in *Typhoon*:

The most recent instance of serious mischief...and useless risk of valuable lives and property by disregard of the rules of our science, occurred in this [China] sea in June (28th and 29th) 1846; in which month the Honorable Company's War Steamer *Pluto*...with a falling barometer and every other indication of a typhoon, steamed directly on her course. ...She of course met the calm centre and shift, with pyramidal sea, and indescribable fury of the winds found there. She lost her funnell, rudder, etc., etc. and was almost foundering when the storm left her. She then put back, and being of course nearly unmanageable drifted on the rocks at Hong Kong, but was saved by the boats of the *Vestal* frigate fortunately lying there. (115-16)

Thus, in the context of seamanship, MacWhirr's two homilies about "facing it," the first delivered to Jukes when he decides not to evade the storm and the second in the eye of it, become ironic because they represent false pride: "A gale is a gale, Mr. Jukes...and a full-powered steam-ship has got to face it. There's just so much dirty weather knocking about the world, and the proper thing is to go through it with none of what old Captain Wilson of the *Melita* calls 'storm strategy'" (34). There is another equally serious obstacle in the text for those who want to identify MacWhirr's stolidity in facing the storm with virtue: his decision not to deviate is tainted by money. Parsimony about the "pretty coal bill to show" is justifiable in normal circumstances but sheer folly in these. It associates MacWhirr's ignorance and lack of judgment with the far darker physical and moral blindness of another captain with an *idée fixe* bordering on obsession, Whalley of *The End of the Tether*. And, like that story, *Typhoon* is also filled with images of darkness and of dollars, linking it emblematically with the corrupting power of treasure, a major theme in Conrad's fiction of these years – from *Heart of Darkness* to *Nostromo*.

Given the case against MacWhirr's seamanship – one that Conrad must have known – why does the omniscient narrating voice set him up as a stalwart figure braving the storm and appearing unruffled by the chaos arround him? The rhetorical surface of *Typhoon* is almost Rabelaisian in tone, overloaded with a language of exaggeration that wavers between the heroic and mock heroic, all in marked contrast to the stolid taciturnity of the man it focuses on; the narrating voice has borrowed all the eloquence in the text, leaving MacWhirr incapable of any but the simplest pronouncements of fact. Was Conrad playing with MacWhirr or with us as gullible readers who might not know how things should be done at sea? Neither, I think. It would take at least another essay to answer such questions properly, but it may be helpful to suggest another possibility here. Throughout his voyage fiction, Conrad both renders the details of his sea world with impeccable accuracy and projects a whole range of attitudes towards it; those attitudes can exhibit chauvinism, political conservatism, traditionalism, romanticism, even sentimentality. They are most often represented in passages with elaborate rhetorical structures, but those passages never cancel or swallow the exact rendering of life at sea that is the baseline of the stories. Let me recall my opening reference to *As I Lay Dying* once again: the words and the deeds may diverge but they co-exist. For example, in *The Nigger of the "Narcissus,"* before Conrad had found Marlow to modulate his attitudes, we find passages praising England in extravagant terms, disparaging the needed reforms in the British Merchant Service introduced by Samuel Plimsoll, distinguishing the virtues of old seamen against the vices of the new, personifying the *Narcissus* as pure bird of the sea that can only be soiled by contacts with the land, and magnifying the virtues of a perfectly ordinary crew:

> Haven't we, together and upon the immortal sea, wrung out a meaning from our sinful lives? Good-bye, brothers! You were a good crowd. As good a crowd as ever fisted with wild cries the beating canvas of a heavy foresail; or tossing aloft, invisible in the night, gave back yell for yell to a westerly gale. (173)

The opening question is, I believe, not rhetorical in the context of the story as a whole; elsewhere I call such attitudes "postures of belief" (cf. Foulke). They represent Conrad searching for certitude rather than finding it because he is never able to ignore anomalies or dismiss inconsistencies. In the case of MacWhirr, who in spite of his steamship command was modeled after several sailing-ship captains Conrad served under, one might expect a range of incompatible attitudes – fondness, exasperation, respect, disdain, imitation, parody. Like Milton, Conrad never stumbled over oxymorons; he embraced them.

Typhoon was never intended to be read simply as a portrait of MacWhirr or as an exemplum for a seamanship manual. Throughout the story Conrad is pushing and stretching the analogy between the direct, confirmable knowledge of seamanship – the kind one could count on – and the more difficult task of finding a course through the instabilities and uncertainties of human experience. MacWhirr, as one might expect, is simplistic and reductionistic, no more the wise mentor Jukes needs than he is a master seaman. His final, repetitious advice to "face it" is no mantra leading to illumination; he has seen the typhoon without reading its meaning. The great rogue wave has no more significance for him than the faulty locks on the doors or the disorder within his cabin, and his changes in attitude are slight – a recognition of the possibility that he might lose his ship and the suspicion that some truth might be found in books after all. Jukes, on the other hand, is undergoing a desperate form of initiation with little imaginative support from either of his two possible mentors. It is frequently the case in Conrad's voyage narratives that the old are neither wise nor of much use to the young. One thinks immediately of Captain Beard and Mahon, who are far less cautious and more foolish than young, green Marlow throughout much of *Youth*. In this instance MacWhirr can provide only some very necessary physical and symbolic support for Jukes, a solid body to grasp on the wing of the bridge and a remote voice through the speaking tube; both confirm the continuing existence of human life but are of no help in coping with cosmic implications of the storm that he neither sees nor feels. "Solomon" Rout has the intelligence and imagination to help but is too far removed from immediate experience of the fury on deck or amongst the coolies; he is busy and enclosed within his own isolated world of orderly machinery. Jukes is the only one on board who has the full experience of the storm and the riot – physically, emotionally, intellectually – and he comes out the other side of it a changed man.

The comic and ironic portrait of MacWhirr sometimes obscures the role of Jukes as the focal point of experience and comprehension for the reader. Typhoons are rare enough in general human experience to require a responsive interpreter. Although Jukes shares some of the immaturity of young Marlow in *Youth* and the narrators of *The Secret Sharer* and *The Shadow-Line,* he has the imagination to see that the fury of the typhoon is "incompatible with the existence of any ship whatever" and to feel as a consequence a "numbness of spirit" – "a searching and insidious fatigue that penetrates deep into a man's breast to cast down and sadden his heart, which is incorrigible, and of all the gifts of the earth – even before life itself – aspires to peace" (41,52). This is the same longing for death which the narrator of *The Shadow-Line* experiences and which is represented in the absolute stillness of exhausted, sleeping men at the end of *Youth* (cf. *The Shadow-Line,* 108 and Moser, 47). Jukes is surely callow when he expects the taciturn MacWhirr to pat him on the back for his genuine exploit in the 'tween decks, but none of this greenness cancels out the depth of his experience of the reality of his accomplishment. In a perfectly formed quest pattern, he endures a preliminary battering and understands the storm's lack of connection with anything human, then sinks into partial paralysis before he is taken to the underworld of the 'tween decks to see the human counterpart of the storm above; there he performs his major task successfully and eventually returns to the bridge to tell his tale to a disinterested MacWhirr, who promptly assimilates Jukes's adventure into a "vague sense of the fitness of things" (85). MacWhirr ultimately further reduces the meaning of what happened in the 'tween decks to a problem in arithmetic, the equal distribution of dollars. That solution is sane and sensible, and far safer than Jukes's notion of letting the Coolies fight for their own among themselves. But far too much has been made of the episode, which is an appendage to the story proper, and a less important one than Marlow's visit to the Intended in *Heart of Darkness.* The distribution of the dollars occurs in the sunlight on deck after the storm. What Jukes needs to deal with is far more essential: he has seen chaos unleashed in human form, and, like Marlow, he cannot shake his vision of darkness. MacWhirr is doubly unfit as a mentor who might interpret this vision because he has not seen it and would not understand it if he had.

The mate's descent, like the rescue of the terrified Wait from the deckhouse in *The Nigger* or Lord Jim's downward trip to inspect the frail bulkhead of the *Patna,* has the special poignancy of entering an enclosed space below the waterline at sea, that chapel perilous of shipboard life which all sailors instinctively dread because its coffin-like entrapment reminds them how tenuous their continued existence always is. When Jukes has successfully faced death and chaos below, he reaps the reward of confidence:

> For some reason Jukes experienced an access of confidence, a sensation that came from outside like a warm breath, and made him feel equal to every demand. The distant muttering of the darkness stole into his ears. He noted it unmoved, out of that sudden belief in himself, as a man safe in a shirt of mail would watch a point. (89)

Conrad's simile from chivalric romance underlines the archetype, but it should not distract us from another essential point about Jukes: from beginning to end, he is the representative of sane, intelligent seamanship. He has enough knowledge and instinct to foretell the typhoon, to the point of entering his prediction in the official log even before he looks at the barometer. He sees the wisdom of dodging it and orders the only effective preparation of the ship for the storm. In the hold with the coolies, he is certainly no reluctant Lord Jim, for as impetuous as his first sudden rush into the maelstrom of the coolies might have been, his quick and precise orders quell the riot. MacWhirr may be an "indomitable" voice at the far end of a speaking tube, but Jukes is always the effective agent of practical seamanship. Thus he has achieved that delicate balance between passivity and activity, seeing and doing, which Conrad equates with "an access of confidence" not only in himself but in the very possibility of meaningful human action in an alien world.

The story goes far beyond portraits of dullness and intelligence, empty gestures and paralysis, in the face of a mighty storm. Its imagery projects a vision far more bleak than any young Jukes is able to assimilate – the total breakdown of civilization as human beings are isolated from each other and language disintegrates into half-heard grunts and howls of rage. Here the thematic parallel between *Heart of Darkness* and *Typhoon* is strongest. The storm itself raises epistemological doubt about the possibility of any meaningful relationship between man and nature – or anything beyond nature which is responsible for it. We first become aware of this menace beyond brute force, though the power of the storm is its agent, in a series of deprivations:the ability to stand, to move, to speak, to be heard, to maintain any sense of communication with other human beings. The storm forces solipsism on everyone who is exposed to it and leaves them only one primal form of communication to break out of it: touch. Thus the boatswain crawls, not walks, to find both Jukes and MacWhirr by grabbing their legs, and Jukes on the wing of the bridge washes back and forth between total detachedness and a close embrace with his captain.

In *Heart of Darkness* Kurtz's eloquence deteriorates under the pressure of the jungle into a single scrawl and a dying phrase. Here language itself begins to disintegrate, first by becoming eliptical as the wind steals syntax from sentences shouted into an ear by a mouth, leaving only a string of dangling phrases to be heard. The second stage of this disintegration is caused by remoteness; men in each compartment lose all connection with those in others, except for the one long, frail link of the speaking tube between the bridge and the engine room. At this stage even those in the same compartment, like characters in Garcia--Marquez's *One Hundred Years of Solitude,* forget the meaning of language, abandoning it or using it more to reassure themselves than to say anything to others. Habits of speech reverse themselves. The normally loquacious and metaphoric Jukes refuses to talk at all to the second engineer as he rushes back and forth between engine room and 'tween decks, and the normally taciturn MacWhirr, the man who believed that "the actualities of the day required no comment" because "facts can speak for themselves," rambles on needlessly to the helmsman (9). Helmsmen are never spoken to, apart from orders, in normal sea practice, and finally the exasperated and overburdened Hackett exclaims: "By Heavens, sir! I can steer for ever if nobody talks to me" (66). In the third stage of language disintegration the words disappear totally as words and sounds begin to inhere in things, becoming the "grouped letters...symbolic of loud exclamations" on the engine-order telegraph or the face of the barometer, "not to be gainsaid, as though the wisdom of men were made unerring by the indifference of matter" (69, 84). Finally, language disappears altogether in non-human but expressive sound, both the "wild and appalling shrieks" of the typhoon itself (47) and the coolie "speaking...like a baying hound...[with] incomprehensible guttural hooting sounds, that did not seem to belong to a human language..." (80).

Thus by stages, and through the kind of expressionistic images we usually associate with Eugene O'Neill's sea plays more than with Conrad's fiction, the great storm gradually deprives the men subject to it of their most human capacities. The coolies in the 'tween decks are reduced to "grunts and growls" matching the savage clamour of the storm outside, and the two are brought together in images of "senseless, destructive fury" – a "ferocity in the blows that fell" from the outside meeting the coolies inside "swarming" on the hatchway ladder "in a crawling, stirring cluster, beating madly with their fists the underside of the battened hatch" (80, 44, 47, 62-3).

This regression back through the stages of human evolution correlates with imagery suggesting the reversal of creation itself. Let there be darkness, this text implies: "The gale howled and scuffled about gigantically in the darkness, as though the entire world were one black gully" (43). Conrad's general preoccupation with black-and-white imagery throughout his early work, and especially in *Heart of Darkness* and *Typhoon*, may be an outgrowth of visual reality at sea, where one sees nothing but black and white conjoined at night – whitecaps on black seas, bright stars as pinpoints of light in a dark sky – and where even daytime reality can be reduced to shades of gray when an overcast sky robs the sea mirror of all other colors. Throughout *Typhoon*, Conrad reinforces the archetypal associations of total darkness by setting the blackness under the typhoon clouds in counterpoint against the dim and ineffectual light of remote stars:

> Through a jagged aperture in the dome of clouds the light of a few stars fell upon the black sea, rising and falling confusedly. Sometimes the head of a watery cone would topple on board and mingle with the rolling flurry of foam on the swamped deck; and the *Nan-Shan* wallowed heavily at the bottom of a circular cistern of clouds. This ring of dense vapours, gyrating madly round the calm of the centre, encompassed the ship like a motionless and unbroken wall of an aspect inconceivably sinister. (82)
>
> Above Jukes' head a few stars shone into a pit of black vapours. The inky edge of the cloud-disc frowned upon the ship under a patch of glittering sky. The stars, too, seemed to look at her intently, as if for the last time, and the cluster of their splendour sat like a diadem on a lowering brow. (83)
>
> The last star, blurred, enlarged, as if returning to the fiery mist of its beginning, struggled with the colossal depth of blackness hanging over the ship – and went out. (88)

Although there is only a tenuous connection between white caps on black seas and the birth and death of stars, the macrocosmic imagery does fit the magnitude of force in wind and water during the typhoon, at least when that force is measured against a human scale. And some otherwise gratuitous Christian allusions link this macrocosmic imagery to apocalypse: the *Nan-Shan* which had sighted "even the coast of the Great Beyond, whence no ship ever returns to give up her crew to the dust of the earth" had come closest to this "coast" on Christmas morning (91, 94).

Unless we are to believe that Conrad was engaged in metaphysical posturing, which seems unlikely between the writing of *Heart of Darkness* and *Nostromo,* we may regard the ironic juxtaposition of the worst of the storm with Christmas as more than a Maupassant effect, and there is other evidence to suggest that the parallel was intended seriously (e.g., anecdotes of near calamity in *Christmas Day at Sea*). Belief in a benevolent Providence does not grow out of living through a typhoon, even if the ship survives. Like *Heart of Darkness, Typhoon* provides an initiation into the extremes of human experience, but there is no contemplative Marlow on hand to register them; like *Moby Dick,* though on a far more modest scale, it questions the human meaning of natural phenomena and whatever may lie behind them. Neither steadfastness nor seamanship can guarantee the survival of ships in such circumstances, and the imagination cannot articulate the unbridled fury of the storm itself within any human system. In such a world neither the myopic vision of MacWhirr nor the imagination of Jukes will serve to interpret experience; speech becomes noise, endurance is reduced to a death wish, and meaning submerges. Just as Marlow never sees the "unspeakable rites" of Kurtz, Conrad never describes the *Nan-Shan* in the dangerous hemisphere of the typhoon.

WORKS CITED

Alston H. *Seamanship; and Its Associated Duties in the Royal Navy.* 1st ed. London: Routledge, 1860.

Bruss P. *Conrad's Early Sea Fiction.* Lewisburg: Bucknell UP, 1979.

Bowen R. O. "Loyalty and Tradition in Conrad," *Renascence,* 12 (Spring 1960), 125-31.

Cooper F. G. "Joseph Conrad: A Seaman's Tribute," *Nautical Magazine,* 105 (1921), 97-101.

Curle R. "The History of Mr. Conrad's Books," *Times Literary Supplement,* (30 August, 1923), 570.

Daleski H. M. *Joseph Conrad: The Way of Dispossession.* London: Faber and Faber, 1977.

Foulke R. "Postures of Belief in *The Nigger of the 'Narcissus',*" *Modern Fiction Studies,* 17:2 (Summer 1971), 249-62; Reprinted in the Norton Critical Edition of *The Nigger of the "Narcissus,"* ed. Robert Kimbrough. New York: Norton, 1979.

Gillon A. *The Eternal Solitary: A Study of Joseph Conrad.* New York: Bookman Associates, 1960.

Hewitt D. *Joseph Conrad: A Reassessment.* London: Bowes and Bowes, 1952.

Johnson B. "Names, Naming, and the 'Inscrutable' in Conrad's *Heart of Darkness," Texas Studies in Language and Literature,* 12 (1971), 387-400.

Karl F. R. *Joseph Conrad: The Three Lives.* London: Faber and Faber, 1979.

Lubbock B. *The Last of the Windjammers.* Vol 1, Glasgow: Brown, Son and Ferguson, 1927.

Lubbock B. *The Colonial Clippers.* Glasgow: J. Brown and Son, 1921.

Moser T. *Joseph Conrad: Achievement and Decline.* Cambridge, Mass.: Harvard UP, 1957.

Najder Z. *Joseph Conrad: A Chronicle.* New Brunswick N.J.: Rutgers University Press, 1983.

Piddington H. *The Sailor's Hornbook for the Law of Storms.* 1st ed., London: Weems & Norgate, 1848.

Said E. *Joseph Conrad and the Fiction of Autobiography.* Cambridge, Mass.: Harvard UP, 1966.

Steel D. *The Shipmaster's Assistant.* London: 1852.

Watt I. *Conrad in the Nineteenth Century.* London: Chatto and Windus, 1980.

Laurence Davies,
Dartmouth College,
Hanover, USA

"Free and Wandering Tales"

> My mind is eased by what you say about Jim's length. It would be to my interest to cut it short as possible, but I would just as soon think of cutting off my head. (Conrad to Meldrum, [30 October 1899]; *CL*, 2, 215)

For those who worked with Conrad – his agent, editors and publishers – the most predictable feature of his fiction was the unpredictability of its length. The sequence repeated itself often enough to make a pattern: the announcement of a new short story on the way, its metamorphosis into a novella, and its extension into a full-scale novel. The books that grew in this way are familiar enough: *Lord Jim, Nostromo, The Secret Agent, Under Western Eyes, Chance, Victory*; if we add the works that merely grew from short story to novella, among them *Heart of Darkness* and *The End of the Tether,* we have listed the bulk of the fiction written in his middle years.

The Secret Agent offers an example. On 13 February 1906, newly arrived in Montpellier, Conrad wrote to assure his agent, J. B. Pinker, that the seductive and unaccustomed Mediterranean sun would not prevent his starting "the story which is provisionally called 'Verloc'." Within eight days, thirteen pages were ready, and despatched to England with a promise of the rest of the story within a week, and a request for twenty pounds. "Don't imagine that the story'll be unduly long," Conrad insisted, "It may be longer than *The Brute* [a pot-boiler that ran to 8,000 words] but not very much so." On 2 March, the shift had begun: "Verloc is extending. It's no good fighting against it. It would take too much time.[1] Any way I think the story is good. And you may tell people [prospective buyers] also that it is authentic enough." Thirteen pages went off on 4 April "with regret but without shame, considering that the conduct of such

153

a story requires no small amount of meditation – not upon
questions of style and so on – but simply upon what is fit or unfit
to be said. ...Moreover the thing has got to be *kept up as a story*
with an ironic intention but a dramatic development" (*CL,* 3,
316-18, 325-6). To Galsworthy on the 9th of April, Conrad was
less confident and, let's say, less meditative:

> As to myself, my dear Jack, I have always that feeling of loafing at my
> work, as if powerless in an exhaustion of thought and will. Not enough!
> not enough! And yet perhaps those days without a line, nay, without
> a word, the hard, atrocious, agonizing days are simply part of my
> *method* of work, a decreed necessity of my production. Perhaps! But if it
> is so, then nothing can repay me for such a sombre fate – not even
> Pinker's satisfaction with the stuff I send to him. 14,000 words was all
> I could achieve. It's simply disaster and there's nothing in them, it seems
> to me, the merest hack novelist could not have written in two evenings
> and a half. (*CL,* 3, 327-8)

Nevertheless, "the stuff" was not abandoned. When, at the
end of May, a bomb hidden in a bouquet of flowers was hurled at
the newly-wed King and Queen of Spain, sparing them, but
annihilating twelve courtiers and standers-by, Conrad woke and
found himself topical. By then he had written around 23,000
words and believed himself close to finishing. The tally had
reached 45,000 by 12 September – he was a meticulous counter
– and still the ending was postponed. It took him, indeed,
another 23,000 words, for which he needed only the next six
weeks. Quite apart from any momentum, any *progression d'effet,*
the story itself might have given him, he was now under serial
contract. The contract, what was more, was with a muck-raking
magazine in New York, *Ridgway's: A Militant Weekly for God
and Country,* whose editor had promised the subscribers "A
Novel Dealing with the Anarchists and Revolutionaries of
London, in which the Diplomatic Intrigue of a Foreign Power
together with Human Selfishness and Anarchistic treachery,
Furnish the Amazing Complications." "The first episode appeared on 6 October, and at the very end of the same month,
Conrad really had reached the last pages. A letter and two
telegrams to Pinker give the atmosphere of the final days:

To morrow *Thursday* I will have the end ready and will send it on either by last train in the evening or by the 7.45 am on *Friday.* Even in that last case you will have time to have the few pages typed before the American mail closes. In any case if the matter is so urgent you could send them by train to South[ampt]on to catch the SS *New York* which is this Saturday's mail boat. You are very patient – and I am very sorry. I would sit up to night but I am gone so stale all of a sudden that it's of no use. But you will have your end by Friday 10am – unless I go to pieces altogether which I don't intend to do. Aren't you sick of me? Yours Conrad. [31 October 1906]

   [2 November 1906, 9.28 a. m.] 38 pages leave by ten train Begin typing at once Another 1500 words to end shall leave at noon by rail With you about 2.40 in time to be typed and catch Southampton mailboat Please wire me at five oclock. (*CL,* 3, 369-70)

   [2 November, 1.04 p. m.] Missed train MS follows[,] Jessie. (Berg Collection, New York Public Library)

It remains to be added that in the following year Conrad prepared the book version of *The Secret Agent,* adding over 30,000 words to what he already had, while his son Borys lay desperately ill with pleurisy and rheumatic fever.

The increments to *Lord Jim* were equally unexpected, and the circumstances of the book's conclusion just as dramatic. Conrad offered "Jim: A Sketch" to old William Blackwood as a piece of 15 to 20,000 words. It had become a projected 40,000 words by the time Blackwood bought it. When Conrad finished, one year later, "with a steady drag of 21 hours," working next to "Cigarette ends growing into a mound similar to a cairn over a dead hero" (*CL,* 2, 284) the total came to 160,000 words. 60,000 of those words had been written in the last two months. What Blackwood had thought would require three instalments of his magazine had required fourteen. "That sort of thing does not happen twice" (*CL,* 2, 413) Conrad told George Blackwood (William's nephew) in 1902, a year that was rounded off with the plans for a story of 15 to 20,000 words called *Nostromo.*

How might one see this pattern of false prophecy, anguish, and reluctant conclusion? Since my destination is cultural, matters of biography had better come first, and first of the first, matters of economic biography.

Word for word, short stories could earn Conrad more money than novels did. Strictly in financial terms, it made more sense to earn a new advance for a fresh title rather than expand work that had already brought him the cash he so often and so badly needed. Again, strictly in financial terms, the time put into a novel, or even a novella, was a high risk investment. A failure to sell serial rights (as was the case with *Falk* and *Romance*) meant a serious loss of putative income – income already spent. Not quite as strictly in financial terms, the unanticipated ballooning of a story could and did inspire editors and agents with feelings of rage, frustration, and the desire to see its author go a long way off. Conrad, then, could hardly be described as acting out of self-interest.

What this chartered accountant's approach fails to consider, questions of artistic inclination aside, is the business of momentum. The Conrad who told Edward Garnett how difficult it was to find a starting-point could not be prodigal with what he did not have. The Conrad who almost always started tentatively, slowly, was not equipped by nature for many starts. Continuing what he started, moreover, kept him away from those periods of indeterminacy between works, the periods when his identity as a writer were most in question. As the merciless interlocutor in one of Miroslav Holub's poems puts it, "You are a poet? Now you're not. You were when you were writing a poem."

Yet the periods when his identity as a writer was firmest, most concentrated – and most dramatic – came as he prepared to finish. Although Ford Madox Ford's stories of ready-saddled horses and couriers waiting to catch manuscripts tossed from a window at three in the morning might have the slightest touch of romancing about them,[2] Conrad's own versions of ending *Nostromo* and *Lord Jim* make impressive narratives, especially in the case of *Nostromo*, where we have two versions – both crackling with immediacy – one circumstantial and novelistic for Galsworthy, the other, meant for Pinker, more obviously, but not, it should be said, more reliably, documentary (*CL*, 3, 156-9).

In these circumstances, all but the most charitable will diagnose an acute case of procrastination. To explain why

Conrad delayed the bursts of concentrated work that he well knew were necessary, one might fall back readily enough on the reasons usually advanced in such cases – perfectionism, laziness, fantasies of omnipotence. One might even claim, in an excess of *post hoc, ergo propter hoc* reasoning, that without a crisis involving untyped manuscripts and latest posting times he could not finish at all. Yet I still wonder about the timing of these crises, for they are not always explicable by outside factors such as contracts and publication dates. It makes better sense to think that Conrad came to a close when his subject was exhausted. Not Conrad, but his subject: I shall take up this clue in a few minutes' time.

Then there is the antipathy to closure itself, an antipathy that may be linked not only to the loss of identity as a writer but also to the loss of any identity whatsoever. In psychoanalytic terms, to postpone ending is to postpone death. Conrad's fascination with death, annihilation, suicide needs only gentle highlighting. Let Marlow be the witness:

> the chilly Antarctic can keep a secret, too, but more in the manner of a grave.
> And there is a sense of blessed finality in such discretion, which is what we all more or less sincerely are ready to admit – for what else is it that makes the idea of death supportable? End! Finis! the potent word that exorcises from the house of life the haunting shadow of fate....While there's life there is hope, truly; but there is fear, too. (*LJ*, 176-7)

In this essay I am concerned with a more public aspect of Conrad's private anxieties and professional manoeuverings. I want to consider his literary practice in relation to other writers of his time. Before locating him in the public context, however, I should say a few words about what actually happens betwen the overture to a Conrad novel and its coda.

The case of *Lord Jim* is unusual only in that a very early stage of the story has survived. Written on blank leaves on an album that had once belonged to his Grandmother Teofila, this first version is held by the Houghton Library at Harvard. There is no need here to jump (or tumble) into the controversies about dating this piece. Whenever they were written, these must be the few pages described in the "Author's Note" of 1917 as begun, then set aside:

> But, seriously, the truth of the matter is, that my first thought was of a short story, concerned only with the pilgrim ship episode, nothing more. And that was a legitimate conception. After writing a few pages, however, I became for some reason discontented and I laid them aside for a time. I didn't take them out of the drawer until the late Mr. William Blackwood suggested I should give something again to his magazine.
>
> It was only then that I perceived that the pilgrim ship episode was a good starting-point for a free and wandering tale; that it was an event, too, which could conceivably colour the whole "sentiment of existence" in a simple and sensitive character but all these preliminary moods and stirrings were rather obscure at the time, and they do not appear clearer to me now after the lapse of so many years.

For all Conrad's emphasis here on the pilgrim ship episode, the Harvard manuscript gives intimations of much more. It touches on major moments in Jim's career: his apprenticeship at sea, a great storm, the embarkation of Muslim pilgrims, life as a water-clerk. There is even a reference to a future time when, in a remote township, he is known as Tuan Jim. "Sketch," then, seems a good name for what we have: it has the form of a literary character sketch – something virtually complete in itself – but it could also be compared to a sketch for the finished painting. The outlines are there. It needs to be fleshed out, highlighted, above all *framed,* but the possibilites are visible.

Turning from the album to the manuscript of the serial version, now lodged with the Rosenbach Foundation in Philadelphia, we see at once the change of scale. What never ceases to surprise me about the majority of Conrad manuscripts is the scarcity of obvious insertions and expansions. (I am ignoring here what happens in the transition from magazine to book; besides offering extra money, publishing in serial form gave Conrad the chance to see what was effectively an entire draft in print.) The holographs are criss-crossed with emendations and reworkings – often aimed at intensifying the effect of what Ian Watt has called "delayed decoding" – reworkings particularly well described by Ernest Sullivan in his unpublished researches on the manuscript of *Youth*,[3] but Conrad always seems to be writing in full; he moves forward not by skirmishes and patrols but on a broad front. By agreeing, like Dickens, to serial publication, Conrad put himself in a position from which there could be no retreat. Material interests have a great deal to do with Conrad's way of writing.

But material interests were not the only ones at work. We are dealing also, I believe, with literary temperament and belief. In other words, the novels have a novelistic texture right from the beginning. To put it another way, *Under Western Eyes* starts with "Razumov," a short story; *The Secret Agent* begins with "Verloc." Any generic barbed wire separating short story from novel was high enough for Conrad to march right under it.

A theoretical aside: some of those who have paced the boundary lines between novel and short story (not forgetting that useful third term, novella) report the demarcation as illusory and others as a formidable barrier. Thus Boris Ejchenbaum, the Russian formalist, writes of the *opposition* between long and short forms.[4] He claims, in other words, that stories always already differ from novels. In Conrad's case, however, the opposite argument seems to work better. I am thinking particularly of Suzanne Hunter Brown's demonstration, using Hardy's *Tess* and a heuristic "Tess," that we can take part of a novel and read it as a short story; conversely, we can take a short story and read it as part of a (hypothetical) novel.[5] Everything depends on the conventions or expectations which author, publisher, and reader invoke.

But towards what place was Conrad marching? To Blackwood, he insisted that he knew his destination: "the end of a story is a very important and difficult part; the *most* difficult for me, to execute – that is. It is always *thought out* before the story is begun" (20 February 1900; *CL,* 2, 252). As if to confirm this statement, we have the references in the original sketch to Jim among the Malay villagers. We cannot assume, however, that right from the beginning Conrad saw a fully-realized Patusan. At the time he was assuring Blackwood, Conrad expected to conclude with Chapters Nineteen and Twenty: the notoriously enigmatic interview with Stein which threatens to swamp the reader in the destructive element of language. At this stage Conrad could only have intended a paragraph or two on Patusan. Critics have often wished that that was all Patusan got.

Whatever one's opinion, there is little dispute about the depth or breadth of the rupture that separates the two parts. Frederic Jameson sees it as the sign of a shift from high to mass culture;[6] Ian Watt sees a caustic rejection of romanticism in Part One and a nostalgic flirtation with it in Part Two.[7] In any case, Conrad has discovered a whole new range of situations to explore. One shrewd comment on his methods comes in Henry James's review of *Chance,* where he identifies it as "a prolonged hovering flight of the subjective over the outstretched ground of the case exposed." According to James, *Chance* "places Mr. Conrad absolutely alone as the votary of the way to do a thing that shall make it undergo most doing."[8] Likewise, Edward Said characterizes the tone of *Nostromo's* final part as one of exhaustion – physical exhaustion and the exhaustion of possibilities: "The immobility that ends *Nostromo* is a sterile calm...in which all action is finally concentrated into a cry of motionless despair. No better ending for the novel could have been written."[9]

I do not think it would be too coercive to claim that *Lord Jim* concerns itself, busies itself, obsesses itself with moral issues, to claim in short that moral issues are the book's intellectual currency. Its currency, not its own economy, I hasten to add. The arguments begin when the assayer-critic tries to find the relative value of the coins, their status as forgeries or genuine pieces, their place of minting, and the authority of the mint. The authority I shall take is Marlow's: "Not clear," he says, "not clear," he repeats. I side, that is to say, with those critics who read this book divergently rather than convergently, as a journey into an only partly-travelled forest rather than an excursion over fields, surveyed, ploughed, and fenced. To cite the "Author's Note" again, this is "a free and wandering tale."

Moral ambiguities and perplexities together with their attendant clouds of epistemological puzzles are perfectly well-suited to the expansive, the concertina-like, form of a novel such as *Lord Jim* or *Nostromo*. To thicken the issues, Conrad could simply create another episode, another partial observer, another reverie. What can exist only very uneasily with these arrangements is the traditional conception of plot as a sequence of cause and effect. We can't say, for example, "Jim obliges Gentleman Brown because Jim does not want to replicate his previous mistakes" when we cannot be sure what, precisely, those mistakes have been. Neither can we expect a vigorous forward movement of the plot or even an ingenious deviation from it when the desire to know what happened is subordinated to the desire to know every imaginable reason why it might have happened. It's as though Conrad undertook "a way to do a thing that shall make it undergo most doing" so that the reader should undergo the most seeing and the most hearing.

Conrad's books could grow in the way they did because he found ways of relegating plot and slowing or dislocating narrative. His practice is almost as much opposed to Aristotelian notions of plot as Brecht's plays are to Aristotelian notions of character and catharsis. Plot is hammered thin in *Lord Jim*, fragmented in *Nostromo*. Because for the last dozen years or so, the word's been overworked, I'd hesitate to use the word *meditation* had not Conrad used it himself: to repeat his words about "Verloc:" "the conduct" (and, I would add, the reading) "of such a story requires no small amount of meditation."

Conrad was only too well aware of the pains his method inflicted. Movement in circles might be as exhilarating for artists as it is for dervishes, but it's a form of torment too:

> I manage to write something nearly every day but it is like a caged squirrel running in his wheel...Sisyphus was better off. He did get periodically his stone to the top. (To the Galsworthys, 14/15 August 1906; *CL,* 3, 349-50)

He might console himself with the idea that a broken, faded, or inchoate plot achieved a stronger mimesis, closer to human experience of disruption, randomness, and imperfection, but in the background he could hear a sometimes real, sometimes imaginary chorus of critics sceptical about his scepticism. Apropos of *The Nigger* he writes:

> As to lack of incident [note the technical word] well – it's life. The incomplete joy, the incomplete sorrow, the incomplete rascality or heroism – the incomplete suffering. Events crowd and push and nothing happens. You know what I mean. The opportunities do not last long enough.
>   Unless in a boy's book of adventures. Mine were never finished. They fizzled out before I had a chance to do more than another man would. (To Garnett, [29 November 1896]; *CL,* 1, 321)

Conrad was not alone in experiencing such feelings. The favorite work of fiction in his circle, for instance, was Turgenev's *From A Sportsman's Notebook*: reflective, descriptive, lyric, elegiac, but scarcely plotted. In another circle, and towards the end of Conrad's career – a career she read quite brilliantly – Virginia Woolf spoke for the insurgents against the tyranny of plot:

> If a writer were a free man and not a slave, if he could write what he chose not what he must, if he could base his work upon his own feeling and not upon convention, there would be no plot, no comedy, no tragedy, no love interest or catastrophe in the accepted style.[10]

To go still farther afield, if we are looking for other books that swell mysteriously from short stories to cavernous and echoing novels, whose themes circle back upon themselves, whose plots are almost infinitely expandable, whose writing exhibits the unexpected delights of thoroughness, where to turn but to Thomas Mann, and above all to *The Magic Mountain*?

The No Man's Land of Modernism is still a place of unexploded shells, muddy craters, barbed wire, and stretcher-bearers. For all the recent attempts to engender distrust of traditional narrative,[11] suspicion of plots and literary plotters appears to span the gender lines. It's not so much that all consciously modern writers look upon plot as a kind of far from necessary evil: that description wouldn't, for instance, do for Ford. But here is one of the few topics on which, say, Hemingway and Stevie Smith, or Mann and Dorothy Richardson might agree.[12] A sense of an ending, a longing for finality – even to the point of Armageddon – pervades the popular fiction of the late nineteenth and early twentieth centuries: witness the cosmic dramas of Marie Corelli and the squads of novels prophesying imminent military or ecological collapse. What distinguishes the "modern" or "modernist" is a turning away from such scenarios of providence and punishment.

It is only appropriate to think of the causes of this revulsion against plot, finality, and certitude as multiple: cultural, political, and philosophical as well as aesthetic. Thanks to the psychologists, human nature became at once more open and more mysterious, and in both cases less suited to traditional literary understanding of character and motivation. Thanks to the feminists, the resolution of a story line in marriage seemed less and less persuasive. Thanks to the psychologists, the feminists, the philosophers, and the physicists, time lost the authority of precision and gained the authority of experience. And, one more speculation in this heterogeneous list, that sense of felt time's power emboldened the novelists to reassert the value of personal time against the domination of historic time. It is tempting to see the relegation of plot as a protest against official history of whatever persuasion, Marxist, Nationalist, Whig, Protestant, Catholic, Positivist, patriarchal – all the triumphalist faiths.

That in turn is a comment leading right back to Conrad, specifically to *Nostromo*. The book offers a variety of histories, personal and public, oral and written, legendary and – comparatively – veracious. Thanks to the disorienting (but not disoriented) splitting up of the narrative, each variety of history comments on the others. On the public scale, Conrad presents two kinds of Latin American histories: those that envision history moving in a straight line, and those that see it as condemned to circularity. The one is represented by the domestic and imported worshippers of commercial and material progress such as Captain Mitchell, by the Marxist photographer, and by the memories of Bolivar the Liberator handed down by Carlos Gould's grandfather. The other, the circular view, is epitomized by the alleged words of the Liberator on his deathbed: "America is ungovernable. Those who worked for her independence have ploughed the sea." Ploughing the sea, of course, is not an occupation restricted to the would-be governors: one thinks as well of Mrs. Gould.

Conrad's sense of Latin America's history – or histories – arose from his experience of Poland.[13] In neither setting does his attitude look at all triumphalist. But it was not only in historical or political terms that he considered the explanatory a mode imposed after the event. T. Fisher Unwin, his first publisher, was a devout man with a confidently Liberal belief in human progress. One can imagine his face lighting up as he read the first two sentences from this portion of a letter – and falling again at the third:

> Everything is possible – but the note of truth is not in the possibility of things but in their inevitableness. Inevitableness is the only certitude; it is the very essence of life – as it is of dreams.... Our captivity within the incomprehensible logic of...accident is the only fact of the universe. From that reality flows deception and inspiration, error and faith, egoism and sacrifice, love and hate. (22 August 1896; *CL*, 1, 303)

"Things" are inevitable, then, but also accidental. As long as Conrad kept his fictional world in motion, they could be both. But once he imposed an ending, they became, if not fixed, circumscribed, and defined by hindsight.

As Edward Said has argued, to begin a work requires courage. So, too, does ending one. At least as much as by a reluctance to abandon his own psychic life, Conrad was moved to postpone his endings by a reluctance to abandon the life of his creations. But he did, he had to, come to an end. When forced by the exhaustion of his created lives to choose between *ewig* and *ad finem,* eternity and ending, he chose the latter. Inspired by my literary elders and far betters, so do I.

NOTES

1. One wonders whether Conrad knew Pascal's apology for not having time to abbreviate a letter.

2. *Joseph Conrad: A Personal Remembrance* (London: Duckworth, 1924), pp. 243-4.

3. Presented at the 1987 conference of the British Joseph Conrad Society.

4. *O. Henry and the Theory of the Short Story* (Ann Arbor: Michigan Slavic Contributions, 1968), pp. 4-8.

5. "'Tess' and *Tess:* An Experiment in Genre," *Modern Fiction Studies,* 28 (1982), pp. 25-44.

6. *The Political Unconscious: Narrative as a Socially Symbolic Act* (Ithaca: Cornell University Press, 1981), pp. 206-7.

7. *Conrad in the Nineteenth Century* (Berkeley: University of California Press, 1979), p. 346.

8. N. Sherry, ed., *Conrad: The Critical Heritage* (London: Routledge and Kegan Paul, 1973), pp. 265, 267.

9. *Beginnings: Intention and Method* (New York: Columbia University Press, 1985), p. 135.

10. "Modern Fiction," *Collected Essays* (New York: Harcourt, Brace, 1967), 2: 106.

11. As in T. de Lauretis, *Alice Doesn't: Feminism, Semiotics and Cinema* (Bloomington: Indiana University Press, 1984).

12. To renew a sense of the variety and multiplicity of modernisms, see B. K. Scott, ed., *The Gender of Modernism: A Critical Anthology* (Bloomington: Indiana University Press, 1990).

13. As Eloise Hay argues in her contribution to this conference. See E. Hay, "Reconstructing 'East' and 'West' in Conrad's Eyes," in volume II, (*Contexts for Conrad*) of this series.

Robert G. Hampson,
Royal Holloway and Bedford New College, University of London,
London, England

Conrad and the Formation of Legends

> Why, in thirty or forty years, were there no books, any great man would grow mythic. (Carlyle, "The Hero as Divinity," *Heroes and Hero Worship*.)

In his book *La Formation des légendes* (1910), Arnold van Gennep observed:

> Fantasy and error are normal, even with us, and...the tendency to distortion...comes into play from the moment of observation. It comes into play particularly when transmission is by means of oral narration.[1]

He accordingly set out to investigate the rules of the genesis, the formation, the transmission and the modification of legends.[2] Francis Cornford, in *Thucydides Mythistoricus* (1907), was concerned with written rather than oral history, but Cornford too remarked on "the transformation which begins to steal over all events from the moment of their occurrence."[3] In the latter part of *Lord Jim*, recounting Jim's period in Patusan, Conrad had already begun to explore this "transformation:" how, in Cornford's words, "fact shifts into legend, and legend into myth."[4]

When Marlow, in Chapter 24, arrives in Patusan, he begins to hear almost immediately quasi-legendary stories about Jim. The headman of the fishing-village, who acts as his pilot up the river, is Marlow's first informant:

> There was already a story that the tide had turned two hours before its time to help him on his journey up the river. (*LJ*, 242-3)

The attack on Sherif Ali's fort is the basis for other legends. In Chapter 26, Jim provides a factual account of this episode, and

167

then, in Chapter 27, Marlow hears how these facts have been imaginatively transformed. In the first version he encounters, "the legend had gifted [Jim] with supernatural powers:"

> Yes, it was said, there had been many ropes cunningly disposed, and a strange contrivance that turned by the efforts of many men, and each gun went up tearing slowly through the bushes, like a wild pig rooting its way in the undergrowth, but...what is the strength of ropes and of men's arms? There is a rebellious soul in things which must be overcome by powerful charms and incantations. (266)

This version of the event is told, however, by Sura, "a professional sorcerer," who clearly has a professional interest in promulgating "occult" explanations.[5] The second version he hears – which is current among "the simple folk of outlying villages" – is itself much simpler: they believed "that Jim had carried the guns up the hill on his back – two at a time" (266). Jim's exploits, to his own exasperation, have been infigurated into the mould of folk-tale. In the same way, Jim's account of his attack upon the stockade is set against the "popular story" that "Jim with a touch of one finger had thrown down the gate" (270). Folk-tale and legend implicitly offer an alternative narrative interpretation of Jim to Marlow's.

The story of Jewel and Jim provides the clearest example of the transformation of fact into legend. Marlow ends his account of this part of Jim's story by recounting what he calls "this amazing Jim-myth" (280). The Dutch "government official" (279) hints at the first version of this "myth," but the hints do not make much sense until Marlow hears of the story "travelling slowly down the coast about a mysterious white man in Patusan who had got hold of an extraordinary gem – namely, an emerald of an enormous size, and altogether priceless" (280). The narrative makes clear that this transformation of the facts is in line with what Cornford was to call "infiguration" (that is, "the moulding of facts into types of myth contributed by traditional habits of thought"), when Marlow, after citing "the famous stone of the Sultan of Succadana" as an analogue, observes that "the story of a fabulously large emerald is as old as the arrival of the first white man in the Archipelago" (280).[6] The second version of the story, provided by the rajah's scribe, is more sophisticated:

> Such a jewel…he said…is best preserved by being concealed about the person of a woman…such a woman seemed to be actually in existence. He had been told of a tall girl, whom the white man treated with great respect and care, and who never went forth from the house unattended. (280-1)

This version shows how the legend is able to assimilate on a second level the factual details which it originally transformed.

Conrad had already touched on such "popular" transformations, the shifting of fact into legend, in "The Rescuer."[7] After his own detailed narration of Lingard's rescue of Hassim and Immada from Wajo, Conrad begins the next chapter with "the traditional account of the last civil war" (*Res,* 83), which is told to travellers visiting Wajo. This includes "the legend of a chief and his sister, whose mother had been a great princess suspected of sorcery," who escaped by magic when their enemies had them trapped "with their backs to the sea:"

> The chief Hassim was gone, and the Lady who was a princess in the country – and nobody knows what became of them from that day to this. Sometimes traders from our parts talk of having heard of them here, and heard of them there, but these are the lies of men who go afar for gain. We who live in the country believe that the ship sailed back into the clouds whence the Lady's magic made her come. Did we not see the ship with our own eyes? And as to Rajah Hassim and his sister…some men say one thing and some another, but God alone knows the truth. (83-4)

In this instance, Conrad and the reader are confident that they also know "the truth," and the effect is to ironize the Wajo narrator's interpretation. There is, however, a further irony about the status of evidence, which potentially rebounds on us. Hearsay evidence, which (in line with our legal practices) is "rightly" treated as invalid, is here probably true, while empirical evidence, which derives its meaning from the observer's pre-conceptions – or, more accurately, their noetic or thought world, is used to support the wrong answer. In *Lord Jim*, on the other hand, Marlow concludes, "there shall be no message unless such as each of us can interpret for himself from the language of facts," and facts "are so often more enigmatic than the craftiest arrangement of words" (340). The implication is, as Allan Simmons points out, that "Sura's version of events – like Marlow's – is but one way of interpreting what the narrative is, ultimately, designed to leave evasive."[8] Nevertheless, despite this scepticism about "the truth," Marlow's narrative interpretation asserts a privileged status relative to the other oral narratives as the narrative that contains them. In *Nostromo*, Conrad's attention to legend and myth moves further towards the play of rival interpretations and competing discourses.

I

Nostromo begins by juxtaposing the historical ("the time of Spanish rule") and the folk-loric (the two *gringos,* spectral and alive...under the fatal spell of their success").[9] As in *The Golden Bough,* we begin with a simple narrative (the *gringos* on Azuera or the priest at Nemi), whose deeper meaning is exposed through the accumulation of analogues: the priest at Nemi anticipates and occludes the "dying god" of Frazer's later narrative just as the *gringos* on Azuera reveal and conceal Conrad's concern with the effects of "material interests" on both the personal and social levels. Furthermore, as Hunter has pointed out, the "two wandering sailors" were themselves motivated by folk traditions of "heaps of shining gold" (4) in the deep precipices of Azuera, and their story is only the most recent instance of a repeated narrative of "adventurers" who have "perished in the search" for this gold.[10] *Nostromo* roots itself in oral narrative and oral-narrative traditions, and it emphasizes, from the outset, its own oral sources: "Tradition has it," "The story goes," "as the sailors say," "as the saying is." The opening chapters are sprinkled with such assertions, that serve to establish the oral culture of Costaguana. The second chapter introduces Captain Mitchell as one of the narrative's own oral sources, as an unreliable "official historian" – a role which is foregrounded in the final chapters of the novel. Chapter 2 silently incorporates what are evidently Mitchell's narratives into its own: the apostrophes – "Nostromo – invaluable fellow...Nostromo, a fellow in a thousand" – clearly derive from a prior, "suppressed" oral narrative provided by Mitchell. To put it another way, Mitchell provides the narrative focalization for this chapter, a focalization signalled by a characteristic attitude and voice; and this use of Mitchell prepares the reader for the novel's shifting focalization, its multiple viewpoints, its play of voices that is also a play of discourses. This is exemplified by the narrative's formal introduction of Mitchell: "'Our Excellent Señor Mitchell' for the business and official world of Sulaco; 'Fussy Joe' for the commanders of the Company's ships, Captain Joseph Mitchell" (11). The history of Costaguana is constructed in this first section from the interplay of different voices, and from what is, in effect, a collage of myths.

These "myths" may be divided into three distinct kinds. First of all, the most obvious mythic element is to be found in allusions to Roman and Judaeo-Christian mythology; and the most conspicuous of these are the names of the ships of the O. S. N. Company – the *Juno,* the *Saturn,* the *Cerberus* etc. As Donald Yelton pointed out, the recurrent classical references in *Nostromo* "extend the historical perspective" and evoke the "optical illusion" whereby "the founders of American republics North and South" saw themselves as "the establishers of new Roman republics."[11] Yelton, however, does not take his analysis quite far enough. Part of the significance of the ships' names is suggested by the narrator's dry comment on the departure of the Goulds' guests, "the three gentlemen from San Francisco" (67), that the *Ceres* was to "carry them off into the Olympus of plutocrats" (68). The O.S.N. steamers are the sign of the new ruling power in Sulaco. It is also important that, as Yelton notes, most of the classical references are Roman rather than Greek. If the new "Occidental Republic" of the later part of the novel seeks to glorify itself by allusions to the Roman republic (Yelton instances the marble medallion "in the antique style" commemorating Decoud and the design for a "bronze Justice" to replace the equestrian stone statue of Carlos IV), the reader cannot forget that the reality is the new Roman Empire of "material interests," the *Pax Americana*. The incongruity of the steamers' Roman names in the South American setting testifies to the imperialist domination they represent, and draws attention to the institutional discourse of neo-colonialism: as "the chairman of the railway board (from London)" (35) tells Mrs. Gould, "We can't give you your ecclesiastical court back again; but you shall have more steamers, a railway, a telegraph-cable" (36).

The other obvious mythic element in the opening section is Judaeo-Christian.[12] As early as Chapter 6, the novel begins that association of Mrs. Gould with the Madonna – "a Madonna in blue robes with the crowned child sitting on her arm" (68) – which is to take on such poignant tones later when juxtaposed to her childless and emotionally-deprived marriage. In Chapter 8, the gorge surrounding the San Tomé mine is described ambivalently as a "paradise of snakes" (105). This ambiguous "paradise" is, nevertheless, destroyed by the re-opening of the mine, and the waterfall "with its amazing fernery" is replaced by the "stream of treasure" (105) pouring from the mountain. It now exists only as an icon in the "watercolour sketch" on the white wall of the Casa Gould. Finally, there is Holroyd, the Christian financier, with his regular endowment of churches, which Mrs. Gould compares to a "poor Cholo who offers a little silver arm or leg to thank his god for a cure" (71) in a Frazerian perception of the "primitive" roots of "civilized" religious behaviour.[13]

The second mythic element relates to the novel's use of legendary figures – whether historical, like Bolivar, Garibaldi and the Duc de Morny, or pseudo-historical like the Costaguana folk-heroes. As Yelton noted, the allusions to historical figures help "to establish the illusion of a historical continuum."[14] But, while creating a sense of history and historical processes, *Nostromo* is constantly shifting from the historical to the legendary. For example, as the narrative proceeds, stories gather around particular characters and elevate them to quasi-legendary status. There are the "strange rumours" (45) of betrayal surrounding Dr. Monygham, the "rumours of legendary proportions" (194) attached to Father Corbelàn and the "extraordinary stories" told of the bandit Hernandez, "of his powers and of his wonderful escapes from capture" (108). Even Guzman Bento, "famed for his ruthless and cruel tyranny," reaches "his apotheosis in the popular legend of a sanguinary land-haunting spectre whose body had been carried off by the devil in person" (47). This story, originated by the priests of the Church of the Assumption in Sta. Marta to explain an absence, the disappearance of Bento's body from the brick mausoleum in the nave of the church, presumably replaces a political narrative, which it would be too dangerous to reveal, by the occult and folk-loric. The priests, like Sura in *Lord Jim*, have a professional interest in supernatural explanations, but this instance also alerts us to the way in which the legendary is used as a displacement or mystification of the political. Something similar happens in the case of Hernandez. If he has the ambiguous regard of the bandit among the country-people of Costaguana, he is demonized in Sulaco. Monygham reminds Gould that "the people here are afraid of Hernandez as if he were the devil:"

> When Hernandez was ranging hundreds of miles away from here the Sulaco populace used to shudder at the tales of him roasting his prisoners alive. (194)

But, when he is needed to protect the inhabitants of Sulaco from Montero, Father Corbelàn urges his appointment as general on the grounds that "Heaven itself wills it" (354), and the fleeing Blancos praise Corbelàn's conversion of Hernandez as "a miracle" (360). The bandit, "whose existence was a protest against the irresponsible tyranny of all parties alike" (353-4), is brought into the political processes of Costaguana under the cover of religion.

Giorgio Viola – "who had been one of Garibaldi's immortal thousand in the conquest of Sicily" (20) – introduces another issue. He sports an iconic "lithograph of the Faithful Hero" (229), Garibaldi, on the wall of the Casa Viola, and justifies his reliance on Mrs. Gould by reminding himself that an English-woman "was allowed to give a bed to Garibaldi lying wounded in prison" (471). Viola both embodies a myth of heroic radicalism, "austere old-world Republicanism" (313), in the competing discourses of the novel and also, as in this last instance, provides an example of living mythically (in the sense that his actions are shaped in accordance with, or at least justified in relation to, a pre-established cultural pattern). An even clearer example of living mythically is provided by Pedro Montero. Decoud, in his letter to his sister, mentions Pedro's ambition "to become a sort of Duc de Morny to a sort of Napoleon" (237). Later, the narrator confirms Decoud's analy-sis by revealing that Pedro had spent his time in Paris "devouring the lighter sort of historical works" about the Second Empire, which had filled his head "with absurd visions" (387). The French Second Empire had supplied the model for his self-conception, and this self-conception had been "one of the immediate causes of the Monterist Revolution" (387). With Giorgio Viola and Pedro Montero, it is not just that Conrad draws on historical sources, but the characters are represented as self-consciously modelling themselves on historical figures. And living mythically involves a displacement and misreading of the political situation in Costaguana, while nevertheless contribu-ting to that situation.

This brings us to the third category: the myths of cultural and political discourse, myths of social formation. There are the myths promulgated by politicians: Don Vincente Ribiera, for example, hails the National Central Railway as a "progressive and patriotic undertaking" (34), while the narrative reveals it as part of the neo-colonial penetration of Sulaco. There are the myths created by the Press in their role as the institutionalized supplement to the oral traditions of the culture: the "Costaguana Press" describes Montero's forest march as the "most heroic military exploit of modern times" (39); conversely, Decoud, in his role as "the Journalist of Sulaco" (159), later cynically fixes upon him the label *"gran' bestia"* (191). Perhaps the clearest example of this kind of myth-making, however, is the work of *The Times's* special correspondent in relation to the new Occidental Republic: he gives it the title "Treasure House of the World," and Hernandez's bandits are reborn as "the renowned Carabineers of the Campo" (480). Indeed, this chapter displays the various "myths" that, in effect, constitute the new Republic.

The careers of most of the major male characters can be plotted in relation to one or other of these categories of myth. For example, when Gould comes to a realization of his own role and identity in Costaguana, the expression of the realization takes a mythic form: after his earlier assertion that "we Goulds are no adventurers" (64), he now accepts that "he was an adventurer in Costaguana" – "only his weapon was the wealth of the mine...this weapon of wealth, double-edged with the cupidity and misery of mankind, steeped in all the vices of self--indulgence as in a concoction of poisonous roots" (365). Gould sees himself as a knight of romance and the mine as some legendary, magical sword. At the same time, his self-definition as "an adventurer" links his career with one of the roles available to the European in South America and recalls the folk-lore tradition, mentioned in the opening chapter, of "adventurers" who have come in search of precious metals. Accordingly, when "Pedrito Montero had Don Carlos led out to be shot – like his uncle many years ago" (477), that particular pattern was almost fatally fulfilled.

In the context of the oral culture of Costaguana, it is understandable that Nostromo should be concerned for his "reputation" and that he should be motivated by the desire "to be well spoken of" (246). Nostromo, however, goes beyond the desire to have a good name: in his construction of his identity upon his public image, he aspires to the status of folk-hero.[15] He conceives of the saving of the silver as "the most famous and desperate affair" of his life: "It shall be talked about when the little children are grown up and the grown men are old" (265). Hunter has noted how Nostromo keeps repeating this phrase ("the most desperate affair of his life"), but misses the point that

these repetitions represent Nostromo's attempt to raise the event
to legendary status: they are both pre-publicity and mythopoeia.
Ironically it is not the saving of the silver but the ride to Cayta
which makes "the Capataz de Cargadores famous from one end
of America to the other" (464). Nostromo's personal myth-
-making is overtaken by the myth-making that surrounds the
creation of the Occidental Republic, in which "the famous ride
to Cayta" becomes an "historical event" (473), one of the
founding myths of the new republic (like Paul Revere's ride in
relation to the United States).[16] There are further ironies:
Nostromo's involvement with the silver proves to be "the most
desperate affair of his life" (321), but not in the way he had
anticipated; and, when Nostromo's legendary status is established, the reader is aware of the gap between his social identity and
the truth.

Decoud too gets caught up in the process of myth-making that
accompanies the creation of the new republic, but Decoud is
a more cynical and successful creator and manipulator of myth.
This was, after all, his professional role as "the Journalist of
Sulaco," but one of his most successful pieces of myth-making
relates to himself. When he and Nostromo part on the island, he
tells Nostromo the message he must deliver:

> You must find the hopeful words that ought to be spoken to the people
> in town...I am looking forward to a glorious and successful ending to
> my mission. Do you hear?...Use the words glorious and successful
> when you speak to the señorita. (300)

Decoud, here, is like a more considerate Kurtz: when Nostromo,
like Marlow, has an interview with the bereaved "Intended," he
has a far more satisfactory script – "he told her how Decoud had
happened to say that his plan would be a glorious success" (489).
Nostromo is able to repeat Decoud's last words, because
(Decoud being a good newspaperman) the last words were
already cynically constructed as a public-relations exercise. As
with Nostromo, there is a gap between the legend and the reality,
but this time the gap is the conscious creation of the subject of the
myth.

The myth-making efforts of Nostromo and Decoud become part of the myth-making involved in the establishment of the new republic. Decoud's vision of the new republic, Nostromo's "desperate ride to Cayta," the reports by *The Times's* special correspondent are all woven into this mythopoeic fabric. In the same way, the "Tres de Mayo" coffee – and the annual ritual of its carriage into town – functions as an act of commemoration, which, at the same time, enforces a national myth and a myth of nationhood; while Captain Mitchell becomes a kind of one-man "heritage industry," presenting his narrative of exciting events, an official history that is entirely innocent (or ignorant) of the true economic and political determinants of events and actions.

In the final chapters, the focus shifts to the private lives of the major characters. For "the last of the Corbeláns, the last of the Avellanos...the last of the Costaguana Goulds" (522), there is no private life, only their role in the public drama. Corbelán asserts his commitment to the cause of "the people;" Gould maintains his "devotion to the great silver mine" (521); Antonia Avellanos continues her father's devotion to the political cause of Costaguana. They are linked by the strength of their devotion ("incorrigible" [521]), but the nature of their devotion does not go unquestioned. Antonia, for example, invokes Decoud's name to support a scheme (the annexation of the rest of Costaguana) which is the opposite of Decoud's own (the separation of the Occidental Province from the rest of Costaguana). A sense of fruitless devotion and corruption pervades these chapters.[17] The former is foregrounded through Monygham: Chapter 11 begins with his monomanic devotion to Mrs. Gould, which has elevated her to the status of a deity ("the sight of that woman...suggested ideas of adoration, of kissing the hem of her robe" [513]), but, at the end of Chapter 13, he is rebuffed by her and forced to admit that "he had been defeated by the magnificent Capataz de Cargadores" (561). She maintains the myth of Nostromo's "unbroken rectitude, fidelity and courage" (561), as Monygham's formulation recognizes, even though she knows it is false. Mrs. Gould herself has experienced the same gap between the legend and the reality. She is a Madonna for Monygham and "the Providence of the Viola family" (513); her compassion is "as famed from one end of the land to the other as the courage and daring" of Nostromo; but she sits like "a good fairy, weary with a long career of well-doing, touched by the withering suspicion of the uselessness of her labours" (520). She comes to doubt the moral role of "material interests" even while she recognizes the sacrifice she has made for them – "her life had been robbed of all the intimate felicities of daily affection which her tenderness needed" (512) – and she has a vision of herself "all alone in the Treasure House of the World" (522), a poignant juxtaposition of private experience and public myth.

It is through Nostromo, however, that the gap between myth and reality is most actively explored. While Ramirez strives to become "a second Nostromo" (515) only to be found wanting, Nostromo sees himself as "a sham" (524) and steadily comes to identify himself not as "the magnificent Capataz" but as "Nostromo the thief" (558). It is this identity he asserts in his relationship with Giselle, and it is "Nostromo the thief" whose loss she eventually mourns (561). Linda's love, by contrast, is given to the legendary figure, "the magnificent Capataz de Cargadores" (552). It is a love which she carries "like an ever-increasing load of shameful fetters" (552) once she learns of his involvement with her sister, but she does not allow her knowledge to challenge the legend. The lighthouse is the shrine of her devotion: "a dome-shaped shrine of diamonds, containing not a lamp, but some sacred flame" (552). And her final cry asserts the myth of "the magnificent Capataz de Cargadores" (566) against the facts, just as Mrs. Gould did in her denial of Monygham's curiosity.[18] This triumph of the mythic over the factual has a parallel on the narrative level: Nostromo's obsession with the silver, which takes priority over his love for Giselle, is explained, in these final chapters, not in historical, sociological or psychological terms, but by reference to the legend of the two gringos. The "fatal spell" (5) of success, which binds the souls of the gringos to their treasure, is echoed by the "accursed spell of the treasure" (540-1) which holds Nostromo. In contrast to *Lord Jim*, *Nostromo* ends by privileging the realm of folk-lore, legend, and myth.[19]

II

The Planter of Malata also explores the area of truth, legend and myth. Conrad wrote the story during November/December 1913 as a break from *Victory,* and there are obvious connections between the two works: Renouard, like Heyst, lives as a "hermit" (*WT,* 25) on an island, and like Heyst he unexpectedly becomes involved with a woman while on a visit to the mainland.[20] The narrative is propelled by Felicia Moorsom's quest for her ex-fiancé, Arthur, which (unsurprisingly) ends by solving the mysteries generated around the absent figure of Renouard's assistant. However, as Stanisław Modrzewski has pointed out, the narrative actually consists of two different, superimposed sequences of events: "one presenting the story of Felicia and Arthur; the other the story of Renouard's love for Felicia."[21] While almost all of the characters "consciously participate" in the first story, a sentimental romance with Felicia in the role of sentimental heroine, the narrative focalization directs the reader's attention towards the second, a self-conscious, modernist version of romantic love.

In his "Author's Note," which is almost completely given over to *The Planter of Malata,* Conrad makes clear his interest in experimenting with "ways of telling a tale" (ix). Modrzewski convincingly demonstrates that the experimentation involved not only a double story, but also a use of characters "not so much as psychologically and morally complex individuals but as representatives of diverse approaches to reality."[22] As in *Victory,* the narrative is constructed and interpreted through the interaction of the different characters' world-views. This is emphasized in the opening section, Renouard's meeting with "the Editor," which foregrounds the question of knowledge. The Kiplingesque Editor takes pride in his office as "the place where everything is known about everybody" (*WT,* 6), but almost immediately he is forced to acknowledge that there was "a certain side" to Renouard "which he could not quite make out" (6). Similarly, his observation that "the only really honest writing is to be found in newspapers" (15) is juxtaposed to a portrait of Renouard in journalese (15-16), which exposes the limitations of the "truth" of newspapers. The mode of knowledge embodied in the Editor stands in sharp contrast to the mode of knowledge involved in Renouard's perception of Felicia. He sees her as "something...pagan" (9) – more specifically as a statuesque classical goddess or (as Owen Knowles suggests) as the statue of a classical goddess that has come to life ("as though she had been a being made of ivory and precious metals changed into living tissue" [10]).[23] Her effect on him is "like the discovery of a new faculty in himself" (12); "her approach woke up in his brain the image of love's infinite grace" (10). In short, Renouard's *coup de foudre* is rendered as an epiphany in which he apprehends a divinity.[24] It recalls Pound's description of Ford's being able to see "the Venus immortal crossing the tram tracks," and Pound's own concern with visionary experience.[25] More important, as in *Victory,* it shows how Conrad uses different narrative perspectives, embodying different world-views, to introduce allegorical and mythic materials that break out of the restraints of realism.

The narrative's attention to different approaches to reality, again as in *Victory,* foregrounds the characters' interpretation (and misinterpretation) of each other. The Editor, for example, misreads Renouard's "air of weariness" and the "augmented dreaminess of his eyes" (occasioned by his distaste for discussing Felicia), because he interprets "according to his own favourite theory" of Renouard's Heystian "detachment from mankind" (26). Renouard, similarly, initially misreads the pragmatic Professor Moorsom as "gentle and indulgent," a man "inapt for action, and more sensitive to the thoughts than to the events of existence" (29) through his stereotyped expectations. The foci of interpretative activity, however, are the characters of Felicia and Renouard. In Renouard's case, the Editor's brief journalistic portrait ("indomitable energy...now working for the prosperity of our country" [15-16]) and Dunster's overheard prediction ("the leading man here some day" [42]) hardly prepare us for the shock of "the tales" current about him. These have created "the legendary Renouard" who is a "ruthless adventurer – the ogre with a future" (74), and this image of Renouard plays a part in the dénouement. Felicia, like Lena, has heard these tales, and, when Renouard finally reveals the truth about Arthur, she responds in terms of the legend: "He is another of your victims?" (73). In Felicia's case, Renouard's visionary perception of her is steadily eroded. After accounts of Renouard's nocturnal visitations from the goddess, the reader's interpretative activity is provoked by an unexpectedly open-ended series of hypotheses about her:

> It was impossible to say if she suffered from anything in the world, and whether this was the insensibility of a great passion concentrated on itself, or a perfect restraint of manner, or the indifference of superiority so complete as to be sufficient to itself. (34)

Her father's later speculation about her produces a similar effect:

> I ask myself if she is obeying the uneasiness of an instinct seeking its satisfaction, or is it a revulsion of feeling, or is she merely deceiving her own heart by this dangerous trifling with romantic images. (41)

It is her father's doubts about her which most effectively challenge Renouard's perception of her: he suggests that she has committed herself to a sentimental quest for Arthur to compensate for her lack of faith in him (39); and, whereas Renouard sees her as "a tragic Venus" rising "not from the foam of the sea" but from a "more formless, mysterious and potent immensity of mankind" (36), her father insists that she has arisen from "the mere smother and froth" (40) of superficial, upper-class society life.

The climactic confrontation between Renouard and Felicia brings together the issues of truth, legend and myth. The meeting is a conflict between rival truths: when Renouard asks her to "understand the truth" in him, he is rebuffed by her assertion that she "stand[s] for truth here" (75). Renouard represents the truth of passion: like Captain Anthony in *Chance,* he experiences the primitive passion of "the age of Cavern men" (45). For Felicia, on the other hand, passion is "an exploded legend:" "she was so used to the forms of repression enveloping, softening the crude impulses of old humanity that she no longer believed in their existence" (77). Renouard is forced to re-appraise his divinity, and to recognize, as Professor Moorsom had said, that she is "merely of the topmost layer, disdainful and superior, the mere pure froth and bubble on the inscrutable depths" (77). She figures an extreme of "civilization" like Mrs. Travers in *The Rescue*. At the same time, like Lena, she has dedicated herself to self-sacrifice: marriage to Arthur would be "a sacred debt – fine duty" (76). But where Lena sacrifices herself, in part, out of love for Heyst, Felicia's project of "reparation" springs from her lack of love for Arthur: Arthur's dying curse on her for not believing his innocence (75) contrasts with Renouard's assertion that he would wear her "for an incomparable jewel" even if she were "steeped to the lips in vice, in crime" (78). That is why she is "not fit" to hear "the truth vibrating" in Renouard's voice (78). She does not perceive the divinity in him which the narrative intimates: his profile "recalled vaguely a Minerva's head" (38), or "the profile of Pallas" (75). And, at the end, she remains in the world of sentimental romance: she is remembered by the "sad story" of "Miss Moorsom – the fashionable and clever beauty," who "found her betrothed in Malata only to see him die in her arms" (84). Renouard, on the other hand, remains in the realm of the mythical and transcedent: he disappears into the sea (like Chatteris at the end of Wells's *The Sea Lady*), swimming "beyond the confines of life" with "his eyes fixed on a star" (85), which is presumably Venus.

III

Through attention to the transformation of fact into legend in *Lord Jim*, Conrad provides, in folk-tale and legend, an alternative interpretation of Jim to Marlow's; at the same time the oral narratives of folk-tale compete with Jim's own construction of his identity according to the narrative conventions of nineteenth-century "light literature." In *Lord Jim*, these possibilities remain implicit and submerged. In *Nostromo*, the folk-loric and legendary explicitly operate as part of a collage of competing discourses on both the personal and the political levels; personal myth-making contributes to, and competes with, political myth-making; legends and myths displace or mystify the political, but are also constitutive of political and national identities. Indeed, while *Nostromo* shows how legends and myths diverge from the self-experience of the legendary of mythicized individual, it ends by privileging the legendary as the master narrative. In *The Planter of Malata*, competing narratives and competing modes of knowledge break out of the constraints of realism into modernist self-consciousness, while the mythic is used to pose the passionate, visionary, the transcendent against various forms of repression and social restraint. From *Lord Jim* through *Nostromo* to *The Planter of Malata*, attention to the folk-loric, legendary and mythic elements discloses an increasing self-consciousness about the interpretation of narrative, and a more subtle interplay of different voices and perspectives in the text.

NOTES

1. Trans. mine. ("*La fantaisie et l'erreur sont normales, mêmez chez nous, et...la tendance à la deformation...agit dès le moment de l'observation. Elle agit davantage encore lorsqu'il y a transmission par récits oraux*") – A. van Gennep, *La Formation des légendes* (Paris: Ernest Flammarion, 1910), p. 160.

2. Van Gennep, pp. 1-2.

3. F. M. Cornford, *Thucydides Mythistoricus* (London: Edward Arnold, 1907), p. 130.

4. Cornford, p. 131.

5. Sura's belief in the "soul of things" and his attendance at "rice sowings and reapings" (*LJ*, 266) bears some similarity to J. G. Frazer's account of "The Rice Mother in the East Indies," which describes practices based on "the simple conception of the rice as animated by a soul like that which these people attribute to mankind." See Sir J. Frazer, *The Golden Bough: A Study in Magic and Religion* (Abridged Edition) (London: Macmillan Co., 1963), p. 544. For an account of Conrad's possible knowledge of Frazer's work, see my essay "Frazer, Conrad and the 'truth of primitive passion'," in R. Fraser (ed.), *Sir James Frazer and the Literary Imagination* (London: Macmillan, 1990), pp. 172-91.

6. Cornford, p. 132.

7. Conrad began work on "The Rescuer" in March 1896; he finished Part I in June 1896 and Part II by March 1898; he put it aside in early 1899 and didn't finish it until 1919. See O. Knowles, *A Conrad Chronology* (London: Macmillan, 1989), pp. 23, 24, 30-2.

8. A. Simmons, *Ambiguity as Meaning in Joseph Conrad's Fiction*, Unpublished Ph.D. Thesis, University of London, 1991, p. 125.

9. My account of *Nostromo* should be seen as a response and complement to A. Roberts, *"Nostromo* and History: Remarkable Individuality and Historical Inevitability," *The Conradian*, 12: 1 (May 1987), pp. 4-17.

10. A. Hunter, *Joseph Conrad and the Ethics of Darwinism* (London: Croom Helm, 1983), p. 124. The discussion that follows was prompted by Hunter's chapter, *"Nostromo*: Heroes and Hobson" (pp. 124-52), and engages with his reading of *Nostromo*.

11. D. C. Yelton, *Mimesis and Metaphor: An Inquiry into the Genesis and Scope of Conrad's Symbolic Imagery* (The Hague: Mouton, 1967), p. 175.

12. I am not forgetting the comparison of General Montero to "some military idol of Aztec conception and European bedecking" (*N*, 122); nor the allusions to "the Old Man of the Sea" and the "ghouls" of the "Arabian Nights" (*N*, 58), which I have discussed elsewhere. See "The Genie out of the Bottle: Conrad, Wells and Joyce" in P. L. Caracciolo (ed.), *The "Arabian Nights" in English Literature* (London: Macmillan, 1988), pp. 218-43.

13. In *The Magic Art*, 1 (1911), Frazer commented on "the abundance of cheap votive offerings" (p. 4) discovered at Nemi; he compared them to "waxen models" of ailing members offered to the Virgin Mary at Kevlaar (p. 77). In a letter to Marguerite Poradowska (15 September 1891), Conrad described the doctrine of atonement through suffering as the "product of superior but savage minds" (*CL*, 1, 95).

14. Yelton, p. 177.

15. For a fuller account of this process, see R. Hampson, *Joseph Conrad: Betrayal and Identity* (Basingstoke: Macmillan, 1992), Chapter 5.

16. Paul Revere (1735-1818), a silversmith and an acknowledged political leader of the Boston working class, took part in the Boston Tea Party and was official courier for the Massachusetts Provincial Assembly. His ride to Lexington in April 1775 (to warn that the British troops were on the march) was raised to legendary status by Longfellow's poem, which was repeated in American textbooks of American history.

17. Consider, for example, how the republican Viola is described as being "king on his island" (*N*, 516).

18. In the same way, Viola dies, clinging to the myth of *Nostromo* despite the evidence of his senses. I am grateful to Keith Carabine for drawing my attention to Linda's cry and its relevance to this study. His edition of *Nostromo* (Oxford: O. U. P., 1984) usefully includes, as an appendix, the serial ending of *Nostromo* so that Conrad's changes of emphasis can be seen.

19. Compare *The Shadow-Line* and *The Nigger of the "Narcissus,"* in both of which sailors' mythic explanations seem to be true: Mr. Burns's belief in the spell cast on the ship by the dead captain, Singleton's belief that James Wait has caused the head winds and that Wait will die with the first sight of land (*NN*, 142), like the "spell" of the silver, resemble the covert plots found elsewhere in Conrad's fiction. See C. Watts, *The Deceptive Text: An Introduction to Covert Plots* (Sussex: Harvester, 1984).

20. For an account of Conrad's permutation of the narrative elements of *Victory* in a subsequent short story *Because of the Dollars*, see my "Introduction" to *Victory* (Harmondsworth: Penguin Books, 1989).

21. S. Modrzewski, "The Consciousness of Cultural Models in *The Planter of Malata*," *The Conradian*, 13: 2 (1988), pp. 171-82.

22. *Ibid.*, p. 176.

23. O. Knowles, "Conrad and Mérimée: the Legend of Venus in *The Planter of Malata*," *Conradiana*, 11: 2 (1979), pp. 177-84. Knowles shows how Conrad adapts Mérimée's fantastic tale *La Vénus d'Ille* to his own purposes.

24. *The Planter of Malata* in this respect bears some resemblance to fantasy literature about "wonderful visitors." Ford Madox Ford's *Mr Apollo* (London: Methuen, 1908) is a particularly relevant example: Apollo visits London; he is assumed to be foreign royalty travelling incognito (*WT*, 15); and it is dangerous to look him directly in the face (*WT*, 73).

25. This occurs in Pound's obituary for Ford, which is reprinted in B. Lindberg-Seyersted (ed.), *Pound/Ford: The Story of a Literary Friendship* (London: Faber & Faber, 1982), pp. 171-4.

Keith Carabine,
University of Kent,
Canterbury, England

Construing "Secrets" and "Diabolism"
in *Under Western Eyes*: A Response to Frank Kermode

Frank Kermode's provocative and influential essay *Secrets and Narrative Sequence* begins with "a simple proposition: we may like to think...of narrative as the product of two intertwined processes, the presentation of a fable and its progressive interpretation (which of course alters it). The first process tends towards clarity and propriety ('refined common sense'), the second towards secrecy, towards distortions which cover secrets" (137).[1] We rightly "place a higher value," he continues, on the kinds of narrative where "there is much more material that is less manifestly under the control of authority, less easily subordinated to 'clearness and effect,' more palpably the enemy of order, of interpretative consensus, of message. It represents a fortunate collapse of authority" (137).[2]

Kermode is rightly attracted to Conrad because "he was," indeed, "certainly aware of the conflict between the proprieties and the mutinous text of interpretation" (137); and *Under Western Eyes*, especially, "is a suitable text" because "the struggle between propriety and secrecy is especially intense" (138-9). This struggle can also be seen in Conrad's "*dedoublement*" which is "sometimes reflected in his characters" (140). "Clearness and effect he sought, out of need and desire too: but there was also the pursuit of interpretations. Hence the doubling...In the hell of composition we see one writer committed to authority, another involved in debauch" (142).[3]

In the remainder of his essay, Kermode seeks to demonstrate "the survival of secrecy in a narrative that pays a lot of attention to the proprieties which, according to its narrator, should be observed 'for the sake of clearness and effect'" (139-40). Kermode claims to find "secret invitations to interpretation"

187

generated by the numerous references to phantoms, ghouls, devils, eyes, "blackness and whiteness, paper and ink, snow and shadow – and to writing itself." These "non-sequential" details and words, he argues, "form associations of their own" that constitute "another plot" (145). And the key to this plot is provided by Razumov's suspicion that the old teacher may be diabolic. That, Kermode maintains, is precisely what he is, "because the secrets of the book are phantoms, inexplicably appearing, ignored, trampled down, turned into lies by the father of lies, a diabolical narrator" (153).

A full reply to Kermode would entail an examination of the many and varied aspects of the novel which he acknowledges, but (largely) ignores – such as "what Conrad...thought about Russia, Slav 'mysticism,' and Dostoevsky; or what Conrad originally planned to write, what he took to be the point of what he did write, and what, having written it, he cut" (141).[4] As I have written elsewhere on these subjects, I prefer to quarrel with Kermode on his own grounds. Hence for the bulk of this essay I concentrate on the three moments when the issue of the narrator's diabolism is directly raised in order to demonstrate that Kermode fundamentally misreads the old teacher's functions and roles in the novel in such a way as to suggest that his narrative schema is itself deeply flawed. If there is a conflict in *Under Western Eyes* between the "proprieties" and "debauch," between the desire for "clearness and effect" and the "pursuit of interpretations," it does not produce "a mutinous text," involving "secrets" and alternative "plots:" rather it generates a multi-layered, multi-voiced, multi-perspectival novel built upon an extraordinary cycle of interpretative demands and failures, embracing tellers, characters and readers ("debauch"), while striving for coherence and "truth" through its intricate collaboration with, and manipulation of its readers ("proprieties").[5] Moreover, Kermode's schema, and especially his conclusion "that the writing of the book...is a work of 'strange mystic arrogance'" (152), suggests that he does not appreciate how one of Conrad's finest narratives works. The narrative of *Under Western Eyes* (like those of *Lord Jim* and *Nostromo*) is extremely playful; it continually glosses its own performance and provides models for reading both itself and its readers, who are subtly embroiled in and, finally, liberated from Conrad's text.

I

Stimulating in his large speculative claims, Kermode surprisingly fails to contextualize the three references to the narrator as devil. The first occurs in Part Second, chapter V, during the only dialogue between the old teacher and Razumov, who speaking colloquially asks, "Who the devil are you?" (186). The second and third references both refer back to this conversation, thus demanding that we re-read it in the light of Razumov's construing (which is Conrad's basic fictional strategy, as we shall see). Hence I consider these later construings first, and then return to their original matrix.

Immediately after their dialogue, the narrator now functioning once again as the editor and transcriber of Razumov's text, reports the latter's wrathful "secret dialogue with himself:"

> "...the fussy officiousness of a blundering elderly Englishman. What devil put him in the way? Haven't I treated him cavalierly enough?...That's the way to treat these meddlesome persons. Is it possible that he still stands behind my back, waiting?"
>
> Razumov felt a faint chill run down his spine. It was not fear...but it was, all the same, a sort of apprehension as if for another, for someone he knew without being able to put a name to the personality. But the recollection that the officious Englishman had a train to meet tranquillized him for a time. It was too stupid to suppose that he should be wasting his time in waiting. It was unnecessary to look round and make sure. (199)

There is in Kermode's terms nothing to advance "sequence" in this passage about devils, "fear," "chill," "another," and "waiting;" but this does not mean that it is "intolerably odd" to relate the details to Razumov's "psychology," for he is as yet not fully aware that his "apprehension" is not for the fussy Englishman, but for Haldin who is "an independent sharer of his mind" (230). And, as usual, every conversation rubs the sore spots of his guilt, rage and self-loathing. (His excessive fear of the old teacher strikes us on a first reading as very odd because we do not know he is a spy, as well as a betrayer – a point I will develop later.) More importantly these details do not contribute to a secret "plot" that the narrator represses; rather Razumov's questions – "What devil put him in the way?" and "Is it possible that he still stands behind my back, waiting?" – draw attention "to writing itself," and engage the reader, in ways that Kermode does not consider. Hence, just as Razumov is unaware that "behind his back" stands the old teacher and his narrative, so both narrator and protagonist are unaware of the secret dialogue forged from both their accounts, between author and reader in Conrad's text. Thus, as ever, we smile ruefully at the narrator's deadpan recording of the pejorative ways in which Razumov construes him. Characteristically, also, we are obliged to review their conversation and so note the huge gap between Razumov's belief that he "treated" the "elderly Englishman" "*cavalierly*" (!) and the reality of both his discomfiture before him, and of his welcoming response ("I like what you said just now.") to his theory that "you people live under a curse." The narrator's innocently portentous "A curse is an evil spell...and the important, the great problem, is to find the means to break it" (194) subserves, of course, one pattern of explanation for both Razumov's and Russia's plight.[6]

In his written confession (Part Four, Chapter IV), composed immediately after his oral confession, and aimed "directly" at Natalia, Razumov once again reverts to his conversation with "the old man." In this "page and a half of incoherent writing" (357) he reviews the history of his desire for revenge, which finally focussed upon Natalia and, fortunately for them both, misfired. Then he enjoins:

> Listen – now comes the true confession. The other was nothing. To save me, your trustful eyes had to entice my thought to the very edge of the blackest treachery...Victor Haldin had stolen the truth of my life from me, who had nothing else in the world, and he boasted of living on through you on this earth where I had no place to lay my head. She will marry some day, he had said – and your eyes were trustful. And do you

know what I said to myself? I shall steal his sister's soul from her. When we met that first morning in the gardens, and you spoke to me confidingly in the generosity of your spirit, I was thinking, "Yes, he himself by talking of her trustful eyes has delivered her into my hands! If you could have looked then into my heart, you would have cried out aloud with terror and disgust...." (359)

Razumov's retrospective and melodramatic account of his secret plot reviews their first meeting, and then alludes to his conversation with "the old man," which followed immediately upon it. The latter is thought to duplicate Victor Haldin's initial role as tempter:

It's certain that, when we parted that morning, I gloated over it...The old man you introduced me to insisted on walking with me. I don't know who he is. He talked of you, of your lonely, helpless state, and every word of that friend of yours was egging me on to the unpardonable sin of stealing a soul. Could he have been the devil himself in the shape of an old Englishman? Natalia Victorovna, I was possessed! (359-60)

"I don't know who he is:" this elegant, meta-fictional joke once again alerts us both to Razumov's unawareness that he is a character and teller in both the old teacher's narrative and Conrad's novel, and to our responsibility to construe meaning from all three. Razumov then proceeds to inform Natalia that because the news of Ziemianitch's suicide had become common knowledge, he was free to enact his atrocious design:

You were defenceless...For days you have talked with me – opening your heart...It was as if your pure brow bore a light which fell on me, searched my heart and saved me from ignominy, from ultimate undoing. And it saved you too...Your light! your truth! I felt that I must tell you that I had ended by loving you. And to tell you that I must first confess. Confess, go out – and perish...

Now I have done it; and as I write here, I am in the depths of anguish, but there is air to breathe at last – air! And, by the by, that old man sprang up from somewhere as I was speaking to you, and raged at me like a disappointed devil. (361)

Conrad makes extraordinary demands upon his readers here, because the old teacher, Natalia and Victor Haldin are characters in Razumov's confession, which rivals and queries the narrator's account. Indeed Razumov's document contains explicit reference to and re-readings not only of his first encounters with Natalia and "the old man" in "the gardens" in Part Second, Chapter IV, but to his oral confession, only hours before, to the pair. Thus *Under Western Eyes*, as ever, announces itself as text constructed upon cycles of counteracting interpretation; and, characteristically, it reminds the reader, as we follow it sequentially, that both our stabs at the "meaning" of any particular moment, and our assessment of the performances and motives of all the characters, are partial and provisional. Conrad's text, then, is cunningly designed, obliging us to re-read the earlier scenes in order to re-assess the narrator's account, the actions, drives and judgments of the characters, *and* the validity of Razumov's impassioned, retrospective construing of them.

The "morning" scene in "the gardens," when Razumov first met both Natalia and "the old man you introduced me to" is the other occasion when the narrator/devil construing is raised by the protagonist. Significantly, this moment constituted Conrad's major impasse during his long troubled composition of the novel. The writing of Part First of "Razumov" took Conrad only three months, but between mid-March to late September 1908, "after much trying and re-trying" "to invent an action, a march for the story," after it switched to Geneva, he only reached the point where Razumov is poised to re-enter the novel; and then he dithered for a further three months over how to effect his re-appearance.[7]

Conrad's compositional problems at this moment were multiple, involving a potential "debauch" that threatened to shatter his narrative and posing particular problems with regard to his presentation and uses of his narrator.[8] The re-introduction of Razumov into the old teacher's account of the "Geneva transactions" proved such a stumbling block because he brings his journal with him! Thus from this moment on, the double time scheme of the novel is always apparent and, hence, Conrad needed to register both the old teacher's and Natalia's responses to, and construings of Razumov, in the *story time* of the former's narrative, when they both responded "in absolute ignorance" to the protagonist's enigmatic gestures, purposes and fate (183).[9] Also Conrad had to decide on Razumov's relations to, and interpretations of *them* as *characters* in his version of events, which tests their construings of him, and of the events that embrace them all. Thus from this moment on, Conrad's text became, willy-nilly, multi-layered in its open clash of voices, accounts, values and interpretations.

With regard to his narrator, Conrad's main difficulty, once Razumov re-entered the text, was to invent an "action" for him that would link him to the protagonist and enable him to perform such multiple and competing roles as eye witness, actor, teller and commentator in relation to the Geneva transactions. (This is the source, incidentally, of the extremely confused and confusing critical debate about the "more or less exasperating riddle of the old teacher's point of view," and of his authority or lack of it in the novel – Kermode's contribution being the most startling and certainly the most ingeniously argued.)[10] These problems of transmission, representation and characterization are negotiated when Natalia confidingly casts her English teacher as one who was "a great support 'in our sorrow and distress'...'I have given him my confidence'" (178). (Only the reader realizes that Razumov is the cause of her sorrow, and that of all the words in the English language "confidence" is the one most likely to trigger a frantic response. "Confidence" drives Haldin, a mere acquaintance, to Razumov's rooms [19], precipitating the cycle of misinterpretation that characterizes Razumov's relationship to everyone he meets.) Natalia's unwittingly "defenceless" appeal to the narrator – Mr. Razumov does not quite understand my difficulty, but you know what it is" (182) – also provides the excuse and the motive for the only conversation in the novel between the pair: during which, according to Razumov's written confession, "every word of that friend of yours was egging me on to the unpardonable sin of stealing a soul" (359-60). And we might add, every word egged Kermode on to endorse Razmov's accusation.

Clearly this conversation requires generous quotation. The old teacher asks:

> "Shall we walk together a little?"
> He shrugged his shoulders so violently that he tottered again...I did not wish to indispose him still further by an appearance of marked curiosity. It might have been distasteful to such a young and secret refugee from under the pestilential shadow hiding the true, kindly face of his land..."Without doubt," I said to myself, "he seems a sombre, even a desperate revolutionist; but he is young, he may be unselfish and humane, capable of compassion, of..." (Conrad's ellipses)

Note that the narrator's presumption that Razumov "seems a sombre...revolutionist" expresses his ignorance in the story time of his own construing and is designed to deceive us as to his "mission" as a Tsarist spy. The passage continues:

> I heard him clear gratingly his parched throat, and became all attention.
> "This is beyond everything," were his first words...I find you here, for no reason that I can understand, in possession of something I cannot be expected to understand! A confidant! A foreigner! Talking about an admirable Russian girl. Is the admirable girl a fool, I begin to wonder? What are you at? What is your object?"
> He was barely audible, as if his throat had no more resonance than a dry rag, a piece of tinder..."As I was saying, Mr. Razumov, when you have lived long enough, you will learn to discriminate between the noble trustfulness of a nature foreign to every meanness and the flattered credulity of some women..."
> "Upon my word," he cried at my elbow, "what is it to me whether women are fools or lunatics? I really don't care what you think of them. I – I am not interested in them. I let them be. I am not a young man in a novel...What is the meaning of all this?"..."What I meant from the first was that there is a situation which you cannot be expected to understand."
> I listened to his unsteady footfalls by my side for the space of several strides.
> "I think that it may prepare the ground for your next interview with Miss Haldin if I tell you of it...The peculiar situation I have alluded to has arisen in the first grief and distress of Victor Haldin's execution. There was something peculiar in the circumstances of his arrest. You no doubt know the whole truth...." [Conrad's ellipses]
> I felt my arm seized above the elbow, and next instant found myself swung so as to face Mr. Razumov.

"You spring up from the ground before me with this talk. Who the devil are you? This is not to be borne!...What do you know what is or is not peculiar? What have you to do with any confounded circumstances, or with anything that happens in Russia, anyway?" (184-6)

Kermode complains that standard accounts of the "plot" of the novel, such as Guerard's, bury "the inconsequential details" (ghosts, devils, phantoms, shadows and so on) into "the psycho-moral significance" (141) of Razumov's character or subsume them too readily into "political readings" "that belong squarely to a tradition of ordinary reading that may be perfectly intelligent" (146). And clearly this sequence positively invites an "ordinary reading." Thus, because we have already had a privileged glimpse into "the pages" of Razumov's self-confession, where he judges Natalia's "appearance" as "a piece of accomplished treachery" (167), and because we see Razumov through the western eyes of the old teacher, during his story "time of absolute ignorance" (183), we are persuaded to relate all of the details of devils and shadows to two main sources: to the "other subjects" the protagonist has "to think about," namely his secret feelings of rage, guilt and shame about his betrayal of Haldin and to the narrator's case that "the pestilential shadow" of Russia now stretches "across the middle of Europe." Again, even on a first reading Razumov's reactions to both Natalia and the old teacher are shown to be hysterical: after all, the former does embody "noble trustfulness," and the only "*accomplished* treachery" we know of is his own, and the narrator's "object" in talking to him "is...to prepare the ground for your next interview with Miss Haldin." So ends what Kermode calls a "Genevan" reading, and psychology, plot, and western eyes are firmly in place.

Meanwhile what "secrets" reside in the passage's references to devilish plots and to writing, that would persuade us, against the evidence of a "Genevan" reading, to construe the old teacher as a "diabolical" narrator? Most of the "secrets" lurk, I think, in the ways, (unacknowledged by Kermode) that the narrative draws attention to "writing itself" by alerting us to a secret author, of whom both the old teacher and Razumov are ignorant. Thus when we re-read the text through the prism of Razumov's later construction, the innocently colloquial "the devil" foreshadows his unconscious, latent diabolical plan to steal Natalia's soul. In other words, when Razumov construes the old Englishman as a pander-devil he inadvertently *transfers* his unconscious desire to possess and destroy Natalia, to her solicitous confidant's "plot," simultaneously affording him an (unwitting) major role in his fervid fiction of temptation and redemption, and we might add, a star part in Kermode's extravagant schema.[11] In a further twist we realize that already latent in Razumov's wild interpretation of the narrator and his hurried dismissal of "women" there lurks a poignant and compassionate irony, confirmed when we read his written confession – namely that his demonic, melodramatic plot, (casting Natalia as a saint and the "old man" as "a disappointed devil"), in a redemptive reversal, triggers his decision to confess.

My observations thus far on the thematic and plot inter-connections occasioned by Conrad's play with the two parallel accounts of the same moment, depend upon a fundamental narratological distinction that is well within the traditions of ordinary reading. This distinction does, however, illustrate one fundamental flaw in Kermode's construction of the narrator's diabolism. Out of the host of opinions ventured in the text as to the narrator's authority, or lack of it, and out of the multiple roles he plays in his own narrative and in Conrad's multi-layered text, Kermode extrapolates and accepts as gospel only one, namely his function as "devil" in Razumov's fervid, secret plot of temptation and release. Moreover, my basic narratological discrimination alerts us to Conrad's distinctive manipulation of his narrative, which Kermode's reading schema fails to credit. Thus Razumov knows nothing about "the old man," other than that he is Miss Haldin's English confidant, who is anxious to talk to him about her fears; correspondingly, the old teacher is ignorant in the *story time* of his narrative of the two most significant facts about Razumov, namely his betrayal of Haldin and his double agency. In other words neither is aware, as they report on each other in the same scene, that each is a character and object of representation in the other's narrative, and in an author's text that incorporates them both. That privilege (as Conrad's lovely joke at Razmov's expense, "I am not a young man in a novel" neatly illustrates) is the reader's, who is ever aware of an author covertly inviting us to tune into nuances, to construe meanings of which the Western teller and Russian sufferer are unaware.

Hence the reader, during these moments, as throughout the text, is always aware whenever the characters speak of, or to each other of what Kermode calls "*dedoublement*" – a *dedoublement*, however, that works in ways opposed to his reading schema. Both the old teacher and Razumov echo a hidden third voice, disclose an unseen presence, coaxing and beckoning us, through the tellers' and characters' persistent misreadings, to construct an alternative account. These demands and our enjoined activity are playfully evident when we cease to attend to aspects of "plot" and "psychology" (as Kermode insists we must), and concentrate instead on the meta-fictional dimensions of the text (which Kermode neglects). Consider, for example, Razumov's frantic questions to the bemused old teacher: "What is the meaning of all this?" "What is your object?" "Who the devil are you?...What have you to do with...anything that happens in Russia, anyway?" Such questions comprise "secret" invitations to "interpretation" that Kermode does not weigh, but which are altogether typical of the design of the novel and its designs upon us. These invitations, however, prompt ambivalent reactions, typical of a narrative responsive to the opposing desires for "clearness and effect" and of interpretative "debauch." On the one hand we detect a cunning artificer, who plays with and communicates behind the backs of his characters' misconstructions, thereby inviting our construction of an order they struggle to attain; and, on the other, the questions remind us that "meaning" is elusive and veiled, that the narrator's generalizations of Russia and women are provisional, and that at every juncture of the whole conversation he also functions in Conrad's text – inadvertently, and much to our awed amusement and bemusement – to *goad* Razumov; who in turn hysterically misconstrues the decent old man who is happy to obey Natalia's request and constrained to obey his author's secret commands. Hence Razumov's "peculiar psychological state" bleeds, as Kermode observes, into "the texture of the book" (149). For Kermode such bleedings "distort the dialogue and are incompatible with any psychology that could be thought appropriate to Razumov, who is always sane" (150). Surely, however, in this scene (as throughout Conrad's narrative) Razumov's precarious and deeply divided "psychology" is ever apparent precisely because we are aware that the guileless characters say more than they know, and, thereby, *simultaneously* enrage him and scour his self-disgust, and so spur him to confession. Again, the "quantitatively large body of text" devoted to souls, ghosts and to "writing itself" may, indeed, "clog sequence," but in noting such incidences we do not register, as Kermode claims, "distortions" (150); rather we are alerted both to the text's intricate design and to the cunning artificer, who deliberately torments his protagonist.

Thus far I have re-read this scene either in relation to our collusion with the author at the expense of all the participants or in relation to Razumov's subsequent interpretation. However this constructive re-perusal is fuelled by the later recognitions that when we first encountered this conversation, we felt privileged because we knew Razumov was a betrayer, but we did not know Razumov was also a Tsarist spy; that, therefore, the old teacher was not only a dupe but a *stooge,* and that we also were hoaxed by the author. The vital fact of Razumov's double agency, as we are coyly told at the beginning of Part Four, "throws light on the general meaning of the individual case" – "general meaning" that we grope to discern, even when the hidden fact is baldly stated. Now when we return to the earlier scenes we realize that Razumov's wild questions – "Who the devil are you?", "Is it possible he still stands behind my back?" – constitute his agonized, entirely unpremeditated response to the old teacher's unintentional threat to his perilously constructed identity of double agent. Thus we realize that the text is composed of a seemingly endless cycle of misinterpretations,

encompassing the tellers, all the characters, and most importantly the reader.[12]

Moreover this cycle refutes Kermode's surprising claim that
Razumov "is *always* sane" (150). Rather, from the moment he
betrays Haldin he is permanently maddened in two ways: by his
loathing for the revolutionary "visionaries" which breeds a "satanic enjoyment of the scorn prompting him to play with the
greatness" of Peter Ivanovitch (228) and all his unsuspecting
interlocutors; and by the sense that he does not belong to
himself, that he is "possessed" by the "phantom" Haldin, who is
"an independent sharer of his mind" (230), and who stole "the
truth of my life from me." His revenge plot against Natalia, as he
admits in his written confession, merely duplicates, and therefore confirms, this "possession."

Conrad's framing tactic, whereby we discover that the whole
middle section of the text hangs upon the answer to Mikulin's
portentous question to Razumov, "Where to?" (99), is a fictional
joke as elaborate as anything in Sterne.[13] All the promises at the
beginning of Part Second (which set up the frame) about
a concern for "certain proprieties to be observed for the sake of
clearness and effect" (100) prove, therefore, to be a hoax,
because our longed-for clarity is veiled from the start.

Kermode then is right to detect a deliberate conflict between
"the proprieties" and a "debauch" of interpretation; but he
underestimates, as I hope to have shown, both Conrad's struggle
to write his novel and the ways in which he purposefully builds
this conflict into our reading experience. Moreover, if there is
a devil in the text the hapless narrator is a poor candidate. We
need instead to grapple with the hoaxing author, who playfully
provides models of, and for, our bemusement and resentment at
his manipulation – models that mischievously rehearse Razumov's construction of the narrator as "devil" – and that escape
Kermode's attention.

Towards the end of Part Third after meeting and deflecting the
approaches of a range of characters in a series of dialogues, all of
which inadvertently disturb and enrage him because they rub the
sore spots of his paper-thin psyche, Razumov privately exclaims:

> This was a comedy of errors. It was as if the devil himself were playing a game with all of them in turn. First with him, then with Ziemianitch, then with those revolutionists. The devil's own game this...(284; Conrad's ellipsis)

At this moment Conrad's *dedoublement* is "reflected" in the predicament and obsessions of one character in search of an author, who mutinously protests the lousy "part" he has been assigned in this very black "comedy of errors." Anticipating the strategies of post-modern novels this moment has great poignancy, because we know that the author "stands behind" his "back, waiting," and that Razumov is precisely "a young man in a novel," he cannot know we are construing. This very awareness of his fictionality invites our sympathy, because our position as blundering readers duplicates his. Moreover this *dedoublement* fits the old teacher; and likewise engages our sympathy for the thankless roles his secret author assigns him, such as stooge, dupe, and over-schematic interpreter of "things Russian," which are ambiguously designed both to solicit our interpretative "debauch" and, by frustrating it, to duplicate our predicament as readers.

To confirm these recognitions, almost immediately after we fully realize we have been conned, Conrad proffers through his narrator, the devil-game model as one way of understanding the "interviews" between the wily Mikulin, and the frantic, isolated Razumov, which are designed to recruit and further entrap him as a spy:

> To the morality of a Western reader an account of these meetings would wear perhaps the sinister character of old legendary tales where the Enemy of Mankind is represented holding subtly mendacious dialogues with some tempted soul. It is not my part to protest. Let me but remark that the Evil One, with his single passion of satanic pride for the only motive, is yet, on a larger, modern view, allowed to be not quite so black as he used to be painted. With what greater latitude, then, should we appraise the exact shade of mere mortal man, with his many passions and his miserable ingenuity in error, always dazzled by the base glitter of mixed motives, everlastingly betrayed by a short-sighted wisdom. (304-5)

From the perspective of Razumov's predicament, psychology and performance – which Kermode deliberately skimps – all the conversations he has endured (and from which Conrad's text is constructed) are indeed "subtly mendacious dialogues." Razumov plays "satanic" games with his interlocutors; they, in turn, persuade him – because they press (inadvertently) upon the secret spring of his guilt and threaten his secret role of spy – to cast them as demonic agents in his own private theatre of temptation. Again, the "mock career" of terrorist hero imposed upon him by the revolutionists, merely duplicates his "unreal" existence and confirms his isolation, thus accentuating his maddened sense of being possessed by "phantoms of the living as well as the dead" (224).

Clearly this model of "the devil's own game" contributes nothing, in Kermode's terms, to "sequence:" rather it re-works the "dispersion of souls, spirits, phantoms, ghosts" (148), and operates as a dark double of Conrad's own games with his tellers, characters and readers. At this point my own argument might seem to veer close to Kermode's, because Conrad mocks both his own procedures and his relationship to his readers. I do not think, however, that the text at this moment can be fitted to either Kermode's case that the book "yields to Russia, misty, spiritual, its significance occulted" (152), or that "for the reading of this book we have the wrong kind of eyes" (153), or that it "despises" and "hates" its readers.[14] After all, the devil-game model is exactly analogous only to the dialogues between Razumov and Mikulin. The latter *is* "subtly mendacious" and a satanic liar, who feigns sympathy for Razumov's "great moral loneliness," flatters his intelligence, and most importantly pretends to share Prince K–'s "mystical" and "artless" (307) belief in God and Providence. "Things are ordered," he assures Razumov, "in a wonderful manner.... You have been already the instrument of Providence...I believe firmly in Providence" (296).[15] For Mikulin, however, "Providence" is a fiction, masking the brutal reality of a "savage autocracy." Hence the old teacher sadly envisages autocracy's most resolute upholders, General T – and Mikulin, "talking over the case of Mr. Razumov,

with the full sense of their unbounded power over all the lives in
Russia, with cursory disdain, like two Olympians glancing at
a worm" (306). Thus Mikulin is cynically ready to condemn his
victim to everlasting secrecy, thereby generating both his terrible
isolation and the corruption of his "soul," and "the quantitatively large body of text" that fascinates Kermode.[16]

Razumov the sceptical man of reason (*razum* is the Russian
root for reason), who feels he "no longer belonged to himself"
(301), because he is in thrall to Haldin's "haunting, falsehood-
-breeding spectre" (304), desperately tries to attach himself to
Prince K–'s and Mikulin's providential plot:

> "And, after all," he thought suddenly, "I might have been the chosen
> instrument of Providence. This is a manner of speaking, but there may
> be truth in every manner of speaking. What if that absurd saying were
> true in its essence?" (301)

Razumov's self-mocking musings remind us that the devil-
-game and providential models are exhibited and reworked to
offer both Razumov and the reader *a way of seeing and
understanding*. Though all of these dialogues between Razumov
and the other characters, including the narrator, are ironic
testimonies to man's prolific "ingenuity in error," we are
increasingly (and on subsequent readings) always aware, that
both the protagonist's fumbling construings and the guileless
remarks of his interlocutors are *precisely crafted* to cut him to the
quick and to stimulate his need for "air," truth and freedom,
and, thereby his escape from the "ghosts" that haunt him. Hence
these "mendacious dialogues," composed of dazzling misp-
risions, half-truths, lies, and silences, in which *all* the characters
(as in Shakespearian drama) always say and communicate more
than they mean, alert us to the author as "providence," deceiving
us while "talking over the case of Mr. Razumov." Conrad,
however, unlike Mikulin, uses his *secret* "unbounded power" to
effect the *emancipation* of this protagonist from the rack of his
suffering and his "prison of lies," Natalia from the toils of
innocence, and the reader from his text.

When he tells Natalia that she is "a predestined victim...Ha! what a devilish suggestion" (349), Razumov shares his creator's power because he can corrupt her soul either by marrying her, or by allowing the revolutionary denizens of the Château Borel "to get hold of you" (350). Torn between conflicting narrative models, between what he calls "the superstition of an active Providence" and "the alternative" of "the old Father of Lies – our national patron – our domestic god" (350), Razumov finds "the means to break" the "curse" by confessing. And, as we have seen, he enthusiastically embraces in the last pages of his journal, the providential model, assigning Natalia the role of Madonna, and the infinitely adaptable narrator the role of devil. He remains, of course, entirely unaware, unlike the privileged reader, that his fate all along lay in the hands of a fictionist, who mimicked in *his* "mendacious dialogues," the strategies of "the old Father of Lies," while *secretly* working as the most "active" of providences.[17]

Conrad's *dedoublement* is, then, evident in the way that these dialogues work upon the reader: on the one hand they deny us the key facts and "subtly" query the authority of all judgments, including those of the hapless *overloaded* old teacher, while on the other they appeal to our narrative desire for meaning and pattern, for what Kermode calls "order, sequence and message." Thus Razumov does not realize that the "old man" he ecstatically construes as a "devil" is an unwitting agent, in a fictional "game" working for his liberation: similarly, the narrator works for our enlightenment, in ways he does not realize, in Conrad's text. The old teacher's hapless fate, then, is to be kept in the dark, while soliciting our vision, and to work for liberation, while remaining trapped in a narrative he writes, but does not control. To the end he struggles, unavailingly, to penetrate the "shadow" of Russia and remains unaware of the "shadow" cast between himself and his narrative by his author's devices and desires. Conrad, therefore, is "dedicated to...secrets;" but they do not as Kermode claims, "form associations of their own" that retain an "occult or questionable shape" (144). Rather both his "dispersion of souls, spirits, phantoms...and so forth" and his *deliberate*

frustration of our interpretative forays simultaneously invite us
to share the "morality" that sponsored his subtly misleading
"dialogues." Moreover this "morality" is expressed with that
massive authority, blended of compassionate irony and mournful pity for our common fate, that characterizes the omniscient
narrators of *Nostromo* and *The Secret Agent*. Precisely because
our own "ingenuity in error" has been exposed, and precisely
because "we" have been *temporarily* "betrayed" (in a plot built
upon a huge betrayal that reverberates throughout every aspect
of the text) "by a short-sighted wisdom," we accept the
narrator's belated invitation to take our "stand on the ground of
common humanity" (293). Thus "with...greater latitude" we
"appraise the exact shade of mere mortal" men, who with their
"miserable" and prolific "ingenuity in error," have passed
before our ken. Hence the text exerts a powerful pressure upon
us to clarify our perspective and to find a norm for appraisal
– a pressure manifest throughout in Conrad's desire to "collaborate" with and to activate his reader even at the risk of
a "collapse of authority."

II

This drive towards clarity is strongly evident in the closing pages
in three inter-related ways: Razumov's need to confess, the
function of Natalia as the first reader of his journal, and the
journal's status in the narrative of *Under Western Eyes*.

Razumov craves confession in order to escape the occult
influence of Haldin and the dreadful cycle of "mendacious
dialogues" that simultaneously manifest his scorn for the
revolutionaries and enthrall him in "a prison of lies." Hence, as
we have seen, his ecstatic construction of Natalia's "voice" as
"divine" (352), and of his transformation of her into a Madonna, a "statue" whose "pure brow bore a light which fell on me,
searched my heart and saved me from ignominy, from ultimate
undoing. And it saved you too" (361). The providential pattern
of release that embraces them both is also manifest when we
learn, finally, the exact nature of the transmission of his journal.

In a remarkable sequence, the old teacher pays a last visit to his beloved Natalia as she prepares to leave Geneva to return to Russia:

> She walked to the writing-table, now stripped of all the small objects associated with her by daily use – a mere piece of dead furniture; but it contained something living, still, since she took from a recess a flat parcel which she brought to me.
>
> "It's a book," she said rather abruptly. "It was sent to me wrapped up in my veil...I've decided to leave it with you...You may preserve it, or destroy it after you have read it. And while you read it, please remember that I *was* defenceless...
>
> "You'll find the very word written there,...Well it's true! I *was* defenceless – but perhaps you were able to see that for yourself...In justice to the man, I want you to remember that I was. Oh I was, I was!"..."My eyes are open at last and my hands are free now." (375-6)

This "flat parcel" may be "still," but it is "living." And as we, like Natalia, hold it in our hands and peruse it with our eyes, it claims the power to open our eyes and to free our hands, as it transforms its first reader's vision of herself and of her world. It enables her to return to Russia determined not to "spare herself in good service" (378), even though she knows that her devotion to freedom and justice are entangled in "the net" of Tsarism and that all ideals are subject to the duplicities inherent in speech and language. This passage devoted to transmission directly echoes and re-works the old teacher's disclaimers in the opening paragraphs of the novel. Thus a text that began with a frank despair of "words," whether used for speech or fiction, as "the great foes of reality" (3), now insists that the "book" we hold in our hands – in marked contrast to Laspara's revolutionary journal *The Living Word,* to Peter's "autobiography" and "other books written with the declared purpose of elevating humanity" (125) and to Razumov's spy report – is indeed, "living, still," because our collaboration has re-activated it.[18] Delivered, wrapped in the veil, symbolic of her suffering, purity and defencelessness, this book demonstrates Conrad's "high gifts of imagination and expression" which "enabled" *his* "pen to create for the reader" a "living form:" a "living form" that attests his desire (most memorably expressed in his "Preface" to *The Nigger of the "Narcissus"*) "to render the highest form of justice to the visible universe" (my emphasis), and to evoke "the latent feeling of fellowship with all creation." He struggles, then, to remove the "veil" that separates "words" from "reality" in order to achieve "a direct grasp upon humanity."[19] Our own bewilderment before the terrible cycle of misinterpretations that constituted our experience of this "book," yields, finally, to a "morality" committed, against all the odds, to release and to action, to "truth" and "light."

However, Conrad's extraordinary commitment to the "recognition of all the irreconcilable antagonisms that make our life so enigmatic, so burdensome, so fascinating, so dangerous – so full of hope" ensures that this powerful drive towards "clarity" and "message" is opposed by his commitment to the "verve" and "debauch" the imagination seeks and generates, and that is located in the very act of writing.[20] Thus Razumov's neatly shaped parable of redemption may testify, as Sophia Antonovna tells the old teacher, in a "message" – enforcing remark, to his "character" (380), but such fictions have already been burlesqued in the rancid, heightened account of Peter Ivanovitch's dual liberation from the beast in man and from the "chains" of Tsarist autocracy by the noble peasant girl, "a liberating genius" (124) who "had selected him for the gift of liberty" (121). The parallels between the two confessions, as I have shown elsewhere, are so close that one almost suspects Conrad of parodying both Razumov's and his own tendency to sentimentalize women.[21] Moreover, Conrad's courageous acceptance of "irreconcilable antagonisms" is most evident in the narrator's deeply felt testimony to Natalia's vision of a world where "at last the anguish of hearts shall be extinguished in love:"

> And on this last word of her wisdom, a word so sweet, so bitter, so cruel sometimes, I said good-bye to Natalia Haldin...wedded to an invincible belief in the advent of loving concord springing like a heavenly flower from the soil of men's earth, soaked in blood, torn by struggles, watered with tears. (377)

If Natalia's dream of "loving concord" were to be fulfilled, divisions and wars would cease. More importantly, fiction would be redundant because "words" would no longer be "the great foes of reality;" rather, once "extinguished in love," they would lose both their multi-accentedness and multi-voicedness, and their ceaseless generation of opposing, bewildering interpretations. Meanwhile, Conrad's devotion to "irreconcilable antagonisms" threatens to tear his narrative apart and to overwhelm his readers with the unimaginable inclusiveness of what we are being asked to piece together – an inclusiveness that spawns the multiple and competing uses, roles and characteristics of his teller.

From this perspective *Under Western Eyes* is perhaps the most quixotic, enthralling and heroic narrative in modern English fiction. We are persuaded to seek meaning against the grain of both the narrator's deceptive certainties and his ignorance and obtuseness; we are induced to "collaborate" in an extraordinary *tour de force* that simultaneously strives to speak the univocal "last word" *and* to register the inherent multiplicity of language; we glimpse providential patterns, and claims to free hands and to open eyes through an agglomeration of "mendacious dialogues;" and we are deceived, ensnared, and manipulated in order to reinforce our compassion for both our own and the characters' "miserable ingenuity in error." A controlled "debauch" indeed then; but in ways, and towards ends, that Kermode's schema does not credit.

NOTES

1. "Secrets and Narrative Sequence" was first published in *Critical Inquiry*, (1980), pp. 83-101. It is reprinted in Kermode, *Essays on Fiction: 1971-82* (London: Routledge and Kegan Paul, 1983), pp. 133-55. All page references in the essay are to this version.

2. Part Second of *Under Western Eyes* begins: "In the conduct of an invented story there are, no doubt, certain proprieties to be observed for the sake of clearness and effect;" and the narrator proceeds, as usual, to confess neither he nor his "work" possesses "imagination" (p. 100).

3. In a wonderful letter (20 October 1911) to Olivia Rayne Garnett about *Under Western Eyes*, Conrad talks about his fear lest "novel-writing becomes a mere debauch of the imagination" (*CL*, 4, 490).

4. Central to Conrad's thoughts about Russia is his polemical essay *Autocracy and War* (1905), where he anticipates several of the narrator's prejudices in *Under Western Eyes*. See H. S. Gilliam "Russia and the West in Conrad's *Under Western Eyes*," *Studies in the Novel*, 10 (1978), pp. 218-233; and L. R. Lewitter, "Conrad, Dostoevsky, and The Russo-Polish Antagonism," *Modern Language Review*, 79 (1984), pp. 653-63. As assistant editor of the forthcoming Cambridge edition of *Under Western Eyes*, I have written a history (unpublished) of Conrad's composition of "my most deeply meditated novel." For brief details of the composition and of Conrad's changes and cuts, see my "From 'Razumov' to *Under Western Eyes*: The Dwindling of Natalia's Possibilities," *The Ugo Mursia Memorial Lectures*, ed. M. Curreli, (Milan: Mursia International, 1988), pp. 147-71; and "More mysterious than ever: Peter Ivanovitch in the MS of *Under Western Eyes*," *Conradiana* (forthcoming). For a full account of the TS see D. L. Higdon (my fellow-editor): "Complete but Uncorrected: The TS of Conrad's *Under Western Eyes*" in D. R. Smith, ed., *Joseph Conrad's "Under Western Eyes:" Beginnings, Revisions, Final Forms* (Hamden, Conn.: Archon Books, 1991), pp. 83-119. Henceforward Smith.

5. In a letter of 14 July 1923, Conrad refers to "my unconventional grouping and perspective, which are purely temperamental and wherein almost all my 'art' consists. This, I suspect, has been the difficulty the critics felt in classifying it as romantic or realistic. Whereas...it is fluid, depending on grouping (sequence) which shifts, and on the changing lights giving varied effects of perspective" (*LL*, 2, 317).

6. It also (secretly) reverses Dostoevsky's thesis that Holy Russia has been contaminated by the curse of Western socialism and atheism.

7. Letter to Galsworthy, 30 November 1908, *CL*, 4, 155. On the basis of this letter Conrad's biographers have mistakenly presumed that he had finished Part Second of the novel. In fact Galsworthy read a "clean copy" of the TS, which ends abruptly in the middle of the Part Second, Chapter IV (p. 160) of the finished novel – with Razumov poised to re-enter the Geneva transactions. Cp. Higdon, note 3.

8. In my articles on Natalia and Peter Ivanovitch I show how, through successive revisions, Conrad strove to use her as "a pivot for the action to turn on," and thereby ensured that she "does not move" and is reduced to a "peg." His decision to shear Natalia's "possibilities" was a "self-imposed limitation," designed to prevent "novel-writing" becoming "a mere debauch of the imagination" (*CL*, 4, 489-491).

9. "The temporal duality...between *erzahlte Zeit* (story time) and *Erzahlzeit* (narrative time)" is discussed by G. Genette, *Narrative Discourse: An Essay in Method*, trans. Jane E. Lewin (Ithaca: Cornell U. P., 1980), pp. 33ff.

10. Cp. J. E. Saveson, "The Moral Discovery of *Under Western Eyes*," *Criticism*, 14 (1972), pp. 32-48. I am currently working on a long generic study of the narrator, which shows that the critical debate about his authority, status, presentation, psychology *et al* is diverse and conflicting, mainly because commentators are unaware of the long, stop-start composition of the novel, during which the old teacher *accumulated* many competing uses, functions, roles and characteristics, in three narratives – his own, Razumov's and Conrad's. He was also useful to Conrad because he curbed his Russophobia and screened his own intense personal involvement in Razumov's tale. See both my essay and Smith's "The Hidden Narrative: The K in Conrad" in Smith (pp. 39-81). We both show how Razumov's fate drew upon Polish memories and deeply disturbed Conrad. During successive revisions, especially the last in the spring of 1910 (after his breakdown when he talked in Polish to the characters in his MS!), Conrad carefully elided the clearest autobiographical traces. Penn R. Szittya's "Metafiction: The Double Narration in *Under Western Eyes*," *English Literary History*, 48 (1981), pp. 817-840 is very fine. He calls the novel "a chronology of interpretative failures" (830).

11. Kermode is, therefore, mistaken when he mocks Guerard for dismissing Razumov's "diabolism" as "an irrelevant intrusion," a "lost subject" and a "vestigial survival" from Conrad's original plan for the protagonist to marry Natalia – thereby "exorcising secrets" Guerard would rather bury (142-3). Conrad outlines this plan in a letter to Galsworthy of 6 January 1908 (*CL*, 4, 8-9). I demonstrate in "'The Figure Behind the Veil':" Conrad and Razumov in *Under Western Eyes*" that Conrad began the novel "trying to capture the very soul of things Russian," only to discover that the "real subject of the story" was, in fact, the *ur*-story of all his accounts of "betrayal, and the subsequent need either to justify, to confess or to be understood." See Smith, pp. 1-2.

12. The best study of this aspect is by P. R. Szittya, "Metafiction: The Double Narration in *Under Western Eyes*," *English Literary History*, 48 (1981), pp. 817-839.

13. Given Conrad's compositional difficulties, as he struggled to effect a transition from St. Petersburg to Geneva, the question can also be construed as a joke at his own expense! Indeed, my model for reading what Kermode calls an "insubordinate text" (138) is consonant with Conrad's compositional practice. His habit was to send batches of holograph to his agent Pinker, who returned them typed. Conrad then reworked this "intermediate" TS, while simultaneously continuing to produce more holograph. He thus "set a precedent to all interpreters," but in ways Kermode cannot credit (137).

14. Cp. D. L. Higdon, "'His Helpless Prey:' Conrad and the Aggressive Text," *The Conradian*, 12: 2 (1987), pp. 108-21.

15. Prince K– is Razumov's father, to whom he turns while Haldin is holed up in his room. The Prince introduces Razumov to the brutal Tsarist, General

T–, as "a most honourable young man whom Providence itself" (44; Conrad's ellipses). A prudential tactic; but he is a sentimental, simple man: Mikulin who mimics him is "said to be astute enough for two" (307).

16. The Mikulin-Razumov dialogues thereby reverse the pattern of the Porfiry-Raskolnikov exchanges, wherein the police chief wants his quarry to confess and to save his soul.

17. Sophia Antonovna tells Razumov that Ziemianitch was "notoriously irreligious, and yet, in the last weeks of his life" he proved to be "a simple ancestor," because "he suffered from the notion that he had been beaten by the devil" (280). Razumov is contemptuous, fascinated and alarmed at Ziemianitch's construction of the beating he gave him. To his question – "you don't believe in the actual devil?" – Sophia responds, "Do you?...Not but that there are plenty of men worse than devils to make a hell of this earth" (281). As always, these image-clusters that loom so large in Kermode's "secret" plot, spur Razumov to confess and relate to Conrad's scheme for his deliverance.

18. As Conrad's correspondence and prefaces plainly show, he anticipated the central tenets of "reader-response" criticism. He knew that his "manner of telling" which was aimed "at stimulating vision in my reader," meant that "the reader collaborates with the author" (CL, 1, 381, and CL, 2, 394).

19. Conrad wrote "A Familiar Preface" to A Personal Record "to explain in a sense how I came to write such a novel as Under Western Eyes" (13 September 1911; CL, 4, 477). In it he confesses that the private "origin" of the novel must be sought in the life of the novelist "who is the only reality in an invented world, among imaginary happenings and people. Writing about them he is only writing about himself." Conrad then reminds us that "the disclosure is not complete. He remains...a figure behind a veil: a suspected rather than a seen presence – a movement and a voice behind the draperies of fiction" (PR, p. xiii; my emphasis). Conrad ensured that the "veil" remained in place when he cut most of the autobiographical passages. Cp. my essay in Smith (note 4).

20. Letter to New York Times, 2 August 1901 (CL, 2, 348).

21. See my essay in Curreli (note 4). Nearly thirty years ago, Thomas Moser sharply observed that the old teacher's mocking summary of Peter's account backfires: "Never did Conrad more effectively satirize his own tendency to sentimentalize women." Joseph Conrad: Achievement and Decline (Hamden, Conn.: Archon Books, 1966), p. 95.

John Crompton,
University of Hull,
Hull, England

Conrad and Colloquialism

As far as I am aware, Conrad's use of the vernacular has not been specifically studied.[1] This seems a potentially interesting topic; especially if one assumes that it is the non-literary, more informal and oral aspects of a foreign language which are the most difficult to acquire, particularly if one is adult when first acquiring the new tongue, and especially if one's immediate linguistic environment is narrow.

I have therefore surveyed Conrad's oeuvre in terms of its colloquiality, and I now present some preliminary findings, which are offered as ideas to be tested, by applying the close textual work which a short paper cannot afford if it is to attempt an overview. The hypothesis offered, which awaits the detailed analysis needed to confirm or refute it, is that Conrad employs certain devices in order to avoid vernacularity, not least in the writing of dialogue, where colloquiality is most expected. This hypothesis rests upon a few simple ideas – these are so obvious that I fear readers will complain that they have long since perceived and taken them for granted.

J. A. Cuddon's *Dictionary of Literary Terms* remarks confidently that: "One can readily distinguish between slang, formal language and colloquial language,"[2] and tells us that:

> A colloquial word, phrase or expression is one in everyday use in speech and writing. The colloquial style is plain and relaxed.[3]

Those who have had to handle *Nostromo, Lord Jim, The Rover* or *The Secret Sharer,* common set texts in England, in high school or with undergraduates, will know that students find Conrad's style very far from "plain and relaxed." My first observation is, in fact, that Conrad's mastery of "formal language" is not in

211

question, and going with this is my second observation, that it is in some ways easier to learn "formal language" than "colloquial language," especially if one makes use of books, precisely because "formal language" can be looked up in dictionaries and derived from texts. Cuddon defines "slang" as:

> the lingo of the gutter, the street, the market place, the saloon, the stable, the workshop, the theatre, [importantly for our consideration] the fo'c'sle, the barrack room and the ranch – indeed almost anywhere where men work or play.[4]

The sexism is obvious. Slang develops wherever women work or play, too. But Conrad worked among men, and here is my advantage as a man: I have experienced the workshop and the barrack room. I have, therefore, an inkling of the lingo of the fo'c'sle.

I do not wish to prolong definitions, but I also believe that, *contra* Cuddon, it is not so easy to distinguish slang, formal, and colloquial language, because the last tends to contain a great deal of words, phrases and idioms which some people would designate slang. For the purposes of this paper, therefore, "colloquial" covers all non-formal usage, including slang, and slang's further reaches of cant and argot. So let us turn to Conrad's early experience of the colloquial.

When Korzeniowski took a berth on the steamship *Mavis* on 24 April 1878 there began a period of almost exactly two years before the mast. Baines and Najder disagree about the date of his first landfall in England, but they agree that when the *Mavis* discharged its linseed at Lowestoft in July 1878, as Baines puts it:

> Conrad had arrived in England, aged twenty, knowing no one and apparently no more than a few words of the language.[5]

I think I know what most of those "few words" were, reminded by Najder that:

> Compared with the riffraff serving in the British fleet, the simple sailors from southern France must have seemed refined.[6]

I can indeed, guess the sort of language that Korzeniowski learned aboard the *Skimmer of the Sea*, the *Duke of Sutherland* and the *Europa*. It must have consisted of seamen's technical jargon, some of which is of course, current idiom, you will not be "taken aback" to learn, and the blaspheming, swearing slang which Cuddon would call "argot:"

> slang or cant...usually refers to the slang used by social outcasts or those who are disapproved of socially.[7]

Or perhaps "cant" would be better:

> The jargon or slang of a particular class, group, trade, calling or profession. Usually associated with pedlars, thieves, gipsies, tinkers and vagabonds.[8]

However defined, the first English that Korzeniowski learned on board ships was almost useless from a literary point of view: not only was it unprintable until recently – Norman Mailer had to use "fug" in place of the dominant lexical item used in the barrack room[9] – but, being essentially a spoken lingo, it does not readily take to the page. The fo'c'sle is, nevertheless, precisely the setting used in *The Nigger of the "Narcissus": A Tale of the Forecastle*.

It is, obviously, in dialogue that colloquialisms are obligatory, and there are three features of the dialogue that I will briefly comment on. Firstly, it is, as it were, assembled from fragments: no one speaker usually has more than a sentence or so, and utterances are often unattributed. There is also a reliance on a few representative speakers, such as Donkin, Knowles, Belfast and Archie. This deliberate reduction of speakers is supported by the fact that some of the men are foreign and taciturn. We never know the names of more than half of the eighteen crew. It is also interesting that the least talkative crewman, Singleton, is the moral arbiter, almost as if Conrad is establishing taciturnity, the withholding of dialogue, as a virtue. Certainly Donkin's loquacity is revealed as part of his essential corruption.

Secondly, it is suitably peppered with printable cant, slang and jargon, and Conrad also manages to suggest accent, especially Donkin's cockney. Wait, by contrast, speaks at times a curiously correct, formal English, which both compounds his dignity and distances the character from conventional stereotypes:

> The captain shipped me this morning. I couldn't get aboard sooner. I saw you all aft as I came up the ladder, and could see directly you were mustering the crew. Naturally I called out my name. I thought you had it on your list, and would understand. You misapprehended. (18)

Thirdly, Conrad hints at what in my barrack rooms was called the "effing and blinding" with various devices. One is to use comparatively harmless epithets and interjections – "damme!" (16), "blooming," "blamed," – and let the reader substitute the probable original. "Skipper-licking" (18) is quite easy, for example: the real usage no doubt suggested that the insulted one was not, figuratively, in the habit of applying his tongue to the entirety of his captain. Donkin is actually allowed the word "bloody" (11). Another technique is the use of the dash, "by–!".

There is, of course, an intriguing language problem about the text as a whole. How could a member of the crew credibly produce such a text at all? But what I want to draw attention to is the fact that Conrad avoids ever having to provide lengthy utterances and, by deploying in short samples, a modicum of the more acceptable slang acquired during his first immersion in the English element, often no more than ejaculations, he achieves a powerful effect.

When on 28 May 1880, Korzeniowski passed his second mate's certificate, he effectively changed his language environment, for however uncertain was the role of third mate, in which capacity he joined the *Loch Etive* on 21 August, he now lived and ate amongst the officers. We might even guess that the reason why his examination lasted so long, as recounted in *A Personal Record,* was because although the examinee knew his business, Captain James Rankin may well have had difficulty with his English and may have doubted whether his shipmates would understand it.

I have no objective evidence for this, but I believe that the officers were of variably higher social class and spoke in a different register. Leggatt and Jim are clergymen's sons, I note. Conrad's own accounts of such officers as Captain MacWhirr, Mr. Baker, Captain Whalley, Captain Beard and the rest, both confirm that their speech was more formal than that of their crews, and make plain that they were not the most subtle and resourceful conversationalists. Their language was, plainly, lacking in variety of subject matter and style. Thus, though it was undoubtedly colloquial, it was limited, and necessarily and desirably so, as Conrad indicates, since imagination and abstraction, the stimulus to and expression of more complex language, were hindrances in this profession, as *Typhoon* shows.

A survey of Conrad's sea stories quickly reveals, indeed, that though the dialogue of the officers comes in longer, more grammatically correct and complete sentences, they, too, do not make long speeches, and the subject matter is, naturally, almost entirely professional, and we may, I believe, deduce that if Conrad's sea writing had depended largely on fo'c'sle and saloon language we would not be discussing him today.

By the time Korzeniowski began to write *Almayer's Folly,* most probably in the autumn of 1889, he had had eleven years of exposure to spoken English, and this was, as Najder puts it "supported by careful, diligent reading of the masters,"[10] in other words of "formal language." But until he finally came ashore, his aural experience of language had been largely limited to (a) the argot of the fo'c'sle, and (b) the rather cribbed, cabined and confined colloquialism of the saloon. He cannot have had, for example much notion of the speech of English women.

Whether conscious or not of his limitations in regard to varieties of colloquial English, my thesis is that part of his genius lay in adopting three main, and interrelated, strategies for outflanking them.

Firstly, as already suggested, he applies the impressionist technique to the dialogue. Assemblages of short utterances, salted with colloquialisms, give an idea, create an atmosphere, without need for extended representations of English speech. Secondly, he employs an intermediary, whose account, though also comparatively colloquial, can be more formal: we assume, for instance, that the narrator of *The Nigger* is *writing,* not recounting his story orally, even though the subtitle's use of "a tale," which carries associations of being a live performance, may be trying to confuse this point. Thirdly, the abundant, even dominant, use of foreign characters and settings means that the reader may not, even must not, expect typically English colloquialisms, precisely because although represented in English, that is not the language the reader is required to imagine as being spoken.

The narrator of *The Nigger* later, as it were, metamorphoses into Marlow. Whatever the other, often discussed, advantages of using Marlow, one obvious benefit of this mysteriously articulate intermediary is his three-fold effect on the dialogue. He compensates for the linguistic limitations of the characters he is relaying, reduces the amount of talk that need be conveyed, and, combining and extending these features, clouds the reader's expectations as to the verisimilitude of the speech itself.

Marlow is, of course, supposed to be telling his tale orally. But the presence of the written frame narrative, immediately compromises the orality, and produces, in effect, a hybrid medium. The result of this is greater manoeuvering-room for Conrad, because it allows him to give the *impression* of colloquiality whilst simultaneously deploying what is actually a quite formal style. Marlow's very first speech in *Youth* may exemplify this:

> Yes, I have seen a little of the Eastern seas; but what I remember best is my first voyage there. You fellows know there are those voyages that seem ordered for the illustration of life, that might stand for a symbol of existence. You fight, work, sweat, nearly kill yourself, sometimes do kill yourself, trying to accomplish something – and you can't. Not from any fault of yours. You simply can do nothing, neither great nor little – not a thing in the world – not even marry an old maid, or get a wretched 600-ton cargo of coal to its port of destination. (*YS,* 3-4)

The rhetoric of this is more complex than its apparently quite simple language may suggest. "You fellows know" is intended to give the impression of face-to-face story-telling and teller-

-listener solidarity: this is, after all, from *Youth: A Narrative*. But the rest of the sentence is only saved from a pomposity that would not be tolerated at a real after-dinner yarn-swapping by its reaching us in writing: "there are those voyages that seem ordered for the illustration of life" and so on. Of course, Marlow's whole narrational career is strewn with just such philosophicalities, and they are a major element in the process of adding depth and breadth to both the events narrated and, vitally for my thesis, the dialogue.

In the first place, Marlow's ostensibly spoken prose has about it the intensity of poetry:

> The sea was white like a sheet of foam, like a caldron of boiling milk; there was not a break in the clouds, no – not the size of a man's hand – no, not for as much as ten seconds. There was for us no sky, there were for us no stars, no sun, no universe – nothing but angry clouds and an infuriated sea. We pumped watch and watch, for dear life; and it seemed to last for months, for years, for all eternity, as though we had been dead and gone to a hell for sailors. We forgot the day of the week, the name of the month, what year it was, and whether we had ever been ashore. The sails blew away, she lay broadside on under a weather-
> -cloth, the ocean poured over her, and we did not care. (11-12)

Is this "plain and relaxed" and thus colloquial in Cuddon's definition? Well, the vocabulary is plain enough, and the idiom hovers on the edge of cliché – "like a sheet of foam" and "for dear life." But the rhetorical devices – "there was for us no sky, there were for us no stars, no sun, no universe – nothing but angry clouds and infuriated sea" – are hardly "relaxed." This is finely wrought, carefully rhythmic, language beyond the usual capability or expectations of spontaneous vocalization. Marlow's narration is, I suggest, usually of a heightened intensity which partly removes it from the realm of the colloquial, while at the same time leaving it accessible to instants of jargon when required – "weather-cloth." The main effect is of surprise, even shock: the domestic image of the caldron of boiling milk is, in its familiarity, a wonderful means of defamiliarization, making us "see."

Another way of perceiving Marlow's narration is to classify it as super, or supra, colloquial – what about "A hungry crowd of shipwrights sharpened their chisels at the sight of that carcass of a ship" (14)? This is plain language honed with metaphor and alliteration beyond the level of ordinary colloquiality. And it is in this special linguistic medium that the sparse items of dialogue are embedded, complete with suitable colloquialisms:

> Well, well! don't talk to me about the intelligence of rats. They ought to have left before, when we had that narrow squeak from foundering. (17)

Thanks to its surroundings, its brevity and its very careful use of sailor-lingo the dialogue acquires extra impact. There is even a little pun included: rats squeak.

I need hardly point out that the same combination of factors, yet further refined, is at work in *Heart of Darkness*. The frame narrative is formal, itself highly wrought and poetic:

> Forthwith a change came over the waters, and the serenity became less brilliant but more profound. The old river in its broad reach rested unruffled at the decline of day, after ages of good service done to the race that peopled its banks, spread out in the tranquil dignity of a waterway leading to the uttermost ends of the earth. (*YS*, 46-7)

Marlow's first utterance this time neatly combines simple language and complex meaning in the famous, gnomic remark: "And this also...has been one of the dark places of the earth" (48). Again, is this colloquial? Yes, it is plain and in some sense "relaxed," but the frame-narrator himself shortly after makes a careful distinction between types of narrative which may carry over into the area of language:

> The yarns of seamen have a direct simplicity, the whole meaning of which lies within the shell of a cracked nut. But Marlow was not typical...and to him the meaning of an episode was not inside like a kernel but outside, enveloping the tale which brought it out only as a glow brings out a haze, in the likeness of one of those misty halos that sometimes are made visible by the spectral illumination of moonshine. (48)

I believe that Marlow's language, as relayed by the frame-
-narrator, is partly what is at issue here, for it is this, its medium,
which envelops the tale and makes its misty halo visible.
Colloquial language does not, I think, possess misty halos to be
made visible. We must, in fact, carefully distinguish between the
vocabulary and syntax of language and its eventual nature and
atmosphere. It may be relaxed and plain in its use of mundane
words, but the overall effect may be, as in the Marlow stories, at
a much higher, more literary, therefore formal, level.

To touch on the third strategy which Conrad uses for
obviating the need for colloquial English dialogue, let us
backtrack to *Almayer's Folly*. Its first two words signal what is
afoot: "Kaspar! Makan!" – a Dutch name and a Malay word.
We are then given Almayer's first-encountered but habitual
dream of wealth, in the conditional:

> They would be rich and respected. Nobody would think of her mixed
> blood in the presence of her great beauty and of his immense wealth. (3)

In English, yes, but what language does the reader imagine
Almayer to be thinking in? Shortly after, we learn that he is
Dutch but speaks English well (5). Later we are told that Nina
spoke to him in Malay (16), and that is obviously the language in
which the Malays themselves converse. When Dain tells Almayer "I speak English a little, so we can talk and nobody will
understand" (53), it confirms that they normally speak Malay.
Lingard presumably speaks English with Almayer:

> Damme, though, if I didn't think you were going to refuse. Mind you,
> Kaspar, I always get my way, so it would have been no use. But you are
> no fool! (11)

Lingard and Captain Ford are, however, readily drawn from the
ranks of Merchant Marine officers, and their speeches are few,
short and suitably terse, an instance of Conrad exploiting his
experience of spoken English.

The overall effect of the novel is, however, that it is, as it were,
a translation: Malay and, or, Dutch thought and speech

rendered in English.[11] This is compounded by the Eastern setting, and this, with the average reader's ignorance of Malay culture, serves to excuse, even require, the overblown language and emotional extremism which would otherwise be more appropriate in Ethel M. Dell or E. M. Hull:

> And so they drifted on, he speaking with all the rude eloquence of a savage nature giving itself up without restraint to an overmastering passion, she bending low to catch the murmur of words sweeter to her than life itself. (69)

Well! The reserved Anglo-Saxon in me wants to say, "I say, steady on, old chap," and the white liberal in me says, "This smacks of racism." The point is, though, that by using exotic characters and settings and limiting greatly the amount of what I will call "first place English," the writer who knew none of the language until he was twenty is able legitimately to excuse himself from using colloquial English. We shall not expect, or want, English slang and idiom when listening to Malays or Netherlanders. And, of course, he pulls off exactly the same trick with *An Outcast of the Islands*. The same avoidance of first place English, deployment of second language speakers, and constant implication that the English is actually a translation, continue throughout Conrad.

In *Heart of Darkness* we must remember that Marlow's contacts with officials and his last interview with the Intended must be assumed to have been in French. What language do Marlow and the Harlequin speak together? In the Francophone Belgian-colonial Congo the most famous utterance in all Conrad, immortalized by Eliot, is actually something of a puzzle. The manager's "boy" would surely not have announced Kurtz's death in English? What French original, if the African had any of that language, has Marlow rendered as "Mistah Kurtz – he dead" (150)?

In *Nostromo* the greater part of the dialogue must, if one stops to consider the matter, be proceeding in Spanish or Italian. Decoud and Nostromo must be speaking Spanish on the lighter, for example. Presumably the Italians speak Italian, the Violas together, and Nostromo with them. The Goulds speak English together – and Conrad curtails their verbal to match their sexual intercourse. Gould's taciturnity increases, indeed, his speeches becoming more and more clipped. Captain Mitchell and Nostromo must speak Spanish. Naturally all groupings of Costaguaneros or Sulacans converse in Spanish. Conrad only occasionally specifies the tongue being spoken, so that the overall effect is a kind of general vagueness about what is the current language of the dialogue – we can simply assume that this is mostly being translated from some foreign lingo for our comprehension. But part of Conrad's genius lies in providing a kind of English which obviates readers worrying about what language is in progress. This actually requires the avoidance of colloquialisms which would, in their Englishness, jar in their inappropriateness in the mouths of foreigners.

This deliberate imprecision operates within the texts within the text. In what language does Decoud write to his sister? Conrad does not say, but readers must assume that he has kindly rendered it for them. Its ironic, facetious tone smacks of the Parisian blague attributed to its writer, so it may be in French. And what of the excerpts we are given from *Fifty Years of Misrule?* We know that Don José speaks English, and so it is possible he has written in that language, but his manuscript may equally be in Spanish and translated for us by the narrator.

The overall effect of its linguistic plurality is to give the impression that the whole of the novel is a translation, that its English is a convenient medium for unifying three or four languages which are being spoken or written. Readers are even given the feeling that they have done some of the translation themselves. By unravelling the snippets left untranslated, we gain a sense that we have done some of the work. *"Un grand bestia," "chica," "esclavo," "hombre de muchas dientes," "tertulia," "Madre de Dios," "va bene," "Misericordia Divina," "padre mio," "hombres finos," "Golfo Placido"* (with the "c" pronounced "s," please, in South American style) – by understanding these and many more such, we feel we are participating in creating the English text.

Much the same cunning use of speakers and settings underlies *Under Western Eyes*. The old teacher of languages is there to translate for us, and thereby keep us reminded that almost all the dialogue is second place English. The whole of Part One is set in Russia, so obviously the English dialogue is Englished. This, as with the overblown, supposedly Malay-rendered style of *Almayer's Folly*, excuses, even creates suitable expectation for such rather fevered dialogue as Haldin's:

> Why be anxious for me? They can kill my body, but they cannot exile my soul from the world. I tell you what – I believe in this world so much that I cannot conceive eternity otherwise than as a very long life. That is perhaps the reason I am so ready to die. (58)

We can accept this because we assume its tone is unexceptionable in a Russian revolutionary speaking Russian. There is, even, something jarring about the use of English colloquialisms: within a few lines of the above Razumov reflects that Haldin is "a slippery customer" (58).

The Russian characters must be speaking their native lingo, not French, and this is confirmed on such occasions as Peter Ivanovitch's introduction of Razumov to Madame de S–. He throws in French phrases: *"Enfin vous voilà," "Un vrai celui-là"* (214). Miss Haldin, we are told, speaks English to the narrator. We shall not, of course, expect a very idiomatic English from her.

A cursory survey of Conrad's works reveals that a large number of his characters are either being translated for us or speak English as a second language. *The Rover* is taking place entirely in French, so to speak, but is given to us in English. And as if aware of his shortcomings in regard to female characters, and especially their speech, it is notable that Conrad applies evading tactics to them, too. He makes them exotic, like Nina and Jewel, or he makes them second language speakers, like Natalia Haldin, or he makes them extremely taciturn.

This employment of second language users is often brilliantly turned to use. Much of the impact of Stein's oracular pronouncements resides in their foreignness:

> Yes! Very funny this terrible thing is. A man that is born falls into a dream like a man who falls into the sea. If he tries to climb out into the air as inexperienced people endeavour to do, he drowns, *nicht wahr?*...No! I tell you! The way is to the destructive element submit yourself, and with the exertions of your hands and feet in the water make the deep, deep sea keep you up. So if you ask me – how to be? (*LJ*, 214)

The fascinating thing about this, as about most of Stein's utterances, is its lack of colloquiality. It is both highly formal – "to the destructive element submit yourself, and with the exertions" – and lacking in slang, cant, idiom. Instead of English vernacularity, of course, Conrad salts his speeches with stage--German – *"nicht wahr?"*, *"Ach,"* *"Gott in Himmel,"* *"ja."* These parallel all the snippets of Spanish and Italian in *Nostromo*. (Is it not interesting that although he could, surely, have readily done so, Conrad never gives us little items of Russian?)

What conclusions can be drawn from Conrad's most ostensibly English novels, *Chance* and *The Secret Agent?* These are especially interesting in terms of taciturn womanhood, because in both novels the still centre is a silent woman. Flora is unable to give voice to herself because she has for most of the novel no established self to speak from or with: Winnie's silence is a necessary product of her situation, which does not bear much looking into. The nearest equivalent elsewhere for these barely speaking women is probably Yanko Goorall in *Amy Foster*: like him, they are virtually strangers in their own country, dependent entirely on patronage. A major element of their appeal is that they are, in effect, in possession of language but denied its use. In their enforced taciturnity they are not unlike young Korzeniowski landing at Lowestoft.

In both these novels, too, other evasive strategies are at work: Marlow is once more the intermediary in the one, and the other is full of foreigners. The very name Adolf Verloc sounds foreign, as if Conrad is nominally undermining his nationality.

Flora is represented to us by Marlow, or by Powell through Marlow. Marlow's blend of sympathy, philosophicalities and formal style performs its function of outflanking colloquiality, at the same time speaking for her and compensating for her silence. In *The Secret Agent* we have perhaps the most wonderful exploitation of linguistic shortcoming in all Conrad, in the use of Stevie. His speech, in essence that of a child, or a foreigner, thus again recalls in its apparent paucity the linguistic competence of the young seaman leaving the *Mavis*. Stevie's most ambitious speech is, "Don't be nervous, Winnie. Mustn't be nervous! Bus all right." Otherwise he is kept to very short iterations: "Bad! Bad!" "Poor! Poor!...Cabman poor, too. He told me himself." These short utterances may seem the epitome of colloquiality in their simplicity, but in their concentration of feeling, reinforced by the terrible irony of Stevie's fate, they acquire a compelling power, culminating in the utterly banal but sapient, "Bad world for poor people." Stevie, too, is, like Marlow, a philosopher.

This is the kind of thing one feels proud of saying in whatever smatterings of a foreign tongue one has come ashore with, so giving one the sense of joining the company of Decoud, Razumov, Heyst, Willems and Stein: *Un monde affreux pour les pauvres; eine schreckliche Welt für den Armen; straszny świat dla biednych.*

NOTES

1. This paper was stimulated by Anne Luyat's suggestion at the 1989 Joseph Conrad Society (UK) conference that I do something on Conrad's language.

2. J. A. Cuddon, *A Dictionary of Literary Terms* (Harmondsworth: Penguin, 1982 [1976]), p. 633.

3. *Ibid.*, p. 128.

4. *Ibid.*, p. 633.

5. J. Baines, *Joseph Conrad: A Critical Biography* (London: Weidenfeld and Nicolson, 1959), p. 60.

6. Z. Najder, *Joseph Conrad: A Chronicle* (Cambridge: C.U.P., 1983), p. 55.

7. Cuddon, p. 56.

8. *Ibid.*, p. 99.

9. N. Mailer, *The Naked and the Dead* (New York: Rinehart, 1948).

10. Najder, p. 115.

11. See also C. Maisonnat, "*Almayer's Folly*: A Voyage Through Many Tongues," *L'Epoque Conradienne*, 1990, pp. 39-49.

Juliet McLauchlan,
Oxford University, Department for Continuing Education,
Oxford, England

Conrad: The "Few Simple Ideas"

Among the most quoted of all Conrad's words are the following:

> Those who read me know my conviction that the world, the temporal
> world, rests on a few very simple ideas; so simple that they must be as
> old as the hills. It rests, notably, *amongst others,* on the idea of Fidelity.[1]

The emphasis is mine, for these "others" are seldom considered
in detail. All too commonly, the word "Fidelity" is simply seized
upon as the central, almost the only, Conradian idea. Quite
commonly, too, it is discussed as largely faithfulness to the task
in hand, solidarity with colleagues, endurance, physical and
moral courage. In *Heart of Darkness,* it is still quite common for
critics to maintain that what prevents Marlow from sinking to
the level of debasement of Kurtz is, precisely, this kind of
faithfulness to a particular task. In fact, much more complex
factors and ideas "save" Marlow.

What *are,* then, Conrad's "few very simple ideas?" He is very
firm: his reader will "know" Conrad's own "conviction" that the
world "rests" on certain ideas, and will *see* these clearly
expressed in his work. So we must assume.

But is it useful to explore these ideas at all? It is currently
fashionable to quote obviously cynical comments on humankind, mainly from Conrad's letters, to prove that he was wholly
cynical, perhaps even pessimistic in the word's full sense,
certainly "existential" in his outlook on life and human nature.
A very nearly nihilistic Conrad is postulated. I shall consider
briefly each concept.

I would argue that Conrad was very aware of (sometimes
inexplicable) conflicts and contradictions within the individual
psyche, so aware that no-one since Shakespeare seems to have

225

seen humankind so clearly in terms of upward and downward
potential. The cynical outbursts in the letters spring, I believe,
from exasperation and anger when he contemplates the mainly
downward tendencies displayed in our temporal world. There is
evidence that Conrad felt some of these conflicts and contradictions within himself, and this may well have contributed to his
more general railings against human nature, when, almost
despairingly, he appears to have given it up as a lost cause. These
are, however, highly personal, mood-of-the-moment outbursts,
to friends. The tone is at times mischevious, mocking, even
hyperbolic, as if meant to shock, or to rid himself of certain
sentiments by expressing them in extreme terms. When Conrad
turns to fiction, however, it is the same reflective, *considered*
Conrad whom we meet in the "Preface" to *The Nigger of the
"Narcissus,"* "A Familiar Preface" to *A Personal Record,* and
throughout the fiction itself. Humankind here inspires concern,
compassion, pity, indignation (on its behalf) "and in minds of
any largeness an inclination to that indulgence which is akin to
affection." (*Chance,* 107). And Conrad never despairs. He
always hopes:

> Joy and sorrow in this world pass into each other, mingling their forms
> and their murmurs in the twilight of life as mysterious as an
> overshadowed ocean, while the dazzling brightness of supreme hopes
> lies far off, fascinating and still, on the distant edge of the horizon.[2]

Though remaining "far off," the "supreme hopes" are still *there,*
their "dazzling [admittedly a rather dubious word] brightness"
unquenched. Thus, although remaining deeply sceptical about
humanity, he was neither cynic nor pessimist. I return to this
point when considering Conrad's existential stance.

But, again, is it useful to explore the simple ideas at all?
Another current critical fashion consists in decrying critical
concern with values or even meaning in any writer's work. So
– even though Conrad may have thought he adhered to certain
simple (elevated) ideas, and even though he assures his readers
that these are to be seen through reading his fiction, neither critic

nor reader has any legitimate business with them. Here we may consider Conrad's moral stance *vis a vis* Shakespeare's. Seeing or reading *Macbeth* or *A Winter's Tale,* we do not need to be told how we ought to respond respectively, to the behaviour of Macbeth or to the Leontes of the play's first three acts. We simply *see* the terrible consequences of what these men are doing. The governing moral stance is *implicit*; we may not be sure what Shakespeare thought or meant himself, but what he seems to do, in effect, is to challenge us to watch human beings in action and see for ourselves whether certain behaviour does not seem to lead convincingly to certain consequences for the central character and for others concerned. (Of course we see much more than that.) As with Shakespeare, Conrad shows an amazing variety of types of human behaviour, shows what seems to motivate people to think and act as they do, finally shows the consequences. When characters behave in certain ways, their lives develop convincingly, as do those of Jim, Kurtz, Razumov, Gould *et al.* There is an implicit moral stance throughout Conrad's fiction. How but by (perhaps unconscious) reference to it, can readers see, as they surely do, Willems's series of betrayals as quite despicable, and as leading him inevitably towards the sort of retributive rough justice administered by Lingard and Aïssa?

Finally, we return to Conrad's existentialism. Difficulties always arise in defining that word. I shall take it as meaning (when applied to Conrad): nothing exists beyond the world (and its universe) as we see it; humankind is on its own; infinitely free and infinitely responsible in coming to terms with it; the heavens are empty. In that sense, yes, Conrad is existential, and consistent in his bleak view of the human lot. I shall discuss below how he seems to weave this view into the two pre--eminently existential works, *The End of the Tether* and *Chance.* Here I would simply say that, sombre as is the context for both works, there are qualifying gleams of something positive, something human. There is the angry and active compassion of Van Wyck, roused by the plight of his old friend. Ineffectual though it proves, Van Wyck's attempted intervention, has led him to an ardent determination to reject, in future, the selfish-

ness of his solitary life. He has been won to some renewed sense
of solidarity with humankind. Then, too, Conrad gave immense
weight to the end of the story, where we see that only the
overwhelming demands of Ivy's life of grinding poverty have
prevented her from recognizing her abiding love for her father.
Genuinely grieving for him, she seems to feel his presence, to see
him "august" in his paternal love and care.

The scope of this paper does not allow full engagement with
the above points but, in the course of it, I hope to demonstrate
that it is worth exploring as far as possible those characteristic
ideas (rather more than a very few) which run right through
Conrad's work.

Fidelity itself, is a great deal more complex than any such
simplistic idea as that suggested above. Among its many aspects
is its close association with the great classical, Medieval,
Renaissance, Polish, and Conradian concept of honour. As
Zdzisław Najder has brilliantly shown,[3] it has long been seen as
a dual one, embodying both "external marks of honour"
(reputation and public recognition) and a "feeling of inner
worth" (a sense of integrity, deep self-respect). The latter springs
from the knowledge that one's conduct is worthy of the
reputation one enjoys, that one's conduct shows a steady
adherence to an ideal of oneself which is based on fundamental
values. This clearly recalls the old chivalric code of honour but,
in Conrad, emphasis is more firmly placed upon the inner sense
of "rectitude." Indeed, this is overriding. No Conradian "hero"
can live with himself, as it were, once he has lost his "integrity."
This is true whether a character realizes his loss (as to some
extent do Gould and Nostromo) or simply feels (as does
Willems) that he has lost any sense of who or what he is.

Conrad often, in fact, presents his ideas by showing clearly the
catastrophic consequences of adopting an opposite basis for
living. Thus, in the case of Willems, we watch his inevitable
downward progression through betrayal: of Hudig's trust; of
Joanna; of Lingard; of Aïssa; until in the end he has utterly
betrayed himself as any sort of honourable man. Betrayal is
consistently shown in Conrad as a direct denial of fidelity to

personal obligations of all kinds, to trust, to ideals, and to oneself. Such types of fidelity are indeed central to Conrad's view of humanity, with betrayal as the deadliest of Conradian "sins."

It is worth looking more closely at Najder's elucidation of the great "ethos of honor," as he calls it. He offers the concept of some "irreversible consequences" which must follow actions of dishonour: a person will actually change qualitatively, perhaps to the point of becoming "depersonalized." He points out that honour must involve fidelity to principles; further, honour "also determines...the kind of principles [one]ought to stick to;" he stresses the absolute stringency of the concept – all must be "judged by [the same] severe standards." There is an underlying assumption that individual and community adhere to identical ideals; and here there is just a hint (hardly more) of a Conradian sense of human solidarity.

What is perhaps most interesting is his discussion of honour *versus* what any Conradian will identify as "material interests." Najder writes:

> The impracticality of honor is most obvious in the disregard for material advantages [and he quotes from Xenophon]: "For if, Socrates, there be one point in which the man who thirsts for honor differs from him who thirsts for gain, it is, I think, in a willingness to toil, face danger, or abstain from shameful gains – for the name of honor only and fair fame."[4]

A Conradian conviction. After pointing out that there was some opposition from Reformation and Counter-Reformation to the ethos of honour, "more momentous" he suggests was:

> the spread of the bourgeois ethos of capitalism, based on work, usefulness, and profit. It brought along more palpably attractive possibilities of vertical social change and drove the ethos centered around honor into a valiant retreat.

In this battle, Conrad remained consistently valiant, and never retreated.

Conrad's second novel, *An Outcast of the Islands,* might almost have been written to illustrate the quotation from

Xenophon – in the negative, of course. Willems is tireless in his pursuit of "shameful gains," hoping to the very end of his life that he may succeed. Of all Conrad's "heroes," Willems is the most completely shameless in this pursuit; it is the very essence of his being. The novel begins with his confident expectation that (without being found out) he can soon pay off a sum he has embezzled. He *is* found out; then, rescued by Lingard, betrays his benefactor and proceeds on his headlong downward path of betrayals. Significantly, he is deflected from his primary aim (temporarily) by his infatuation with Aïssa. While in the grip of his lust, nothing else seems to him to be of any consequence; yet he does wonder if he is seeking happiness in the right way. Trying to justify his betrayal of Lingard, he considers:

> He was ashamed of his state of mind...Were these scruples?...scruples were for imbeciles. His clear duty was to make himself happy. Did he ever take an oath of fidelity to Lingard? No. Well then – he would not let any interest of that old fool stand between Willems and Willems' happiness. Happiness? Happiness meant money. Much money. At least he had always thought so till he had experienced these new sensations. ...(142)

Willems is a brilliant portrayal of a totally dishonourable man, who becomes, in Najder's suggestive word "depersonalized" in that he loses all sense of his identity, until, finally his downward path of betrayal leads him to an inevitable death. I can think of no other work of fiction which so clearly shows the negative link between a man's lust for money (and the power he hopes it may bestow) and his honour. Conrad pursues this theme in a number of works, but in *An Outcast of the Islands* it is absolutely central.

In his first novel *Almayer's Folly,* the case of Almayer is qualitatively rather different: true he dreams of an "opulent existence" and "a life of splendour," of "the big mansion in Amsterdam," "the earthly paradise of his dreams," and believes he will be "made king amongst men by old Lingard's money," but he seems most of all attracted by dreams of Nina's glittering social life and by "the indolent ease of life – for which he felt himself so well fitted" (16-17). His folly consists less in greed as such than in his totally destructive tendency to live in dreams which are altogether illusory and, worse, to try to impose his vague plans upon his daughter.

Neither Almayer nor Willems appear to feel any sense of solidarity with others. All motivation is centred on self, if we consider that for Almayer Nina is simply an extension of self.[5] Other characters who appear to be motivated only by a mean and obstinate pursuit of wealth are the Manager in *Heart of Darkness* and Massy in *The End of the Tether*. The Manager's thirst for gain is so compulsive as to rob him entirely of heart, soul, and any recognizably human sentiments. The emptiness of his nature is encapsulated in his mode of entertaining himself when on leave: "riot[ing] on a large scale – pompously. Jack ashore – with a difference – in externals only." In these characters there is outright rejection of solidarity; others exist only to be exploited.

Both the Manager and Massy become malevolent in their obsession with gain, behaving ruthlessly towards anyone who gets in the way. Massy's thirst for gain is even more obsessive. Conrad has never represented so savagely the sheer obsession with wealth for its own sake as he does in the unlovely person of Massy. Malevolence and greed motivate him, and he bends all his efforts towards winning a fortune through gambling. Characteristically, he places no reliance on personal qualities or hard work. His total reliance on chance is combined with the idiotic conviction that he can detect some system in the way the numbers come up. Hence all his efforts are spent in trying to discover this. His sole ambition is now "to do nothing, nothing whatever, and have plenty of money to do it on" (*YS*, 268). He sees wealth only in terms of inactivity and power over others.

> the notion of the absolute idleness of wealth he could very well conceive. He revelled in [the idea of]...walking about the streets of Hull...his pockets full of sovereigns...[his family and former] chums would render him infinite homage...His word would be law [he imagines, as he recalls] the joyful cringing and the curiously respectful looks of the "trashy" white men...His heart had swelled within him [Satanic echoes here]. This was the true power of money – and no trouble with it, nor any thinking required either. (268-9)

This discussion would not be complete without some reference to Kurtz – but Kurtz stands alone, quite apart from any of the greed-obsessed, mean figures we have been considering, despite his obvious obsession with the ivory. This is because that rapacious, voracious lust for the ivory itself is only one element in his multiple obsessions (all self-deluding): with his wilderness, his power, his people, his intentions, his greatness, his future – with all those passions which make him hollow at the core and emptied of genuine human emotions. Then, too, he differs totally from any of the others (especially, in the context, from the Manager) in that he has started with elevated ideals and altruistic intentions. The others are quite incapable of the kind of conflict Kurtz suffers between a "loathing" which cannot quench an overwhelming "desire" to indulge his various passions.

On a deeper level altogether, Gould and Nostromo become obsessed with material interests, Gould with the successful operation of the mine, Nostromo with becoming rich "slowly" through drawing in secret upon his illicit treasure of silver. Both suffer from the catastrophic and irreparable loss of "feelings of inherent worth" (Najder's phrase). Both lose, too, any capacity for love. As between the two men the second loss is qualitatively different. The tragedy of Gould is, in part, that the Gould marriage has been potentially a rich one, based upon mutual love, respect, and, at the beginning, apparently shared ideals. Gould's growing obsession simply displaces his natural feelings and robs him of a capacity for love. Nostromo's obsession robs him of any sense of fidelity and honour in both public and private relationships. The measure of his deep corruption is his betrothing himself to Linda while loving Giselle (*only* because of his fear that Giorgio may bar him from access to his treasure), with the atrocious suffering thus caused to Linda Viola and (to a lesser extent, Giselle). Similarly, Gould's corruption is measured by the suffering of Emilia Gould. Both men prove unfaithful in the deepest sense, causing far more lasting pain to the women concerned than could any ordinary infidelity. Both Nostromo and Gould lose all sense of solidarity with other human beings, becoming indeed solitary, imprisoned, even "depersonalized" within their obsessions. Gould's tragedy goes deep in that he started with ideals, even altruistic intentions, and comes too late to a shattering awareness of his own corruption. Ironically both enjoy an enhanced reputation, but this is no compensation for their awareness of their corruption, total loss of self-esteem, and the accompanying loss of any capacity for a shared love. In *Nostromo,* Conrad shows no example of a shared love. But he gives us something even more interesting. In the unlikely person of Dr. Monygham, we see a man who possesses an "inexhaustible treasure" upon which he can live:

> Dr. Monygham had grown older, with his head steel-grey and the unchanged expression of his face, living on the inexhaustible treasure of his devotion drawn upon in the secret of his heart like a store of unlawful wealth. (504)

This offers a wonderful contrast to Nostromo, who draws secretly upon his illicit store of wealth, but cannot live on it (indeed dies for it). Further, the doctor is being truly sustained by his own active devotion to Emilia Gould; he needs not to be loved, simply to love. Having lost, years before, all sense of honour through his betrayal (under torture) of innocent people, the doctor regains true self-respect by courageously risking his life at the time of the silver riots. Here we come to see a positive interdependence between a man's personal sense of honour and his capacity for devotion to a person and to a principle (even when, as here, the principle may be in doubt). Conrad shows a sort of "virtuous circle" in Dr. Monygham: his faithful devotion to Mrs. Gould gives him the strength and courage to risk his life for her. In direct contrast to Gould and Nostromo, he never enjoys a good reputation but his full compensation consists in his regained self-esteem – together with that "priceless" and "illuminating" inner treasure, the selfless love, upon which he lives. The doctor's regained self-respect springs from his awareness of renewed solidarity in one of its vital aspects, in hard-won oneness with humanity's higher ideals.

Thus, Najder's quotation from Xenophon has been most illuminating. As shown above, Conrad consistently shows that a man's "thirst for gain" readily becomes obsessive, and must squeeze out all capacity for genuine sentiment, or concern for others – hence, there is loss of any true human solidarity.

Here we note that Najder calls attention to the gradual democratization of the ethos of honour, as it came to apply to a broad concept of "human dignity," applying to all classes, and often embodied in Conrad's "little" people. Captain Beard has "rectitude of soul" (a supreme Conradian accolade) and other positive qualities: he is a loving husband, a perceptive judge of men (employing the young Marlow), a captain who effortlessly maintains his authority under almost impossible conditions and pushes himself to the point of exhaustion in the struggle to save his first command. It is true, too, that his loyalty to the interests of his company is comical – yet it is genuine. We could make an almost endless list of "little" people who prove their virtue and moral stature throughout Conrad's fiction: Ransome, Singleton, Don Pépé, Father Roman, the boilermaker, young Powell, Tekla, the Fynes (though in a limited way). Within the compass of their larger or smaller roles all acquit themselves worthily. All possess a strong intuitive sense of human solidarity.

Apart from those already discussed, none of Conrad's major figures is disproportionately concerned with financial gain or the power resulting from wealth. For Jim, Razumov, Heyst, Jasper, together with the "sea" figures of *The Secret Sharer, The Shadow-Line, Typhoon* and *The Nigger of the "Narcissus,"* wealth is never a major concern. Marlow himself never expresses the slightest interest in material gain and, as narrator, is consistently sardonic about the pursuit of material interests, notably in *Heart of Darkness* and most of all *Chance*. In the latter, the City as the necessary setting for de Barral's financial activities and failure, together with the blatant "interests" of the governess, the East End cousins, and other "shore people" (though *not* the Fynes) typify the sordid "shore" life from which Flora de Barral must escape. The "sea" virtues attributed to Captain Anthony are exactly those which Conrad most values and, significantly, Anthony has not the slightest interest in material gain as such. Lingard is an interesting case. Of course, he has been and is an adventurer, in consistent pursuit of gain, and he becomes enviably rich (to people like Almayer and Willems). But, in none of the three novels in which he figures is his wealth of any overriding importance as a factor of moral issue. True, he makes his living through trading, and does well, but he is in no way obsessed. This is most obvious in *The Rescue* in which we see him as a young man. At the heart of the novel is "the point of Honour" *versus* "The point of Passion," as the title of part V puts it. Lingard is a man who prides himself on his reputation as a man of honour, which is fully deserved. It is the essence of his being. A passion quite different from a lust for gain, overmasters, for a time, this man and his judgement and, worse, dulls his moral sense and renders him literally forgetful of his moral obligations. Jörgenson, despairing, blows up the *Emma,* causing the death of Lingard's "heart's friends" and others. Lingard's hopes, plans, and all his own self-esteem are destroyed; realizing the depths of his betrayal of trust, he becomes "a prey for ever to infinite remorse and endless regrets" (*Res,* 398). Renouard is yet another central figure whose obsession and moral downfall have nothing to do with pursuit of material gain. Obsession with the worthless Felicia Moorsom leads him to practise a wilful deception. He finds that he cannot live with the consequent loss of his "rectitude." This, and not his disillusioned but continuing infatuation with the girl, is what makes his suicide inevitable. Renouard is an interesting case in another way. A confirmed solitary, he has never had any sense of solidarity with humankind – quite the contrary. Losing the illusion which alone sustains him, he simply has no identity, nothing to live for.

How far have we come? How far we traced those "few very simple ideas?" Najder's "ethos of honor" has been illuminating, but it does not take us all the way. Najder lists some of the qualities associated with the ethos: duty, solidarity, fidelity, courage; he stresses the rigour of the concept, by which all must be judged *and* judge themselves. However, the whole concept does not take in all the ideas which appear to have concerned Conrad deeply.

First, it does not explicitly include any full sense of solidarity, as conceived by Conrad. At its simplest, solidarity has perhaps long been acknowledged as a virtue in a team, an army, (latterly) an union, or any group which is pursuing fixed aims and must co-operate closely in carrying out specific tasks necessary to success. Conrad, of course, sees this as all-important in the context, say of a ship's crew. But in its full sense, Conrad extends it much further, as we see his reflections on the concept in the "Preface" to *The Nigger of the "Narcissus."*

The very details of the wording at the beginning of the "Preface" imply the writer's own adherence to a human solidarity which is all-inclusive, universal. Conrad, from the start, is with the rest of "us" even when considering the roles of the thinker and the scientist. These plunge into "ideas" and "facts" and, "emerging...make their appeal to those qualities of our being that fit us best for the hazardous enterprise of living." They address "our" interests, "our common sense...intelligence...desire of peace, or...of unrest...prejudices...fears...egoism" as they concern themselves with our minds, bodies, ambitions, and "our precious aims." Though "otherwise with the artist," he too appeals to *us* and to "that part of our being...which is a gift and not an acquisition – and, therefore, more permanently enduring." Then there is a wonderful broadening out, to include many basic qualities of humankind: "our capacity for delight and wonder...sense of mystery surrounding our lives...sense of pity and beauty, and pain." All these are *our* characteristics. Then the sense of solidarity swells into "the latent feeling of fellowship with all creation – and to the subtle but invincible conviction of solidarity that knits together the loneliness of innumerable hearts, to the solidarity in dreams, in joy, in sorrow, in aspirations, in illusions, in hope, in fear, which binds men to each other, which binds together all humanity – the dead to the living and the living to the unborn." For us, and for the writer, then: "for, if any part of truth dwells in the belief confessed above, it becomes evident that there is not a place of splendour or a dark corner of the earth that does not deserve, if only a passing glance of wonder and pity" (viii). This is a declaration of all-inclusive solidarity, beginning with the dedicated writer and "bind[ing]" or knitting individuals to one another and to "the visible world." Solidarity in this full sense is what Conrad's writing is about. In "A Familiar Preface" Conrad considers the "human," again broadly and inclusively: "The comic, when it is human, soon takes upon itself a face of pain; and some of our griefs (some only, not all, for it is the capacity for suffering which makes man august in the eyes of men) have their source in weaknesses which must be recognized with smiling compassion as the common inheritance of us all." Later, "the sight of human affairs deserves admiration and pity. They are worthy of respect, too."[6] So far we have noted numerous references to the concept of solidarity, sometimes in a positive sense, sometimes in terms of a "sin" against it. If the latter, these are clearly linked to other Conradian failings which are likely to lead to grave disregard or outright rejection of solidarity with others whether those close to an individual, or to humankind more broadly.

This leads to further consideration of other Conradian ideas not specifically covered by "the ethos of honor." It does not embrace specifically what we might call the softer virtues: love, compassion, imaginative insight (intuition), all that can be defined as truly "human" in relationships – although we have clearly seen an implied connection between obsession with material gain and loss of concern for others. Nor does it extend to other characteristically Conradian preoccupations: lack of imagination (Amy Foster, Captain MacWhirr, in very different ways); too much imagination (Almayer, Jim, Falk, *et al.*); a tendency to try to live by illusions (Almayer, Renouard, Freya and Jasper, most characters in *Nostromo* except Decoud, whose own illusion is that he has none); self-delusion (closely related to previous point, and epitomized in "old Nelson, or Nielsen" whose wilful blindness and total selfishness are shown to be totally destructive).

Nor does it deal directly with sheer malevolence, sadism, cruel manipulation or exploitation – that is, evil which is external to an individual's inner conflicts. And finally, it takes no account of the supreme indifference of the universe in which man must confront the "poignant problem of conduct on this earth" or "how to be." It is that "knitting-machine" of the famous letter to Cunninghame Graham in which there are no divine or other supernatural sanctions to intervene or guide us.[7] Conrad does not seek to escape its bleakness by embracing any form of nihilism. Instead his fiction is pervaded with a rigorous moral imperative, so rigorous as to recall the rigour of the ethos of honour but also to lead towards a more determined pursuit of others of the "few very simple ideas."

Here it seems relevant to cite a comment from Bertrand Russell:

> What interested [Conrad] was the individual human soul faced with the indifference of nature, and often with the hostility of men, and subject to inner struggles with passions both good and bad that lead towards destruction.[8]

Many of Conrad's "heroes" do have to confront the indifference of nature, and the hostility of men, and most are indeed "subject to inner struggles with passions both good and bad that led towards destruction." This may well recall Conrad's comment in his "Author's Note" to *Nostromo* that "events" in that great novel "flow[ed] from the passions of men short-sighted in good and evil" (xvii). Conrad's "interest" in humanity's "struggles," with internal and external forces seems to have acted as an effectual antidote to his losing himself in nihilism. The "destruction" Russell refers to may or may not involve physical destruction, but is more likely to be most poignant when it is moral destruction (Gould, Nostromo, Razumov); or perhaps most poignant of all may be the inner conflict which we endure along with the characters themselves, as, above especially, in the case of Captain Whalley.

Captain Whalley is an excellent example of many aspects of Russell's statement. His growing blindness brings him face to face with the indifferent forces of nature within himself. More profoundly he is confronted with the total "cosmic indifference" of a universe where, despite the most earnest prayers to, and belief in Providence, all prayers remain unanswered and Whalley comes to feel that he has been abandoned by his God. In the sheer inhumanity of Massy he has to face an almost superhuman malevolence, for Massy is endowed with qualities which are specifically satanic:

> A temper naturally irritable and an amazing sensitiveness to the claims of his own personality had ended by making of life for him a sort of inferno – a place where his lost soul had been given up to the torment of savage brooding. (*YS*, 269)

To his "blunt brain" all his difficulties seem to have been caused by "the malevolence of men." Yet, he is malevolence itself.

Captain Whalley, trusting, naive in his belief in God and man, honourable, loving and generous as husband and father, is Massy's exact opposite. The contrast is developed in detail, with Massy as the embodied negation of every Conradian virtue. Within Whalley, the rigorous ethos of honour comes into direct conflict with the softer virtue of paternal love and care. In Whalley's heart, the latter ultimately triumphs. Yet after concluding his deal with Massy, Whalley's conscience has been uneasy. He consoles himself with only one thought:

> [In case of anything Ivy will receive] all of his money. *Integrally*. Every penny. He was not to lose any of her money, *whatever else had to go – a little dignity – some of his self-respect*. (214) My emphasis.

Conrad himself, in a letter to David S. Meldrum (in the early autumn of 1902), referred to Whalley's earlier failure to be open with Eliott, adding: "A character like Whalley's cannot cease to be frank with impunity."[9] Indeed he cannot. He cannot escape his own severe self-judgement. Nor can he escape his terrible "punishment," although this comes about through the apparent indifference of the heavens (which seem to be rather empty than vengeful) and the actions of Massy as an external malignant force, rather than through any more direct "judgement."

The other work in which Conrad is supremely concerned with
the indifference of the universe is *Chance*. I shall not repeat here
material which I have elsewhere developed in detail,[10] but return
briefly to it (before I conclude by considering Conrad's own
compassion, imagination, intuition, and related qualities). The
novel is based on a sustained antithesis: land values *versus* sea
values. "Shore people," whether financially motivated malevolent, or well-meaning but limited, can do little to help Flora de
Barral, but drive her to despair, misery and, almost, to death.
Her own father, released from prison, becomes a figure of evil
and death in her life, a force which, as it were, invades the
Ferndale, where Captain Anthony has brought her in an attempt
to rescue her from the horrors of her shore existence. Anthony
can do so only through those cherished Conradian qualities
which he is made to embody. They are the "sea" values of fidelity
to duty, fine seamanship, courage, rectitude, but go further, to
include compassion, and both the passion and the tenderness of
love. Indeed within the novel's tight metaphorical structure,
Anthony comes to represent a large generous active concern for
humanity's suffering, as embodied in the frail figure of Flora.
His sense of solidarity becomes immense. Anthony's "amazing
and startling dream [is to] take the world in his arms – all the
suffering world – not to possess its pathetic fairness but to
console and cherish its sorrow" (347). At the end of the book
Marlow listens "amazed and touched" as Flora recounts her:

> finest adventure in the world. I loved and I was loved...All the world, all
> life were transformed...How good people were...Roderick was so
> much liked everywhere...[knowing] kindness and safety, [she saw] the
> most familiar things...lighted up with a new light, clothed with
> a loveliness I had never suspected. The sea itself...do you know how
> strong, how charming, how friendly, how mighty...(404)

Anthony's qualities enable him to give to Flora a life relieved of
suffering and brightened with real happiness – but only for
a time. In *Chance* where Conrad is deeply concerned with "the
simple but poignant problem of conduct on this earth,"

compassion and love are essential to this partial solution
– partial because of the indifference of the universe.

Razumov is a very special case. Through the pressures of the
bleak and lonely circumstances of his personal life he has become
in effect a solitary – not misanthropic, not inherently selfish,
simply forced to rely upon his own efforts to gain a real sense of
identity and a purpose in life. Haldin bursts into his life
demanding the precise sort of solidarity which Razumov seems
uniquely unfitted to accept or offer. Instead the demand shocks
the young man of reason into anger, hatred, a despairing and
abiding resentment which extends almost to real misanthropy.
Ultimately, and wholly against his conscious will, his love for
Natalia grows so as to effect a total change of outlook. It leads him
into a kind of solidarity such as he has never felt, not a political
solidarity, but a solidarity so strong as to make him realize that in
betraying a fellow human being he has betrayed himself.

It is now the role of Marlow as a figure of concern, intuition,
and continuing interpretation which I wish to consider. This will,
I believe, take us very near to Conrad himself, his ideas, and even
to his whole aim in writing. I start with the wonderful "scene" in
Chance in which Marlow is interpreting (for his imagined
auditor) the nature of Flora de Barral's experience when the
governess first asks "violently" whether

> she imagined that there was anything in her, apart from her money to
> induce any intelligent person to take any sort of an interest in
> her,...[and then tells her] viciously [that] she was, in heart, mind,
> manner and appearance, an utterly common and insipid person. (109)

Marlow has already surmized that Flora has recovered from this
only because "luckily,...people...are for the most part quite
incapable of understanding what is happening to them." This, he
sees as "a provision of nature." At this point, the listener "struck
in" sarcastically to ask whether

> [our] inestimable advantage of understanding what is happening to
> others is also a provision of nature...And what is it for?...that we may
> amuse ourselves gossiping about each other's affairs? You, for instance,
> seem...

Marlow ignores the jibe, continuing

> from the same provision of understanding there springs in us compas-
> sion, charity, indignation, the sense of solidarity, and in minds of any
> largeness an inclination to that indulgence which is next to affection.
> (107)

This closely resembles Marlow's consistent approach to Flora's
life-death problems in *Chance*. Here we see an especially good
example of one way in which Conrad involves the reader in
Marlow's developing argument as he interprets the situation.
His listener's challenge is made directly to Marlow within the
narrative, but extends right to Conrad himself (Why write
literature?) and to his readers (Why read literature?). It leads into
the subsequent wonderful Conradian statement about, I take it,
his whole aim in writing with, again, much stress on solidarity in
the truest sense.

Except in *Youth,* it is always *understanding* which Marlow
seeks and (to the extent which understanding comes) interprets.
Understanding is a complex concept. Marlow achieves it only
gradually through a painstaking process. It comes as the
culmination of attempts to *see* truly, and its perhaps unlikely
starting-point is simple, human curiosity – but a curiosity far
removed from any negative act of prying into the affairs of
others. *Chance* gives to it an essential role as an awakening of
interest, a first necessary movement towards actual concern and
towards that active compassion which Marlow mentions. Conrad calls de Barral "incurious," and this is symptomatic of his
inward-looking, ultimately destructive nature. His lack of real
interest in his daughter's past suffering or present feelings is
heart-breaking to the girl. Fellow-qualities, such as a lack of
intuition, lack of insight, seem to accompany *in*curiosity.
Primarily, it springs from lack of imagination, for, without that,
one can never see into another person or an unfamiliar situation.
Imagination, intuition and growing insight combine in Marlow,
as narrator, supremely in *Chance* where he is far from being the
garrulous, misogynistic bore of critical mythology.

Of course, Conrad regularly employs Marlow-like figures in

similar roles, notably Dr. Kennedy in *Amy Foster,* d'Alcacer in *The Rescue,* the narrators of *Falk, Freya of the Seven Isles, Karain,* and others, who see (to a greater or lesser extent) more of what is happening than those involved in their own story, interpreting (to a greater or lesser extent) for the auditor/reader. By contrast, in *Under Western Eyes,* the teacher of languages is shown to have, so little imagination or insight that the reader has the unusual and rather pleasurable experience of appreciating more of what is going on than the obtuse narrator.

Overall, this device of a narrator who sees, imagines, exercises his gift of intuition, and may gradually interpret what is happening, is very satisfying. The process of his seeing and understanding is itself fascinating; the final understanding may be incomplete, *or* total and convincing, but it always imparts some of that "compassion, charity, indignation, the sense of solidarity...[and even] an inclination to that indulgence which is akin to affection" (*Chance,* 107). All these qualities *are* of course, Conrad's. He endows his narrators with that curiosity, imagination, intuition, compassion, and understanding which truly "make [us] see." However detached the writer may seem to be from his narrators, all the great insights, all the great values spring from his ideas, those cherished ideas upon which the temporal world rests. They doubtless resemble closely those "working truths on this earth," to which he refers elsewhere.[11]

To Conrad, the writer's connection to his work is so close that, when he is writing about things, inclinations, people, the writer "is only writing about himself."[12] The insights and ideas of Conrad's narrators are part of Conrad and he specifically rejects a role detached from life or from his artistic creation:

> I would not like to be left standing as a mere spectator on the bank of the great stream carrying onward so many lives. I would fain claim for myself the faculty of so much insight as can be expressed in a voice of sympathy and compassion.[13]

Here in the deepest sense Conrad expresses his profound sense of solidarity with humankind. It is his reason for writing, to express that solidarity and to extend it by sharing his myriad insights with the rest of *us*. Clearly, he wishes to be, and is, deeply involved. His aims are high. Among them, the search for "truth" recurs throughout the "Preface" to *The Nigger of the "Narcissus."* In "A Familiar Preface" he senses that the danger for the writer is a loss of "the exact notion of sincerity...[of his] coming to despise truth itself as something too cold...not good enough for his insistent emotion," and thus descending from "laughter and tears...to snivelling and giggles." Wishing to "reach the very fount of laughter and tears," he writes firmly that "A historian of hearts is not an historian of emotion, yet he penetrates further" (xviii-xix).

And what of the reader in all this? What *will* he come to "know" of Conrad's ideas? If Conrad succeeds in "mak[ing] you see," "you shall find there according to your deserts: encouragement, consolation, fear, charm – all you demand – and, perhaps, also that glimpse of truth for which you have forgotten to ask" ("Preface," *NN*, x).

He also speaks of the necessity for the artist's "complete, unswerving devotion to the perfect blending of form and substance," and seems to mean much the same thing when he stresses the vital importance of "the manner:"

> The manner in laughter, in tears, in irony, in indignations, and enthusiasms, in judgments – and even in love; the manner in which, as in the features and character of a human face the inner truth is foreshadowed for those who know how to look at their kind.[14]

For "those who know how to look at their kind" – supremely for Conrad himself, for his penetrating narrators, and for his readers "according to [our] deserts." We can, if we will, see and share many of Conrad's "few very simple ideas."

We shall then conclude, I think, that it is Conrad's developed insights into the complexities and contradictions of humankind which prevent him (as a man or, supremely, as a writer) from foundering in cynicism, pessimism, or nihilism – insights together, of course, with that "voice of compassion" in which he consistently expresses them.

NOTES

1. "A Familiar Preface," *PR*, p. xix.

2. *Ibid.*, p. xvi.

3. Z. Najder, "Conrad and the Idea of Honor," in *Joseph Conrad: Theory and World Fiction*, ed. W. T. Żyła and W. M. Aycock (Lubbock: Texas Tech University, 1974), pp. 103-14.

4. Najder quotes from Xenophon, *Works*, trans. H. G. Dakyns, (London: 1897).

5. See also J. McLauchlan, "Almayer and Willems: – 'How Not to Be'," *Conradiana*, 11: 2 (1979), pp. 113-41.

6. "A Familiar Preface," *PR*, pp. xvi, xix.

7. *CL*, 1, p. 425.

8. B. Russell, *Autobiography, 1914-1944* (London: Allen Unwin, 1967), p. 208.

9. *CL*, 2, p. 441.

10. See J. McLauchlan, "Cosmic Indifference and Human Concern," *L'Epoque Conradienne* (1978).

11. "A Familiar Preface," *PR*, p. xii.

12. *Ibid.*, p. xiii.

13. *Ibid.*, p. xv.

14. *Ibid.*, p. xix.

John Lester,
Havering College of Further and Higher Education,
Hornchurch, England

Conrad and Music

The impact of one art upon another is always an interesting phenomenon, especially when the first is created essentially to be performed and heard whilst the other is written to be read. Music and literature engage two different senses yet each has served as an inspiration to the other. The dramatized word combines with music in opera, but for music to meet literature within the pages of a book is a less obvious liaison in an unpromising rendezvous. Does the master of words automatically appreciate the master of notes? Though Conrad's main objective was to make us *see,* he was also concerned with making us hear.

Music and Conrad are not often closely connected, as the mere handful of essays on the subject testifies. Despite describing it as the "art of arts" in his "Preface" to *The Nigger of the "Narcissus"* (*NN,* xiii), the role of music in Conrad's correspondence is a minor one. Few composers are named. There are two passing references to Wagner and one appreciative mention of Meyerbeer of whom Conrad writes, "I suppose that I am now the only human being in these Isles who thinks Meyerbeer a great composer: and I am an alien at that and not to be wholly trusted."[1] Giacomo (or Jakob) Meyerbeer, a German composer, was an important figure in French opera from 1831 till his death in 1864; Wagner, of course, was also a composer of operas. Otherwise there is a brief mention of Ravel but only because Conrad met him once or twice, confessing that "We got rather thick together last time he was here."[2] There is nothing about his music, though.

This scanty information at least suggests an interest in opera, and Conrad seems to confirm this when writing to Sir Hugh Clifford about the latter's *Downfall of the Gods*:

247

What a tremendous subject for a great, a really great opera! And pray
don't think it mean praise. No great poem for music has been written
yet; subjects of course are lying about. What I mean to say is that here is
a subject, the subject of *the* Great Oriental Opera, worked out.
Absolutely done! The simplicity of the highly dramatic action, the
picturesquely imposing background, the irresistible blind movements
of the crowd and the tragic fatality of the *passion charnelle* – all is there
to inspire some musician of the future, great enough to express the very
spirit of the East in the music of the West. I never thought that the day
would come on which I would wish I had been born a great composer.
Then indeed we would have collaborated – to be abused of course by
every yapping musical critic on the press, but with the certitude of
leaving behind us a magnificent achievement.[3]

The comment "I never thought that the day would come on
which I would wish I had been born a great composer" is
significant here, since it hints that Conrad had no profound
interest in music as music (opera, of course, has a significant
literary element). When, during his thoughts on *The Titanic
Inquiry,* he is critical of one of the officials, likening him to
Pooh-Bah and referring to "a felicitous opera-bouffe of the
Gilbertian type" (*NLL,* 239), it is the librettist (Gilbert) he
mentions, not the composer (Sullivan). That he did occasionally
attend concerts is made clear by a letter to Garnett, but that the
motivation was more social than musical is also apparent since
he writes, "I shall turn up on Tuesday at the concert. There is
nothing I desire more than to be made known to Mrs. Garnett"[4].
John Conrad reports that there was a piano at the Conrad home
and that guests of musical talent (including Paderewski) were
invited to play it.[5] Whether the host himself played is not
mentioned.

Most of Conrad's references to music, then, are operatic.
After finishing *Almayer's Folly,* for instance, he wrote to
Marguerite Poradowska:

I shall soon send you the last chapter. It begins with a *trio* – Nina, Dain,
Almayer – and it ends with a long *solo* for Almayer which is almost as
long as the solo in Wagner's *Tristan.* Enough! You will see! – but I very
much fear that you will find the thing mawkish.[6]

Opera also attended the conclusion of *An Outcast of the Islands*:

> It is my painful duty to inform you of the death of Mr Peter Willems late
> of Rotterdam and Macassar who has been murdered on the 16th inst at
> 4 p. m. while the sun shone joyously and the barrel organ sang on the
> pavement the abominable Intermezzo of the ghastly Cavalleria.[7]

(*Cavalleria Rusticana* by Mascagni, first performed in 1890, is
the work referred to.)

It is opera that so impresses Lingard in *The Rescue,* the "story
acted to music" that he sees seeming to him to be "More real
than anything in life" (300–1). This, at least, is positive, even
though it reflects the Rajah Laut's fading grip on a reality that
will prove all too grim by the finale. Indeed Jeffrey Meyers,
following the Meyerbeer lead, suggests strong influences from
opera on the plot of the novel.[8]

There is a brief operatic interlude in *Almayer's Folly*:

> Babalatchi stretched himself yawning, but Lakamba, in the flattering
> consciousness of a knotty problem solved by his own unaided
> intellectual efforts, grew suddenly very wakeful.
>
> "Babalatchi," he said to the exhausted statesman, "fetch the box of
> music the white captain gave me. I cannot sleep." .
>
> At this order a deep shade of melancholy settled upon Babalatchi's
> features. He went reluctantly behind the curtain and soon re-appeared
> carrying in his arms a small hand-organ, which he put down on the table
> with an air of deep dejection. Lakamba settled himself comfortably in
> his armchair.
>
> "Turn, Babalatchi, turn," he murmured, with closed eyes.
>
> Babalatchi's hand grasped the handle with the energy of despair, and
> as he turned, the deep gloom on his countenance changed into an
> expression of hopeless resignation. Through the open shutter the notes
> of Verdi's music floated out on the great silence over the river and
> forest. Lakamba listened with closed eyes and a delighted smile;
> Babalatchi turned, at times dozing off and swaying over, then catching
> himself up in a great fright with a few quick turns of the handle. Nature
> slept in an exhausted repose after the fierce turmoil, while under the
> unsteady hand of the statesman of Sambir the Trovatore fitfully wept,
> wailed, and bade good-bye to his Leonore again and again in
> a mournful round of tearful and endless iteration. (*AF,* 88-9)

The pair have just been plotting Almayer's murder and, though Lakamba seems content, the description inclines us to Babalatchi's view that what is going on is a monotonous dirge. The music is produced mechanically (like the *Cavalleria* Conrad complained of) and the overall effect (Lakamba's delight notwithstanding) is negative.

The role of music is generally negative in Conrad's work in fact, though, ironically, it is positive *in absentia* in *The Nigger of the "Narcissus"* where Archie's concertina, which usually accompanies the songs (and helps the morale) of the crew, is stilled by the influence of the dying James Wait (36). When sweet and melodious music is present (as in *Il Conde*) it accompanies a mugging. In *A Personal Record* the author has little time for the banjoist who interrupts the progress of *Almayer's Folly*:

> When he did not play the banjo he loved to sit and look at it. He proceeded to this sentimental inspection, and after meditating a while over the strings under my silent scrutiny, inquired airily:
> "What are you always scribbling there, if it's fair to ask?"
> It was a fair enough question, but I did not answer him, and simply turned the pad over with a movement of instinctive secrecy. I could not have told him he had put to flight the psychology of Nina Almayer, her opening speech of the tenth chapter and the words of Mrs. Almayer's wisdom which were to follow in the ominous oncoming of a tropical night. I could not have told him that Nina had said: "It has set at last." He would have been extremely surprised and perhaps have dropped his precious banjo. (*PR*, 4)

Music here, then, is regarded as an intrusion into Conrad's own art, though, while the musician "lowered a tender gaze on his banjo," it enables the writer to recall that, being beside a quay in Rouen, he is near the café "where the worthy Bovary and his wife...had some refreshment after the memorable performance of an opera which was the tragic story of Lucia di Lammermoor in a setting of light music" (5). This, though, is primarily a literary reference (to Flaubert) rather than a musical one to Donizetti.

Lucia di Lammermoor is also mentioned by the Costaguanan official Charles Gould has to deal with in *Nostromo,* who, by attributing the work to "the divine – ha! – Mozart," thus displays his false pretensions to Western culture (as Jeffrey Meyers points out).[9] Since the military band he is listening to is "braying operatic selections," the quality is far from being "Exquisite, delicious" as the devious official maintains (*N*, 90). He is thus wrong about the composer and the quality and (for all we know) about the work as well (since his comments elicit no response).

The earlier mention of mechanical music reminds us immediately of *The Secret Agent* and the meetings of Comrade Ossipon and the Professor at the Silenus Restaurant, where the wonders of science (a prime target in the novel) provide "an upright semi-grand piano near the door," which "flanked by two palms in pots, executed suddenly all by itself a valse tune with aggressive virtuosity. The din it raised was deafening" (*SA*, 61). This piano is impertinent and dominant (just like science), producing not music but a "din" that interrupts (and thus takes precedence over) human communication – in this case question (Ossipon) and answer (Professor). Its mechanical jauntiness, exhibited on each of is appearances, is out of keeping with the tone and the subjects of the discussions it intrudes on, showing perhaps the indifference of science to things human. Here, for instance, is its next outbreak of activity, cued by the Professor's assessment of the damage one of his bombs would do in the establishment:

> The piano at the foot of the staircase clanged through a mazurka with brazen impetuosity, as though a vulgar and impudent ghost were showing off. The keys sank and rose mysteriously. Then all became still. (67)

This preludes the horrific images of death and mutilation conjured up in Ossipon's mind as a reaction to the other's statement. (The composer of the mazurka, by the way, is not mentioned but could be Chopin – probably the only composer of mazurkas known to mechanical piano manufacturers in England – about whom Conrad is surprisingly reticent.) The music comes nearer home when Ossipon ponders the Professor's

advice to fasten himself upon Mrs. Verloc (it being assumed that
Verloc is dead):

> The lonely piano, without as much as a music stool to help it, struck
> a few chords courageously, and beginning a selection of national airs,
> played him out at last to the tune of "The Blue Bells of Scotland." The
> painfully detached notes grew faint behind his back while he went
> slowly upstairs, across the hall, and into the street. (79)

Now there is pain connected with the sound. At the end, when
Ossipon is guiltily obsessed by Winnie Verloc's suicide, "The
mechanical piano near the door played through a valse cheekily,
then fell silent at once, as if gone grumpy" (310). That the piano
is personified (exhibiting a gamut of emotions from impetuousi-
ty, cheek and courage to loneliness and grumpiness) indicates the
paucity of other human feelings present, particularly in the
ruthless fanatical Professor and his indifference to the tragedy
that has engulfed Winnie. Despite its personification, however,
the piano is still mechanical, incapable of putting feeling and
soul into its music, condemned to repeat identical performances
of its limited repertoire.

Mechanical music (music subjected to science) acts as an
encroachment rather than an accompaniment to human life but
(also in *The Secret Agent*) the human composer at the house of
Michaelis's lady patroness is not seen in the best of lights under
the shrewd eyes of the Assistant Commissioner. That high
official "saw his wife in a small group by the piano. A youngish
composer in pass of becoming famous was discoursing from
a music stool to two thick men whose backs looked old, and
three slender women whose backs looked young" (222). The
feeling here is that the "youngish composer" thinks rather a lot
of himself since he is "discoursing" to an audience (of no
individuality), though at least this piano won't play without him.

There is a piano, too, in the Intended's drawing room in *Heart
of Darkness,* standing "massively in a corner; with dark gleams
on the flat surfaces like a sombre and polished sarcophagus"
(*YS,* 156) – music linked with death. In *Falk,* meantime, the
unfortunate Miss Vanlo, confronted by the solid presence of the

silent Scandinavian, "couldn't tell for the life of her what to do with such a man, so she would keep on playing the piano and singing to him evening after evening till she was ready to drop" (*TS*, 179). Music becomes here a desperate means of filling time, of entertaining, though the fact that "poor Miss Vanlo could only sing sentimental songs to the strumming of a piano" (207) – note the "strumming" – suggests that she is not an accomplished performer, just a desperate one.

A more talented and enthusiastic pianist is Freya in *Freya of the Seven Isles*. For Freya the piano is a means of proclaiming her passion for Jasper Allen, a defence against the unwelcome attentions of Heemskirk and a weapon to drive the Lieutenant on his way when, in confusion, he takes his hasty leave. The important role of the piano in the story is indicated early on by the account of its arrival and its description as a "beautiful rosewood monster...certainly the heaviest movable object on that islet since the creation of the world:"

> The volume of sound it gave out in that bungalow (which acted as a sounding-board) was really astonishing. It thundered sweetly right over the sea. Jasper Allen told me that early of a morning on the deck of the *Bonito* (his wonderfully fast and pretty brig) he could hear Freya playing her scales quite distinctly. (*TLS*, 151)

In stormy weather, however:

> Freya would sit down to the piano and play fierce Wagner music in the flicker of blinding flashes, with thunderbolts falling all round, enough to make your hair stand on end; and Jasper would remain stock still on the verandah, adoring the back view of her supple, swaying figure, the miraculous sheen of her fair head, the rapid hands on the keys, the white nape of her neck – while the brig, down at the point there, swayed at her cables within a hundred yards of nasty, shiny, black rock-heads. Ugh! (152)

The narrator's concern at the recklessness of this passion expressed by piano, is prophetic, of course. He has already commented that Freya's "upright grand" nearly wrecked one of his boats while it was being brought ashore (an incident not calculated to endear it to a seaman) and here he repeats the association of the piano with shipwreck. For Freya it acts as an extended voice, an outlet for proclaiming her emotions. When the lecherous Heemskirk begins to make his unwelcome advances, she uses the instrument as a musical barricade:

> And when Heemskirk, still without looking at her, began resolutely to crush his half-smoked cheroot on the coffee-tray, she took alarm, glided towards the piano, opened it in tremendous haste, and struck the keys before she sat down.
>
> In an instant the verandah, the whole carpetless wooden bungalow, raised on piles, became filled with an uproarious, confused resonance. But through it all she heard, she felt on the floor the heavy prowling footsteps of the lieutenant moving to and fro at her back.... Freya, aware that he had stopped just behind her, went on playing without turning her head. She played with spirit, brilliantly, a fierce piece of music, but when his voice reached her she went cold all over. (194)

In the end, though, it takes a slap to deter Heemskirk. The sudden ceasing of the music causes her father, old Nelson, to rush in "quite excited" and say, "Only this minute you were playing a tune and...." But Freya is never simply "playing a tune" (the comment simply shows Nelson's lack of awareness). When Heemskirk leaves, trying to sneak away in the early morning, she puts him to full and undignified flight:

> She frowned, discovered it, dashed at the piano, which had stood open all night, and made the rosewood monster growl savagely in an irritated bass. She struck chords as if firing shots after that straddling, broad figure in ample white trousers and a dark uniform jacket with gold shoulder-straps, and then she pursued him with the same thing she had played the evening before – a modern, fierce piece of love music which had been tried more than once against the thunderstorms of the group. She accentuated its rhythm with triumphant malice. (205-6)

In quick succession, then, the piano becomes a savage beast and a firearm. Whether the "modern, fierce piece of music" is one of the Wagner works that she knows is not clear (he died in 1883) – it may depend on how modern is "modern." That, though, is by the way; the important point is the impact that this and subsequent piano music has on Heemskirk:

Then a piano began to play near by, very plainly, and he put his fingers to his ears with no better effect. It was not to be borne – not in solitude. He bolted out of the chartroom, and talked of indifferent things somewhat wildly with the officer of the watch on the bridge, to the mocking accompaniment of a ghostly piano. (209)

Music, then, incites Heemskirk's own act of triumphant malice – his deliberate wrecking of Jasper's boat – and to its melancholy aftermath. Music and shipwreck, linked earlier (prophetically), are linked again.

If the piano has an unfortunate career in Conrad's fiction, the strings fare little better. In *The Shadow-Line* the crazed previous captain, "shut up in his cabin and wedged in a corner of his settee against the crazy bounding of the ship, played the violin – or, at any rate, made continuous noise on it" (*TSL*, 60). As his health fades, the sound diminishes accordingly to become "only a feeble scratching." His final act is to throw the instrument overboard (60). The violin thus records madness, fading physical health and, on its departure, the prefiguring of death. The song is over, so to speak, but the malady lingers on – in the fever that strikes at the crew – and there are echoes in the story of *The Flying Dutchman* (another Wagner opera).

We have yet to find any soothing music and are unlikely to discover any in *Victory*, despite Schomberg's claim that "a little good music" is available at his table d'hôte through the ladies' orchestra of Zangiacomo (*V*, 49, 67). Here are violins in force:

The lamentations of string instruments issued from the building in the hotel compound...Scraps of tunes more or less plaintive reached his ears. They pursued him even into his bedroom, which opened into an upstairs verandah. The fragmentary and rasping character of these sounds made their intrusion inexpressibly tedious in the long run. Like most dreamers, to whom it is given sometimes to hear the music of the spheres, Heyst...had a taste for silence...(66)

One needs, however, to be present to gain the full effect:

The uproar in that small, barn-like structure...was simply stunning. An instrumental uproar, screaming, grunting, whining, sobbing, scraping,

squeaking some kind of lively air; while a grand piano, operated upon
by a bony, red-faced woman with bad-tempered nostrils, rained hard
notes like hail through the tempest of fiddles. The small platform was
filled with white muslin dresses and crimson sashes slanting from
shoulders provided with bare arms, which sawed away without respite.
Zangiacomo conducted. ...Heyst, quite overcome by the volume of
noise, dropped into a chair. In the quick time of that music, in the
varied, piercing clamour of the strings, in the movements of the bare
arms, in the low dresses, the coarse faces, the stony eyes of the
executants, there was a suggestion of brutality – something cruel,
sensual, and repulsive.
"This is awful!" Heyst murmured to himself. (68)

Conrad claims, in his 1920 "Author's Note," that this
orchestra was based on a smaller one that played "strident
music" in a South of France café (XV). "The Zangiacomo
band," however, "was not making music; it was simply mur-
dering silence with a vulgar, ferocious energy" (68). After the
interval, during which Heyst first makes contact with Lena, the
entertainment resumes:

Heyst winced in anticipation of the horrible racket. It burst out
immediately unabashed and awful. At the end of the platform the
woman at the piano, presenting her cruel profile, her head tilted back,
banged the keys without looking at the music.
    Heyst could not stand the uproar for more than a minute. He went
out, his brain racked by the rhythm of some more or less Hungarian
dance music. (81-2)

Why Hungarian? Is this choice arbitrary or deliberate? Are
there any potential composers (Liszt, for instance)? Could
Conrad's ear distinguish between different European musical
characteristics? Was Hungarian dance music in vogue when
Conrad was in Marseilles – in that French café, for example?
    Whether this is a detail worthy of attention, or merely a detail,
music appears here as an instrument of violence. The imagery
moves from a creature in pain to a storm to simple aural assault;
the women are initially described by their uniform clothing and
active arms – there is no sense of humanity being attached. The
injunction to mingle with the clientele suggests that the music is

(or could be) a cloak for more immoral entertainment; significantly Lena, the only one pretty enough to be propositioned,
is reluctant to engage in any extra-musical activities.

The music itself is described here as a violent act; in *Nostromo*
there are reminders that music is used to inspire and accompany
violence. It is a military band that "plays sometimes in the
evenings between the revolutions" (*N,* 11); the spot where it
plays is the place where Ribiera's mule expires and exacerbates
an already critical situation. The band also plays the Sulaco
garrison off to war but it is Decoud who directly connects music
and violence:

> But to return to my noises; there used to be in the old days the sound of
> trumpets outside that gate. War trumpets! I'm sure they were trumpets.
> I have read somewhere that Drake who was the greatest of these men,
> used to dine alone in his cabin on board ship to the sound of trumpets.
> (174)

Music (religious music at that) is made to condone violence,
moreover, when the infamous dictator, Guzman Bento, commands "the celebration of a solemn Mass of thanksgiving...sung
in great pomp in the cathedral of Sta. Marta" (139), and a more
fundamental form of church music (church bells) welcomes the
equally bloodthirsty Monteros to Sulaco (381).

There is, however, another musical background to the events
of *Nostromo*; most evident during the earlier, more official visit
of President Ribiera:

> and away to the left, from where the crowd was massed thickly about
> a huge temporary erection, like a circus tent of wood with a conical
> grass roof, came the resonant twanging of harp strings, the sharp ping
> of guitars, with the grave drumming throb of an Indian gombo
> pulsating steadily through the shrill choruses of the dancers. (123)

Here is the music of the ordinary people (in contrast to the
military band); music to dance by – a far more pleasant and
natural accompaniment, even (it later appears) during hos-
tilities:

In the patio littered with straw, a practicante, one of Dr. Monygham's native assistants, sat on the ground with his back against the rim of the fountain, fingering a guitar discreetly, while two girls of the lower class, standing up before him, shuffled their feet a little and waved their arms, humming a popular dance tune. Most of the wounded during the two days of rioting had been taken away already by their friends and relations, but several figures could be seen sitting up balancing their bandaged heads in time to the music. (363-4)

Music plays a defiant role here – a positive force in the midst of suffering, still capable of rallying the people, or at least distracting some of them momentarily from their current woes. Whatever the political situation in Sulaco, the guitars are still heard (the gallant secret messenger, Bonifacio, carries one on his back [94]), and it may be significant that the *practicante* tries to "conceal his guitar hastily" at the sight of Charles Gould, suspecting, perhaps, that devotion to the San Tomé silver mine leaves no room for music. The furtive action certainly suggests that, if Gould is thought to disapprove of the simple scene, he has not accepted the culture and customs of the country in which he was born – he remains an outsider.

In *Nostromo* there is the "tinkling" and the "strumming" of guitars whilst, in *Karain*, "Jackson jingled an old guitar and sang, with an execrable accent, Spanish love songs" (*TU*, 20), and "twanged the guitar and gasped out in sighs a mournful dirge about hopeless love and eyes like stars" (21). This does not sound melodious and seems to anticipate the doleful tale of Karain, upon whose arrival the "jingling vibration" is suddenly (and perhaps mercifully) halted – an echo, perhaps of the banjoist in *A Personal Record* (see above). For "excellent music" one must accompany Il Conde "after dinner to listen to the band in the public garden, the Villa Nazionale:"

This magic spot, behind the black trunks of trees and masses of inky foliage, breathed out sweet sounds mingled with bursts of brassy roar, sudden clashes of metal, and grave vibrating thuds.

As he walked on, all these noises combined together into a piece of elaborate music whose harmonious phrases came persuasively through a great disordely murmur of voices and shuffling of feet on the gravel of that open space. An enormous crowd immersed in the electric light, as if in a bath of some radiant and tenuous fluid shed upon their heads by luminous globes, drifted in its hundreds round the band. Hundreds more sat on chairs in more or less concentric circles, receiving unflinchingly the great waves of sonority that ebbed out into the darkness. The Count penetrated the throng, drifted with it in tranquil enjoyment, listening and looking at the faces. (SS, 277)

The music is once more attended by violence, however, for as the Count moves away from the crowd, he is held up at knife-point:

"The clarionet," he declared solemnly, "was finishing his solo, and I assure you I could hear every note. Then the band crashed *fortissimo* and that creature rolled its eyes and gnashed its teeth hissing at me with the greatest ferocity, "Be silent! No noise or–" (280)

The whole sinister drama takes place to the sound of music. The assailant's savage manner accompanies "a slow movement of solemn braying by all the trombones, with deliberately repeated bangs of the big drum" and the actual robbery is performed "to the sweet thrilling of flutes and clarionets sustained by the emotional drone of the hautboys..." (282). "Great waves of harmony" are "flowing from the band" as the Count prepares for death rather than to hand over his ring. Instead he finds (on opening his eyes) the robber gone and the band "executing, with immense bravura, the complicated finale. It ended with a tremendous crash" (283-4).

Sweet music, then, but with a frightening accompaniment. Wind and brass are prominent for a change and the only piano to be mentioned is back at Il Conde's Sorrento residence (274). The music is harmonious; the action is not. In the early pages Il Conde recalls that "mimes and flute players" were the amusements of the Romans (271) and his accurate recollection of the music being played while he is robbed reflects his sensitivity to things of gentle beauty and repugnance for things brutal – both present in this case, bringing the Count face to face with the other side of life. This harsh reality makes the beautiful music seem unreal and an illusion.

In its literal state, then, music does not appear to advantage; metaphorically it fares little better. In *Almayer's Folly* it is said of Almayer after Nina has gone that "Henceforth he spoke always in a monotonous whisper like an instrument of which all the strings but one are broken in a last ringing clamour under a heavy blow" (192-3). In *An Outcast of the Islands* the buzz of a persistent fly, swatted at in vain by Almayer and Lingard (symbolizing their ineffectuality) is likened to "a far-off string orchestra" (169); in *The Secret Agent* there comes from Sir Ethelred's mouth "a subdued rolling sound, as from a distant organ with the scornful indignation stop" (138). Only in *Nostromo* is the metaphorical usage positive:

> the engineer-in-chief...had contemplated the changing hues on the enormous side of the mountain, thinking that in this sight, as in a piece of inspired music, there could be found together the utmost delicacy of shaded expression and a stupendous magnificence of effect.
>
> Sir John arrived too late to hear the magnificent and inaudible strain sung by the sunset amongst the high peaks of the Sierra. It had sung itself out into the breathless pause of deep dusk before...he shook hands with the engineer. (40)

This passage shows that Conrad was able to appreciate music, or (at least) the attributes of good music. (How significant it is that Sir John, representing a material interest, arrives too late to enjoy the marvellous effect here!) The author clearly did not like mechanical renditions or bad performances and generally the music in his work is unmelodious, suggesting that he may have encountered quite a few. His pianists are nearly all female, ranging from the fiery competence of Freya to the thumping indifference of Mrs. Zangiacomo. Music is functional for Babalatchi in *An Outcast of the Islands* (where his song ensures that Aïssa and Willems will not doze while the blind and murderous Omar is about [138]) and also for the salesman from Baltimore in *The Rescue* who considers that "musical instruments, this side up with care" (98) would be a suitable label for a box containing firearms. Lastly (and perhaps whimsically) there does seem to be an echo of the tonic sol-fa about the names Doramin in *Lord Jim* and *Sofala* in *The End of the Tether*.

This, then, adds perhaps another bar or two to the unfinished symphony of Conrad's attitude to music and his use of it. Very few composers are mentioned by name and it is nearly always opera that attracts his attention – the works of Wagner, Meyerbeer and Verdi. Whether the handful of articles about Conrad and music constitutes a movement yet remains to be seen. That there are other movements as yet unresearched and unwritten seems clear; we have progressed to date no farther than the beginning.

NOTES

1. Letter to John Galsworthy, 18 June 1910, *CL*, 4, 338.
2. Letter to Eric Pinker, 9 April 1923, *LL*, 2, 303.
3. Letter to Sir Hugh Clifford, 22 June 1911, *CL*, 4, 451-2.
4. Letter to Edward Garnett, 22 February 1896, *CL*, 1, 263.
5. *Joseph Conrad: Times Remembered* (Cambridge: C.U.P., 1981), p. 161.
6. Letter to Marguerite Poradowska, 2 May 1894, *CL*, 1, 156.
7. Letter to Edward Garnett, 17 September 1895, *CL*, 1, 245.
8. "Conrad and Music," *Conradiana*, 23 (1991), pp. 190-3.
9. *Ibid.*, p. 184.

Ray Stevens,
Western Maryland College,
Westminster, USA

A Milch-Cow's Overview of Sailing Ships, and Other Conradian Narrative Perspectives in the Lighter Later Essays

> There, on fine mornings...the ship's children, some controlled by nursemaids, others running loose, trooped forward to pay a visit to their cow, which looked with mild big eyes at the small citizens of our sea community with the air of knowing all there was to know about them. (*Ocean Travel; LE,* 56-7)

Conradian criticism is filled with commentary about the author's narrative perspective, especially the role of Marlow in *Heart of Darkness,* the various voices of *Lord Jim,* and the dualism of personality in *The Secret Sharer.* Much criticism of prose fiction of the last fifty years has focused on this topic, especially fiction that wrestles with the realities or relativities of psychological states of mind and searches for meaning in the inner recesses of character. Conrad knew the inability of the uninitiated to understand complex actions by complex individuals, just as he knew the inevitable sense of alienation that forces the misunderstood to try to escape the judgment of those not "one of us." Most often discussed in Conrad's fiction are *Lord Jim* and the intricate web of characters who try to explain Jim's actions both to Marlow and, through Marlow, to us. Some explain glibly; some, like Gentleman Brown, explain maliciously; some, like Stein, explain with, shall we say, Lepidopteran certainty. And of course there is Marlow, whose insatiable curosity compels him to amass various opinions ultimately leading to an open-endedness belying the application of easy explanations to inscrutable human behavior.

Thus Jim retreats ever more into the recesses of the East, until the consequences of his actions, of his tortured psyche, and of the opinions of others – consonant with the duplicitous deeds of Gentleman Brown and Cornelius – destroy him. And in *The Secret Sharer* Leggatt swims away, seeking a new life on an alien shore. The search for understanding the narrative complexities in Conrad has been varied and long standing. Thirty-five years ago a critic argued that, because Marlow sits on the *Nellie* in the lotus position during his narration in *Heart of Darkness,* a Buddhist perspective must inform the interpretation of narrative technique.[1] Since then students have occasionally become redundant seeking new formulas to express old truths, as William Scheick does for *Lord Jim* in his recent *Fictional Structure and Ethics*:

> This pattern of triple layers of narrative – recording narrator, formulating Marlow, and nearly inarticulate Jim – constitutes the principle of order, or narrative-structure, imposed on a chaotic plot-structure replete with chronological ambiguities, syntactic obfuscation, and distorted perspectives.[2]

Conrad avoided such narrative complexities – real or imagined – in *Last Essays,* which has been neglected by critics focussing on Conrad's narrative method, except for occasional comments of dismissal.[3] To refresh memories, *Last Essays* is that posthumous volume of writing containing twenty miscellaneous essays beginning with *Congo Diary,* written in 1890, and concluding with *Legends,* which remained unfinished on Conrad's desk when he died in 1924.

At least six essays can serve as a primer to illustrate Conrad's narrative method in a way that makes John Keats's opinions about Shakespeare's creation of character – his "negative capability" letters to George and Thomas Keats (21-7 December 1817) – and elaborated on in another letter to Richard Woodhouse (27 October 1818)[4] – at least as applicable in interpreting Conrad's narrative technique as contemporary theory. If Conrad does not simply fill others' bodies, as Keats might argue, at least he travels with them, treating them in his essays with a Wordsworthian and Coleridgean certain colouring of the imagination, whereby ordinary things should be presented to the mind in an unusual aspect; and, further, and above all, to make these incidents and situations interesting by tracing in them, truly though not ostentatiously, the primary laws of our nature: chiefly, as far as regards the manner in which we associate ideas in a state of excitement.[5]

In the creative explorations of the past that constitute most of the *Last Essays,* especially those recalling his life as mariner, Conrad became more playful and discursive than in his earlier more consciously aesthetic writings, enlivening his lighter later autobiographical narratives with imagined perspectives of historical navigators and other creatures of the imagination who traveled with him.

These mental travelers range from a writer of a preface to a cookbook oscillating ironically between dyspepsia and gastronomic content; to a milch-cow observing the antics of itinerants aboard a ship bound for Australia; to a novice writer whimsically recreating a walk through London with Stephen Crane. Of course other, more sober, perspectives prevail: Conrad sees through the eyes of a teenage gunner on the *HMS Ready* the strafing of a German airship and recreates some of his earlier voyages through the eyes of fellow travelers Vasco Nuñez de Balboa, Abel Tasman, John Franklin, and James Cook. Finally, he comments in a personally intertextual way in *Geography and Some Explorers* on his trip to the Congo – recalling his experience through Wordsworthian "spots of time:"[6] first, in his romantic association with a map of Africa as a school boy in Poland; second, in his actual experience there; and third – filtered perhaps through Marlow in *Heart of Darkness,* through Wordsworth communing with his sister Dorothy a few miles above Tintern Abbey, and through Nelly Dean narrating to Lockwood the story of Heathcliff and the residents of Thrushcross Grange and Wuthering Heights – in recreating an image of himself smoking a pipe of peace near Stanley Falls.

A brief examination of six *Last Essays* will illustrate Conrad's narrative technique as he 1) demonstrates ironically the antithetical method of argumentation in *Cookery*; 2) differentiates between factual and fictional writing in *Outside Literature*; 3) illustrates perhaps unwittingly a favorite way of creating character in *The Unlighted Coast*; 4) develops a Wordsworthian "certain colouring of the imagination" in an impressionistic recreation of his first meeting with Stephen Crane; 5) shows the way in which narrative techniques involve autobiographical spots of time in *Geography and Some Explorers*; and 6) goes one ironic length better than Leigh Hunt in his approach to animal intelligence in *Ocean Travel*.

Take dyspeptic and malnourished North American Indians. Conrad's appetite for the ironic and absurd had almost fifteen years to digest these creatures of his culinary imagination. *Cookery,* a brief preface to Jessie's *Handbook of Cookery for a Small House,* was written in January 1907; it was first published in late 1921. In this trifle, one might recall the truism that some writings, unlike Scotch whiskies, do not improve with age. *Cookery* also might recall the truism that in minor works, one can often find illustrations by which to interpret the artistic method of major works, as one can find in Lord Byron's biblical dramas clues to his personal ethical dilemmas not always evident in his most frequently read works.

Written hastily as an appetizer for a cookbook that he hoped would relieve his indigestible monetary problems, *Cookery* is interesting stylistically because it demonstrates Conrad in blatantly obvious fashion developing character ironically through antithesis.[7] Conrad contrasts himself, the completely domesticated and gastronomically contented British husband, to wild Indians of North America, whose collective dyspepsia create chaos:

> The noble Red Man was a mighty hunter, but his wives had not mastered the art of conscientious cookery. And the consequences were deplorable...[They] were great warriors, great orators, great masters of outdoor pursuits; but the domestic life of their wigwams was clouded by the morose irritability which follows the consumption of ill-cooked food...Victims of gloomy imaginings, they lived in abject submission to the wiles of a multitude of fraudulent medicine men – quacks – who haunted their existence with vain promises and false nostrums from the cradle to the grave. (218-9)

Beginning typically with a "moral point of view" – here the view that cookery books, unlike other written works, are truthful and "above suspicion" – Conrad's whimsical and ironically fictive voice works antithetically as he theorizes that physiological factors motivate psychological ones. The implied questions of the Socratic dialectical method work logically and silently in the text.

Even though Conrad's is not the eleemosynary fest that Fielding presented in the introductory chapter of *Tom Jones,* with its calipash of literary theory extended through all eighteen books and its calipee of extended ironic control, Conrad's preface is at least an appetizer for stylistic study. Rushed for funds, however, Conrad leaves his Indians eternally dyspeptic and aesthetically undeveloped: in 1907 he had to return to *Chance*; and in 1921 he was beginning to think seriously about *The Rover.*

In *Outside Literature* Conrad continues with antithesis,[8] contrasting creative to factual writing. One of Conrad's responsibilities as second mate on the *Torrens* was to record each day's events in the ship's log; and he recalls that duty almost thirty years later in the note inscribed on the privately printed copy of *The "Torrens"* that once was in the Keating collection.[9] Thus his awareness of the importance of precision in the use of written English preceded his entry into fiction. *Outside Literature*[10] addresses the need for the "ideal of perfect accuracy" in notices sent to mariners to aid in proper navigation. Such concise utilitarian prose differs from the equally concise maxims of La Rouchefoucauld, which "open horizons...plumb the depths...make us squirm, shudder, smile in turn" (59-60). But equally important for both styles is narrative voice.

Conrad illustrates this contrast by violating the canon of accuracy that mariners insist on as his imagination transcends objectivity momentarily, and as the reality of factual record blurs into impressionism as he recalls a moon-faced clock staring at him while he takes the examination. Conrad concludes:

> Henceforth I had to begin...to write prose myself...And yet I never learned to trust it. I can't trust it to this day...A dreadful doubt hangs over the whole achievement of literature. (65)[11]

The reader in turn contributes to Conrad's ironic intent by recalling, as Hans Van Marle has pointed out in "Plucked and passed on Tower Hill: Conrad's Examination Ordeals"[12] that Conrad recorded incorrectly the details of his licensing examination.

Two essays illustrate perhaps excessively the truth of Conrad's observations in *Outside Literature: Stephen Crane,* which H. L. Mencken[13] and others have critiqued unfavorably; and *The Unlighted Coast,* which functionaries in the Admiralty Office did not bother even to publish when Conrad sent a report on his November 1916 tour aboard the *HMS Ready.*

In *Stephen Crane,*[14] Conrad discusses their friendship in an anecdotal rather than critical style, defending Crane against charges of intemperate behavior and discussing sympathetically Crane's relationship with Cora. Conrad recalls their first meeting in October 1897, joining impressionistic and stream-of--consciousness techniques by referring to time specifically on three occasions[15] to give a Carlylean phenomenal framework to noumenal creations, lugubriously contrasting several places that frame an intellectual communion transcending physical circumstances. The afternoon was a "care-free instant" that "had a character of enchantment about it" (151). After reminiscing about the introductory line of Crane's *Open Boat* – "None of them knew the colour of the sky" – Conrad shifts suddenly to color the evening impressionistically:

> After the Green Park the next thing I remember are the Kensington Gardens, where under the lofty and historical trees I was vouchsafed a glimpse of the low mesquite bush overspreading the plum-coloured infinities of the great Texas plains. Then after a long tramp...the only things I carried off were impressions of the coloured rocks of Mexico (or was it Arizona?) and my first knowledge of a locality called the Painted Desert – there came suddenly Oxford Street. (150-1)

Conrad slips into another era; into an earlier impression of himself; and into a narrative style of impressionism from a style of nostalgic reminiscence. He just as easily slips out again.

The Unlighted Coast, not published until 1925, was originally

written in late 1916 as a document designed to give the
Admiralty Office the benefit of Conrad's sea experience, and of
his twelve day experience aboard the *HMS Ready* in war time.
The Admiralty was not impressed[16] by Conrad's brooding
recapitulation of impressions of events on the *Ready,* which
recreates the most significant spot of time in the life of a young
sailor.[17] Under stress, many moments become one continuous
moment, and prose often becomes purple.[18]
    Intriguing stylistically is Conrad's transition from self to
other. Leaving the darkness of the North Sea on the deck of the
Ready, Conrad enters the light of the officer's cabin to meet the
young man who, Conrad argues, becomes "one of us." Rather,
by literary legerdemain Conrad becomes "one of him" – a young
man who had recently fired the ship's gun at a German Zeppelin.

> The memories of my twenty sea years crowded upon me, memories of
> faces, of temperaments, of expressions. And looking at him, all I could
> say to myself was – How like! (79-80)

"How like!" Conrad recalls a face, a temperament, an
expression; he identifies with the person, in this instance the
youth who had ten minutes "of unforgettable anguish, something like the anguish of a man whose eternal salvation would
depend on the soundness of his judgment." Action of youth
blends with wisdom of age: Conrad goes from self, to gunner,
back to self, back to gunner, and concludes morally *in propria
persona*: "Rare, like drops of water in a desert, are such
opportunities for the watchers of the lightless shore" (85-6). Less
rare as Conrad aged and as he struggled to find new subject
matter, are such obvious illustrations of technique that once
came easily, especially an essay that in another context might be
mistaken for a short story.
    Conrad paused while working with *Suspense* to write *Geo-
graphy and Some Explorers,* which recounts his adventures at sea
within the context of great explorers. He focuses especially on his
voyages through the Torres Strait as captain of the *Otago,* and
up the Congo on the *Roi des Belges.* In doing so, he relives the

adventures of those who preceded him, especially of Vasco
Nuñez de Balboa, Captain James Cook, Abel Tasman, Sir John
Franklin, and Conrad's earlier self.

First, Conrad enters into a narration of the discovery of the
Pacific as implied recollections of literature lead to historical
reminiscence and, in turn, to his entry into the experience itself.
A discussion of the calm of the Gulf of Panama repeats the
experience of Coleridge's Ancient Mariner and the horrors on the
slave ship of Melville's *Benito Cereno*. The passage could also
serve as marginal gloss for Keats's sonnet "On First Looking into
Chapman's Homer." Conrad recalls Balboa's (or, as Keats would
have it, Cortez's) surmise, "silent, upon a peak in Darien,"
overlooking the Pacific, recalling that navigators in the days of sail
dreaded the calm Gulf of Panama, where "one might be caught
and lie becalmed for weeks with one's crew dying slowly of
thirst.... I would rather face the fiercest tempest than a gulf pacific
even to deadliness, a prison-house...of torture for...crews." (6-7)

Experiences with Franklin, Tasman, and Captain Cook
follow. Conrad emphasizes the continuing and repetitive experience of *The Voyage of the "Fox" in the Arctic Seas* as Conrad
recalls having absorbed Sir Leopold McLintock's book, published the year (1857) he was born, telling of McLintock's attempt
to find Franklin and his lost ships, the *Erebus* and the *Terror,*
which had disappeared while Franklin was seeking the Northwest Passage.[19] Conrad had read a French translation by the
time he was ten; by thirteen he was writing essays on Arctic
geography, studying and drawing maps, which "brings the
problems of the great spaces of the earth into stimulating and
directing contact with sane curiosity and gives an honest
precision to one's imaginative faculty" (19). It might be noted
that this echoes the discussion of *Outside Literature.*

Such youthful activity gave insight into the life of great
explorers "who were my first friends," and "not the characters of
famous fiction" (22). An interesting inversion this: the romance
of truthful geography, not the imaginative truth of romance,
became a creative force in Conrad's life long before he began to
write fiction.

Recreation of these experiences comes to fruition in his two most memorable voyages – through Torres Strait and into the Congo. "One day," Conrad records, while loading the *Otago* in Sydney bound for Mauritius

> the deep-lying historic sense of the exploring adventures in the Pacific surged up to the surface of my being. Almost without reflection I...wrote a letter to my owners suggesting that, instead of the usual southern route, I should take the ship to Mauritius by way of Torres Strait. (26)[20]

Conrad rejoices in retrospect, because

> what would the memory of my sea life have been...if it had not included a passage through Torres Strait...right on along the track of the early navigators? (27)

This adventure – which recaptured those of Torres, of Tasman, and of Cook – was valedictory to sea life as active master mariner. Even though Conrad would spend five more years at sea and in the Congo, he records – in this essay at least – that no sea experience gave him the satisfaction and sense of imaginative fulfillment that his command in the Torres Strait did.[21]

The entrance to and exit from the thirty-six hour trip through the Torres Strait was marked by the presence of two wrecked ships, the *Honolulu,* and an unknown American ship. The pairing of these two ships repeat the pairings of Captain Cook's *Endeavour* and *Resolution* and of Franklin's *Erebus* and *Terror.* Conrad enters the character of Captain Cook almost completely, as he had Franklin's earlier. He spotted a small island, which to him

> was a hallowed spot, for I knew that the *Endeavour* had been hove-to off it in the year 1762 for her captain...to go ashore for half an hour. What he could possibly want to do I cannot imagine. Perhaps only to be alone with his thoughts for a moment...It may be that on this dry crumb of the earth's crust which I was setting by compass he had tasted a moment of perfect peace. I could depict to myself the famous seaman navigator,

a lonely figure in a three-cornered hat and square-skirted laced coat, pacing to and fro slowly on the rocky shore, while in the ship's boat, lying off on her oars, the coxswain kept his eyes open for the slightest sign of the captain's hand. (30-1)

Conrad concludes: "Thus the sea has been for me a hallowed ground, thanks to those books of travel and discovery which have peopled it with unforgettable shades of the masters in the calling which, in a humble way, was to be mine, too" (31). Despite a mixed metaphor and perhaps an overstated case, his conclusion is paradigmatic, as he shifts from himself to become Captain Cook, then in succession back to himself, to Captain Cook, to the coxswain, and to himself once again as he recalls reliving their experiences in his.

Perhaps most exemplary in *Geography and Some Explorers,* however, is Conrad's entry into his own persona in a three-fold recollection of his experience in the Congo. First, he recaptures the excitement he felt when, as a schoolboy in Poland, he pointed to the map, saying that one day he would visit the white spot that would become his heart of darkness. He recalls the boys who were with him in school.[22] This repetition of individual involvement in exploration – from observer to participant – is evident throughout the essay. The first image of exploration recalls his nights in the Congo; later he remembers camping where the

thundering mutter of the Stanley Falls hung in the heavy night air of the last navigable reach of the Upper Congo...Away in the middle of the stream, on a little island nestling all black in the foam of the broken water, a solitary little light glimmered feebly, and I said to myself with awe, "This is the very spot of my boyish boast." (24-5)

As he re-enters the loneliness of his youth, "awe" replaces "boyish boast," and childhood experience in Poland is relived in adult experience both in the Pacific and at his desk in Kent:

What an end to the idealised realities of a boy's daydreams! I wondered what I was doing there, for indeed it was only an unforeseen episode, hard to believe in now, in my seaman's life. Still, the fact remains that I have smoked a pipe of peace at midnight in the very heart of the African continent, and felt very lonely there. (25)

Of course, the record in his letters and in various studies indicate that, if Conrad actually did feel lonely there, he must have done so while wondering why he had told his school-mates that he would one day go to the Congo; questioning how he ever came to be there; and wondering whether or not he would get out alive. But only in the Congo, apparently, because Conrad explains that elsewhere in his maritime adventures, he

> never felt lonely, because there I never lacked company. The company of great navigators, the first grown-up friends of my early boyhood...commanded my profoundest loyalty, and perhaps it is by the professional favour of the great navigators ever present to my memory that...I have been permitted to sail through the very heart of the...Pacific. (25-6)

Simplistic though Conrad is, his narrative theory is clear, consonant with Wordsworth's belief in *Lines Composed a Few Miles Above Tintern Abbey,* in its theme of the power of reminiscence and personal continuity of experience; and with *The Prelude,* in its emphasis on the physiological and psychological effect of spots of time that create the autobiography that leads to literature.[23] As Wordsworth said in *The Prelude,* Book XII:

> There are in our existence spots of time,
> That with distinct pre-eminence retain
> A renovating virtue, whence, depressed
> By false opinion and contentious thought,
> Or aught of heavier and more deadly weight,
> In trivial occupations, and the round
> Of ordinary intercourse, our minds
> Are nourished and invisibly repaired;
> A virtue, by which pleasure is enhanced,
> That penetrates, enables us to mount,
> When high, more high, and lifts us up when fallen.
> This efficacious spirit chiefly lurks
> Among those passages of life that give
> Profoundest knowledge to what point, and how,
> The mind is lord and master – outward sense
> The obedient servant of her will. Such moments
> Are scattered everywhere, taking their date
> From our first childhood. (lines 208-25)

A final absurd example is Conrad's entry into the surmise of a milch-cow in *Ocean Travel*. Conrad writes briefly about the ways that passengers on sailing ships, in contrast to steam ships, acclimate themselves to life on board. But he wonders: how do the livestock acclimate themselves to a sea voyage? Like donkeys on the El Dorado expedition in *Heart of Darkness*, a milch-cow for a moment ascends over other animals. Of all the

> feathered and four-footed company the most important item was the milch-cow...It was the last living thing that came on board, already boxed and in its travelling stall, and displaying a most praiseworthy composure even while spinning in mid-air at the fore-yard-arm before being landed on the fore-deck against the mast, to which its straitened habitation was secured for the passage with lashings of chain and rope fit to withstand the heaviest weather we were likely to encounter.... There on fine mornings...the ship's children, some controlled by nurse-maids, others running loose, trooped forward to pay a visit to their cow, which looked with mild big eyes at the small citizens of our sea community with the air of knowing all there was to know about them. (56-7)

Those who find powerful symbolic significance in every word that Conrad writes might note that he encapsulates in one milch-cow our whole tradition of the mountain-top experience, from Satan spiraling in to tempt Adam, as Milton has it in *Paradise Lost, IV*; to Moses on Mounts Sinai and Pisgah; to all the gyres and winding staircases of Yeats. Others might see in this final example of Conradian irony and absurdity, however, the stylistic approach of John Galsworthy interpreting outer manifestations of character; of Tolstoy entering the world-view of a dog in *Anna Karenina,* or of Leigh Hunt entering the world-view of a fish in his sonnets on "The Fish, The Man, and The Spirit;" or of the psychological simplism of the office-mates of Melville's Bartleby the Scrivener; rather than of Conrad at his best. Absurd as the example is, however, it should remind the reader that Conrad often explores external characteristics or actions, reflects on a deeper psychological or spiritual significance, and returns to them, as with Marlow sitting in the lotus position on the *Nellie* recalling the physical characteristics of

Kurtz writing his moral document while doing immoral things in Africa; or Marlow recording Lord Jim's enigmatic physical characteristics through three layers of narrative.[24]

You will recall that, in *Paradise Lost,* Book II, in the great debate among the forces of pandemonium, Milton structures philosophical arguments based on four points of view, beginning with antithetical ones: Moloch (Let us have open war against the powers of Heaven), and Belial (Let us accept defeat with what grace we still have). These in turn are followed by gradations of the antithesis: Mammon (Let us seek "our own good among ourselves."), and Beelzebub and Satan (Let us win by aggressive deceit); simplistically stated here. This is standard logical argumentative technique in the Greek dialectical tradition, gloriously elevated in *Paradise Lost*: take antithetical positions, and seek symphonic variations on a theme by asking the questions that the text implies, as Browning does, for example, in *The Ring and the Book.*

The logic informing much of Conrad's most creative and imaginative work has not received enough critical attention: for example, use of antithesis in the Greek dialectical tradition that seeks gradations of opinion framed by antitheses, framed by that certain coloring of the imagination necessary for works of art. This becomes increasingly obvious when we study Conrad's major works in the light of the record of his manuscript revisions and of his letters, noting especially the tortuous way that his major texts often grew, and the way in which he, like Keats, often analysed and theorized about his art and the art of others.

The six essays examined briefly here suggest paradigmatically some of Conrad's basic approaches to narrative technique in 1) using antitheses in *Cookery* and *Outside Literature*; 2) developing spots of time and a certain coloring of the imagination in *Stephen Crane* and *Geography and Some Explorers* to reminisce about and associate with travelers as they evolve into creative incidents and texts, and as the characters grow to complement each other creatively and aesthetically; 3) becoming for a moment a young gunner on the *Ready* in *The Unlighted Coast*; and 4) playfully creating an ironic context that allows

Conrad to give a milch-cow an overview both of sailing ships and of life in *Ocean Travel.*

Conrad explained his narrative technique to Ernest Rhys in 1922: "I have my psychological aim, first of all.... Then I look about for some event, some personal adventure...some catastrophe, 'pour motiver' my characters,"[25] and he told a reporter from the *Christian Science Monitor* on 19 May 1923 that he did not "gather material," but wrote "in retrospect of what he saw and learned during the first 35 years of his life."[26] Significantly, Conrad returned in the *Last Essays* to a consistent pattern of narrative technique that he first exhibited in his development of the *Sapphire's* Captain Johns of *The Black Mate,* but perhaps also, one might speculate, of the forty-two year old Captain Richard Jones of Bath whom Conrad knew as commander of the *Falconhurst* during his five-day tour of duty in 1886.[27]

NOTES

1. W. B. Stein, "The Lotus Posture and the *Heart of Darkness*," *Modern Fiction Studies,* 2 (Winter 1956-57), pp. 235-7.

2. (Athens: University of Georgia Press, 1990), p. 139.

3. See for example F. R. Karl, *Joseph Conrad: The Three Lives* (New York: Farrar, Straus and Giroux, 1979), p. 883; and Z. Najder, *Joseph Conrad: A Chronicle* (New Brunswick: Rutgers University Press, 1983), p. 422.

4. D. Perkins, ed., *English Romantic Writers* (New York: Harcourt, Brace Jovanovich, 1967), pp. 1209, 1220.

5. W. Wordsworth, "Preface to the Second Edition of the *Lyrical Ballads*," in Perkins, p. 321.

6. J. Wordsworth, M. H. Abrams, and S. Gill, *The Prelude 1799, 1805, 1850* (New York: Norton, 1979), pp. 429-30.

7. Conrad wryly commented to Ford Madox Ford that *Cookery* was "a mock serious thing into which I dragged Red Indians and other incongruities." (Letter of 25 January 1907; *CL,* 3, 410). See also Ford's account in *Return to Yesterday* (London: Gollancz, 1931), pp. 239-40. As Ford suggests, Conrad was ambivalent about both his preface and the cookbook itself. Conrad was interested in the revenue that the project – enhanced as it would be by the increased value that his preface would add to it – might bring; yet he was aware of its obvious literary insignificance. His stance in the essay was at least in part a mask to conceal his ambivalence about the project.

8. This is not an attempt to force yet another Procrustean antithetical or dialectical schema upon critics of literature. Rather, it is primarily an attempt to demonstrate that Conrad is using one of the most common human methods of argumentation. That such a method is occasionally adapted to fit various philosophical schemata attests both to its prevalence and to its importance.

9. G. T. Keating, compiler, *A Conrad Memorial Library: The Collection of George T. Keating* (Garden City, New York: Doubleday, Doran, 1929), p. 377.

10. First published in the Manchester *Guardian*, 4 December 1922.

11. Conrad had developed this idea much earlier in such places as his review of H. Clifford's *Studies in Brown Humanity* (published in *Academy*, 23 April 1898), in which he distinguishes between a book devoted to literal truth, in this instance Clifford's observations as Governor of Malaya, and Conrad's Malayan fiction.

12. *Conradiana*, 8: 2 (1976), pp. 99-109.

13. *Dial*, 76 (January 1924), pp. 73-4.

14. Written hastily at the request of Thomas Beer for Beer's study: *Stephen Crane: A Study in American Letters* (New York: Alfred A. Knopf, 1923).

15. Their communion began sometime after 4 p. m. when S. S. Pawling, who had introduced them, left; it concluded about 11 p. m. In between, Conrad remembers that Jessie awaits him at home.

16. Zdzisław Najder speculates that it was not published "possibly because it contained no trace of propaganda and not even much optimism" (422). In addition, the Admiralty was much more concerned with the logistics of the day-to-day operations of World War I, and sought prose that was useful and informative, prose "outside literature."

17. He was to use the same theme later in *Dover Patrol*.

18. Take for example the following: "The land had turned to shadow. Of all scourges and visitations against which mankind prays to Heaven, it was not pestilence that had smitten that shore dark. It was war; with sudden death, another of that dreaded company, full of purpose, in the air, on the water, and under the water...it was as hard to believe in the existence of this prowling death as in the dauntless, tense life of that obscured land. That mere shadow – big with fate" (74). One can imagine the M'Choakumchilds and Gradgrinds of the Admiralty mumbling in frustration: "Mr. Conrad, all we want is facts."

19. Franklin's travels encapsulate nicely the nautical world of Conrad's *Geography and Some Explorers*. Conrad knew from his reading of Fox's book and other sources that Franklin had served as governor of Van Dieman's Land (Tasmania) as an interlude between two earlier voyages to the Arctic and the disastrous last one that ended in 1845.

20. The owners reminded Conrad that the Strait often became becalmed during that season of the year. This continues the stylistic pattern of repetition – recalling the season of calm in the Gulf of Panama.

21. Conrad's trip was far from idyllic, however, as he had recorded earlier in *The Shadow-Line*; and as others, notably N. Sherry in *Conrad's Eastern World* (Cambridge: C. U. P., 1966), pp. 246-9, have examined in detail.

22. Of course this is only one of various works where he recaptures that experience.

23. E. Said in *Joseph Conrad and the Fiction of Autobiography* (Cambridge: Harvard University Press, 1966), is one of many to have discussed this theme.

24. This is by no means an exhaustive catalogue. For example, in *The "Torrens,"* Conrad develops the life of a passenger who was convinced that he would die if he had to continue his sea voyage to Australia, recording the exterior events of the situation, but entering into the man's mind as well.

25. *Bookman* (New York), LVI (December 1922), pp. 402-08.

26. "Americans Kind, So Why Lecture?," p. 2. Quoted in: M. Ray, ed., *Joseph Conrad: Interviews and Recollections* (Iowa City: University of Iowa Press, 1990), p. 189.

27. See E. Bojarski and R. Stevens, "Joseph Conrad and the *Falconhurst*," *Journal of Modern Literature,* 1: 2 (1970), pp. 197-208. For a discussion of the problems of dating *The Black Mate,* see Najder, pp. 338-9.